Learning Habits

What makes some students thrive while others struggle? This exciting book reveals how teachers can help young people become expert learners—curious, resilient, and capable of thinking for themselves.

Drawing on educational and psychological research, this book explores three key themes—how we learn, the challenges of thinking, and habit formation—providing a clear practical framework to help students develop more effective, lasting learning habits. It explains how students absorb and forget information, the limits of working memory, the importance of self-control, and how cognitive biases affect decision-making alongside strategies to foster critical thinking. Providing actionable guidance for supporting learning in school and at home, this book includes:

- Memorable stories of real experiences and case studies designed to create an emotional impact and help ideas about learning habits "stick" with readers.

- Student-friendly demonstrations of scientific experiments which can be downloaded from www.routledge.com/9781041096382, showing surprising and counterintuitive aspects of how we learn, think, and form habits.

- Chapter summaries, images, and a dedicated scenarios chapter to make the key messages easy to follow, revisit, and apply.

With additional guidance on the role of AI in education and using technology effectively, this is essential reading for teachers and parents wanting to help children and young people develop effective, sustainable learning habits.

Richard Wheadon has nearly 20 years of teaching experience. He previously oversaw teaching and learning in a large comprehensive school and was recently awarded a Fellowship by the Chartered College of Teaching. He has presented at education conferences in the United Kingdom and abroad.

Learning Habits

How to Develop Independent and Successful Learners

Richard Wheadon

LONDON AND NEW YORK

Designed cover image: © Getty Images

First published 2026
by Routledge
4 Park Square, Milton Park, Abingdon, Oxon OX14 4RN

and by Routledge
605 Third Avenue, New York, NY 10158

Routledge is an imprint of the Taylor & Francis Group, an informa business

© 2026 Richard Wheadon

The right of Richard Wheadon to be identified as author of this work has been asserted in accordance with sections 77 and 78 of the Copyright, Designs and Patents Act 1988.

All rights reserved. No part of this book may be reprinted or reproduced or utilised in any form or by any electronic, mechanical, or other means, now known or hereafter invented, including photocopying and recording, or in any information storage or retrieval system, without permission in writing from the publishers.

For Product Safety Concerns and Information please contact our EU representative GPSR@taylorandfrancis.com. Taylor & Francis Verlag GmbH, Kaufingerstraße 24, 80331 München, Germany.

Trademark notice: Product or corporate names may be trademarks or registered trademarks, and are used only for identification and explanation without intent to infringe.

British Library Cataloguing-in-Publication Data
A catalogue record for this book is available from the British Library

ISBN: 9781041096399 (hbk)
ISBN: 9781041096382 (pbk)
ISBN: 9781003651079 (ebk)

DOI: 10.4324/9781003651079

Typeset in Melior
by codeMantra

Access the Support Material: www.routledge.com/9781041096382

Contents

Foreword by Kate Jones — vii
Preface — ix
Acknowledgements — xi

Introduction—What Does a Successful Independent Learner Look Like? — 1

1. How Do We Learn? — 7
   The Role of Cognitive Science? — 7
   Working Memory Is Limited — 9
   Why Do We Need to Remember? — 10
   WHIP, Pitcher's Mound, Double Play, Pickoff, Bullpen, Sacrifice Bunt — 13
   Why Is Remembering So Hard? — 13
   Why Students Forget—And What Can We Do About It? — 20
   The Importance of Schemas — 24
   Desirable Difficulties Dilemma — 30

2. The Challenges with Thinking — 39
   The Role of Bias in Learning — 39
   Overcoming Bias — 55
   The Psychology behind Our Statistical Blind Spots — 59
   Nudge Theory — 63
   Noise—Measuring Variability in Learning Habits — 69

3. The Challenge of Change — 77
   The Curse of Self-Gratification — 77
   The Misunderstand of Motivation — 83
   Counting What Counts: Motivation Through Measurement — 89
   How Habits Are Born — 91

4. Creating Better Learning Habits — 96
   The Habit Loops — 96
   Making the Unconscious Conscious — 99
   Design for Success: Start Small, Shape the Space — 104
   The Power of Believe — 111
   Belonging: The Missing Link in Habit Formation — 116

5. AI: Can We Outsource Effort without Losing Learning? 129
   The Hidden Cost of AI Convenience 129
   Harnessing AI for Learning: Principles Grounded in Cognitive Science 133
   Applying Cognitive Science Through Adaptive Flashcards 134
   AI Tutors in Education: Promise with Precautions 135
   Feedback: Why It's Not What AI Says, But What Students Do 139

6. The Path to Expertise: Accelerating Learning Habits 144
   How Novices and Experts Think Differently 144
   The Case of Overconfidence 150
   How Do We Make Decisions? 153
   Developing Better Mental Models 158
   Using Scenarios to Accelerate Learning Habits 163
   Metacognition and Self-Regulation 181

7. Conclusion 189

   Glossary of Stories 191
   Index 193

Foreword

Kate Jones

Much has been written about the science of learning and what this can look like in the classroom (I am one of several teacher authors that have contributed to this field). The key principles from cognitive science have been widely adopted across education. The evidence base has been widely discussed, debated, and cited in national policy and documentation. The conversation about effective teaching continues, but the book *Learning Habits* by Richard Wheadon is timely, as it shifts the focus from teaching practice to student learning, thinking, and habit formation.

I genuinely believe this book brings something new, fresh, relevant, and (most importantly) something helpful to the educational discourse. Wheadon shares his vast experiences as a classroom teacher, leader, and parent and combines this with an extensive evidence base. I believe the combination of evidence, experience, and enthusiasm is essential to ensure teaching and learning strategies are implemented and embedded effectively, inside and outside of the classroom.

There is regular discussion of making learning stick, but what does this actually look like? What is stickiness when it comes to learning? Wheadon explains this with ease and simplicity, despite the complexities of learning. How can schools share the knowledge and insight from cognitive science with their students, parents, and the wider school community? Again, Wheadon helps to make this possible with practical advice, suggestions, and scenarios. Cognitive science principles and approaches are viewed through the lens of the learner, not just the teacher, and this is also necessary.

I am sure every reader will have their own highlights and areas of interest as they work through each chapter. My personal highlights were the discussions of artificial intelligence (AI) and the different cognitive biases that can be present. At the time of writing, AI feels like something that can be very powerful and transformative to teaching and learning, but it is not without its concerns and fears. Wheadon approaches AI in a helpful, pragmatic, and practical way. The cognitive biases are expertly explored, and they are something educators and learners should not only be aware of but also understand and be able to recognise. The reflective questions and discussion points throughout this book make this an ideal text for a staff CPD library and one to be shared across the school community.

Wheadon ensures the reader (whether they be a teacher, student, or parent) can gain insight, knowledge, and a range of strategies to develop learning habits that ultimately help, not hinder, learning, thinking, and overall progress. I apologise for the spoiler, but I wanted to finish this foreword with a key takeaway, a quote from the author, which captures the essence of this book:

> At the heart of it all is a powerful idea: with the right knowledge, strategies, and habits, anyone can become an expert learner.

Kate Jones is Senior Associate for Teaching and Learning at Evidence Based Education. She is also a best-selling author, an international keynote speaker, and an experienced classroom teacher and leader.

Preface

In *The Tipping Point*, Malcolm Gladwell (2000) introduces the concept of "stickiness" as one of the key factors to ensure an idea or trend spreads rapidly and becomes widespread. Stickiness refers to the ability of an idea, message, or piece of content to "stick" in people's minds and compel them to act on it or share it. The stickier something is, the more likely it is to have a lasting impact, whether that's in the form of changing behaviours, influencing opinions, or spreading through a community.

Key characteristics of stickiness include:

1. **Memorability**: For an idea or message to be sticky, it must be memorable. If people can easily recall it or it resonates with them on an emotional level, they are more likely to adopt it or pass it along to others. This involves making the content simple, relatable, and emotionally engaging.

2. **Emotional Impact**: Stickiness is often tied to how strongly something resonates emotionally with individuals. Ideas or messages that evoke strong emotions—whether positive or negative—tend to stick more effectively. For example, stories of personal struggle and triumph often resonate with people and are more likely to be remembered and shared.

3. **Simplicity and Clarity**: Simple messages are more likely to stick than complex ones. This is why catchphrases, slogans, and short stories are often more effective than long-winded explanations. The key is to convey your message in a way that's straightforward and easy to digest.

4. **Practicality**: For ideas or behaviours to stick, they need to be actionable. People are more likely to act on something they can understand and apply right away. This is why "how-to" content or practical advice tends to have higher stickiness—people want to know what they can do with the information.

5. **Surprise or Uniqueness**: When something surprises people or is unexpected, it often sticks. A surprising or counterintuitive idea tends to capture people's

attention more than something that feels obvious or familiar. In Gladwell's book, he talks about how surprising elements can create memorable moments, making the idea more likely to spread.

There are parts of this book that are very personal, and that decision was intentional, with the goal of making it memorable. My own stories, along with the various case studies in this book, are intended to have an emotional impact on the reader. Many of these stories are designed to be read directly by students—preferably as a whole class with a teacher, or at home with a parent—in the hope that these ideas on how to help them develop learning habits will stick. At the back of this book, there is a glossary of each of the stories so that you can go directly to them.

Student-friendly versions of some of the scientific experiments aimed at teaching students about learning, thinking, and habit formation, can be downloaded from the Routledge website www.routledge.com/9781041096382. These experiments are designed to surprise students into understanding concepts about learning that are often counterintuitive.

Finally, the chapter summaries, images, and chapter on scenarios are designed to make the key messages of this book clear and simple to follow and revisit.

I do hope you enjoy reading this book as much as I enjoyed putting it together, and that you—either as an educator or a parent—act as the intermediary to the true audience of this book: the children I hope to help become successful, independent learners.

Reference

Gladwell, M. (2000). *The tipping point: How little things can make a big difference*. Little, Brown and Company.

Acknowledgements

First and foremost, I want to express my deepest gratitude to my wonderful wife, Ceri, and our two amazing daughters, Mali and Megan. Without their love, patience, and encouragement, this book simply wouldn't exist. Ceri has lovingly carved out the time and space for me to write, and as you read through these pages, I hope it becomes clear that my girls are the heart and inspiration behind everything in this book.

I am also truly thankful to the many Headteachers and Deputy Headteachers who have guided and shaped my understanding of education over the years—Stephen Morris, Jane Cooper, Jane Water, and Sen Galagedera, your influence has been invaluable.

And to my dear friend and former colleague, Mitchel Mills—thank you for the countless hours of thoughtful conversation and shared passion for teaching and learning. Your friendship and insights have meant the world to me throughout this journey.

Introduction–What Does a Successful Independent Learner Look Like?

Imagine a student sitting in their first university lecture. They are diligently listening to the lecturer, trying to keep up while taking notes on key ideas. Twenty minutes in, the lecturer is still speaking at a relentless pace, and the student starts to feel overwhelmed and lost.

But this student is prepared. *Cognitive overload,* they think. *Not a problem.* Instead of continuing to take exhaustive notes, they shift their focus, jotting down only the concepts that feel unfamiliar. They recognise gaps in their prerequisite knowledge and make it their goal to identify these gaps, planning to revisit and address them after the lecture.

When the lecture ends, they don't feel discouraged. Instead, they are energised by the challenge ahead. Using a variety of resources, they begin to piece together the new information, interrogating their notes and linking them to their prior knowledge they are pulling from their long-term memory. However, they realise that their notes, while helpful, are disorganised and need restructuring. To make the material stick, they organise their notes into a more logical order relevant for the material of the lecture. In this instance they choose to use a mind map; this is a deliberate choice as there is no hierarchical structure to the content of the lecture.

Once their notes are complete, they feel confident in their understanding of the lecture's content. Yet they know learning has not happened just yet. The next step is crucial: creating flashcards and developing a structured plan to revisit the material systematically over the coming weeks.

Let's look at another scenario: imagine a student has left school and started an apprenticeship as a plumber. Four weeks into the course, everything has been going smoothly. However, they now face their first real challenge.

They accompany their supervisor to a house where the customer reports an issue—the toilet flush isn't working properly, and the cistern isn't filling fully after each flush. The supervisor takes a quick look and identifies a fault with the flushing mechanism. The student has observed their supervisor fixing similar issues several times before, so the supervisor invites them to take the lead.

Confident in the steps they have practised over the past month, the student begins by scanning the various parts of the system. However, they soon encounter a problem: the flushing mechanism looks completely different from anything they've seen before. At this moment, they realise their mental model of the problem is limited to the designs they have previously encountered.

Now, they face a decision. Should they ask their supervisor for help? Should they search for a YouTube tutorial on this exact design? Or should they try to apply their existing knowledge to solve the problem independently?

Before going any further, as an educator reading this book think about a student in your classroom who might one day find themselves in a similar situation. As a parent reading this book consider a situation your child might be in similar to the one above. How do you think they would react? Would they take a considered approach, or might they resort to a less productive response? Some students, when confronted with difficulty, look for excuses and slowly withdraw from the challenge. Unfortunately, some would rather become the "class clown" than admit they are struggling. Others might disengage entirely, wandering the corridors rather than facing the challenge.

Returning to the scenario, the former student weighs their options and decides to start by applying what they already know. They examine the mechanism, searching for familiar elements.

The first step is identifying the inlet valve, the component that controls the flow of water into the cistern. They flush the toilet and carefully observe where the water enters. They notice that the cistern only fills about halfway before stopping. As they continue to watch, they see a ball float rising with the water—something they haven't encountered before. However, they quickly make a connection: the ball is attached to the inlet valve, and once it reaches a certain height, the valve closes.

They now understand the root of the problem—the ball float is triggering the inlet valve too soon, preventing the cistern from filling completely.

Although they've successfully diagnosed the issue, they don't yet know how to fix it. But that's okay. They recognise that learning is the process of acquiring knowledge and skills through study, experience, and instruction. They understand that this is the moment to seek guidance.

They explain their findings to the supervisor, who confirms their reasoning and demonstrates the solution. The supervisor adjusts a small screw near the inlet valve, raising the ball float and allowing the water to flow properly again. Watching closely, the student has an idea. They ask if they can reset the ball float to its original position and attempt the adjustment themselves.

This moment—where they take an active role in their learning—marks an important shift. They are no longer just following instructions. They are problem-solving, refining their understanding, and building independence.

These scenarios exemplify the habits of an expert learner. It is my belief that one of our primary goals as educators should be to develop expert learners in our classrooms. As a parent if your goal is for your child to lead a successful life then developing the traits of an expert learner will give them an excellent chance.

While the idea of developing expert learners might seem ambitious, it is entirely achievable. In his book *Outliers*, Gladwell (2008) popularised the idea that mastery in a field requires approximately 10,000 hours of practice. Students in the United Kingdom spend around 1,000 hours per year in school, amounting to roughly 13,000 hours over 13 years of statutory education; this doesn't account for the time students spend on their education outside of school or the support parents can contribute to achieving this goal.

With this time at our disposal, we, educators and parents, have a unique opportunity to guide our students in becoming expert learners. This book will outline a practical, step-by-step approach to making this vision a reality. For the remainder of this book, I will refer to children as students. Although the primary audience is educators, the structure of the book is designed to allow parents to work directly with their child or children on the key themes discussed.

This book will explore three key themes: **learning, thinking**, and **habit formation**.

We begin with learning (Figure 0.1). In this section, I will share what I have learned from 20 years in education about how learning happens. I will explain why it is essential to teach students about the science of learning, and I will guide readers through the last 60 years of research in a way that is meaningful and accessible to students. This chapter draws on a range of influential research to explore why knowledge fades and how learning can be made more effective. George Miller's (1965) work on the limitations of working memory, along with Bennet Murdock's (1962) free recall experiment, provides insight into the cognitive constraints that contribute to forgetting. Their findings help explain why newly learned information is often lost without reinforcement or structure. I also examine the 2005 research by David Hambrick and Frederick Oswald, which highlights the role of prior knowledge in learning—a concept that aligns closely with Frederic Bartlett's (1932) seminal work on schemas and their influence on the way we interpret and store new information. The chapter concludes by introducing David Ausubel's (1968) theory of meaningful learning, emphasising the importance of helping students relate new ideas to what they already know.

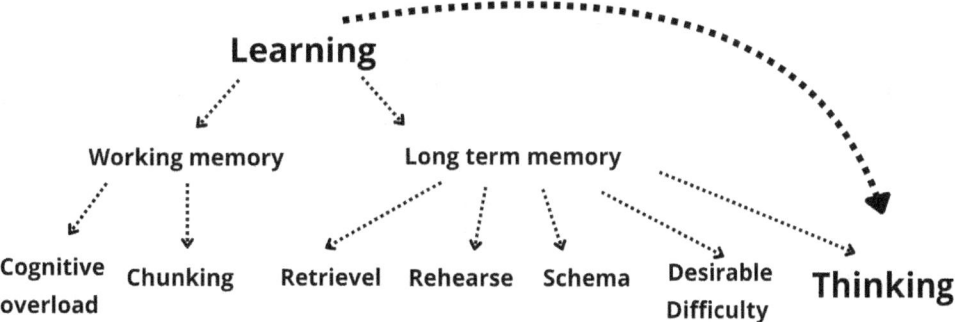

Figure 0.1 An overview of the cognitive processes underpinning learning

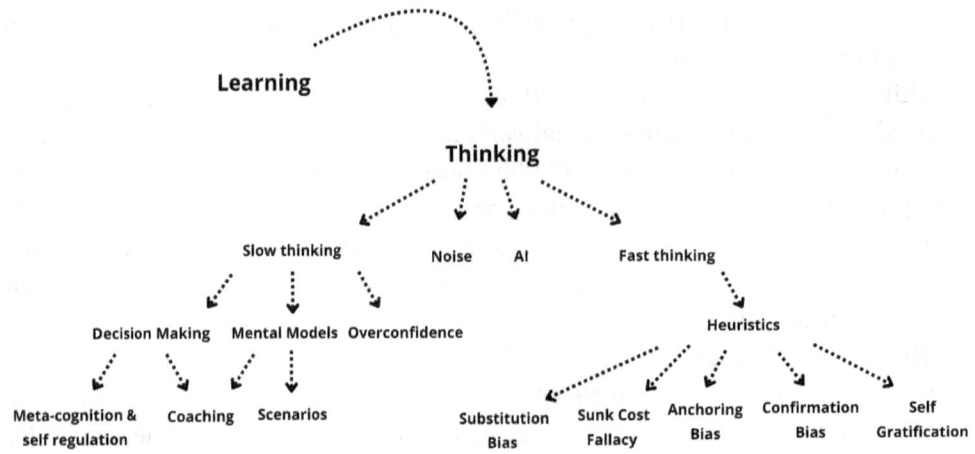

Figure 0.2 Key themes in how thinking influences learning and decision-making

The second theme is thinking (Figure 0.2). For students to learn something new, they must engage in deep, effortful thinking—but fostering this kind of cognitive engagement is not always straightforward. Although it may seem intuitive that thinking hard improves learning, cognitive biases frequently interfere with this process. This section draws heavily on the work of Nobel Prize winner Daniel Kahneman (2011), whose research highlights the ways in which intuitive, automatic thinking (System 1) often overrides slower, more deliberate reasoning (System 2). These cognitive shortcuts can prevent students from processing information deeply, leading to misconceptions or shallow understanding. I will provide clear examples of common biases—such as confirmation bias and availability heuristics—illustrate how they appear in everyday decision-making, and explain how they can obstruct learning. Crucially, I will also suggest practical strategies to mitigate the influence of these biases in classrooms, as well as methods for measuring and monitoring variation in student decision-making across educational settings.

The third theme is habit formation (Figure 0.3). Knowing what effective learning looks like is one thing; developing the habits to sustain it is another. Everyone reading this book has, at some point, set out to improve themselves and failed—whether through dieting, learning a new language, or picking up a musical instrument. Students are no different. This section draws on popular works such as *Atomic Habits* by James Clear (2018), *The Power of Habit* by Charles Duhigg (2012), and *The Tipping Point* by Malcolm Gladwell (2000) to explore how we can help students build habits that support long-term learning. I will use both stories and research to show how habits are formed, how small changes can lead to significant outcomes over time, and how these insights can be applied in educational settings to support sustained, effective learning behaviour.

Drawing on the core themes of learning, thinking, and habit formation explored throughout this book, I will examine how AI intersects with these areas and the implications it brings, and I will propose a framework to help students engage

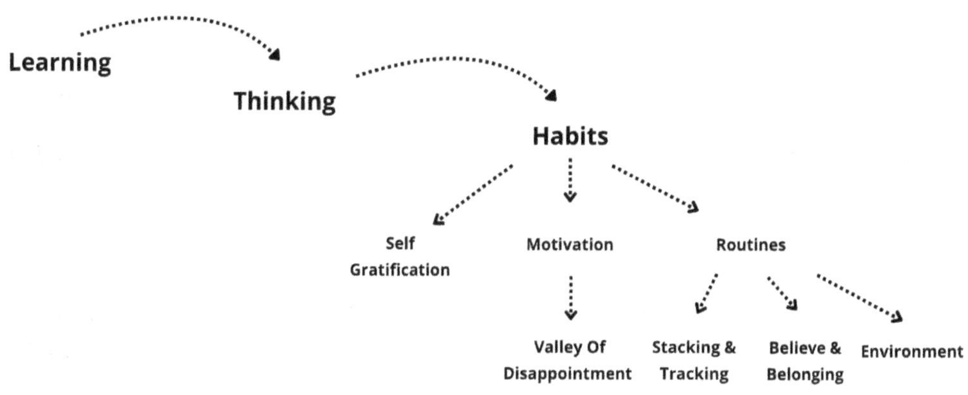

```
         Learning
                            Thinking
                                            Habits
                            Self         Motivation        Routines
                         Gratification
                                      Valley Of    Stacking &   Believe &    Environment
                                    Disappointment   Tracking   Belonging
```

Figure 0.3 An overview of the key elements of habit formation

meaningfully with AI—anchored in cognitive science—to ensure they develop effective habits for learning.

I will present a model of expertise based on the work of Dreyfus and Dreyfus (1986), which outlines the progression from novice to expert through stages of increasing competence and intuition. This model helps us understand how students can move beyond rule-following towards more fluid and adaptive thinking. I will also discuss how overconfidence—often seen in early or intermediate stages—can hinder true expertise by giving learners a false sense of mastery. Additionally, I will explore Gary Klein's (1999) work on naturalistic decision-making, which illustrates how experts draw on patterns and experience to make effective decisions in complex, high-stakes environments. This type of decision-making is a useful benchmark for the kind of judgement and adaptability we want students to develop as they prepare for life beyond school.

Finally, this book will examine how to accelerate the development of students' mental models of learning in order to fast-track their journey towards independence. A mental model is how we understand or imagine how something works—an internal map that helps us navigate the world, solve problems, and make decisions.

One key way to speed up the building of mental models is through the use of scenarios. Scenarios act as practice runs for the brain: they create imagined situations where students can predict outcomes, make decisions, and experience cause and effect. By working through scenarios, students are not just absorbing facts; they are actively organising knowledge, building connections, and developing a deeper understanding with the overall goal to connect the three key themes, earning, thinking, and habit formation, to develop successful independent learners.

References

Ausubel, D. P. (1968). *Educational psychology: A cognitive view*. Holt, Rinehart & Winston.
Bartlett, F. C. (1932). *Remembering: A study in experimental and social psychology*. Cambridge University Press.

Clear, J. (2018). *Atomic habits: An easy & proven way to build good habits & break bad ones.* Avery.

Dreyfus, H. L., & Dreyfus, S. E. (1986). *Mind over machine: The power of human intuition and expertise in the era of the computer.* Free Press.

Duhigg, C. (2012). *The power of habit: Why we do what we do in life and business.* Random House.

Gladwell, M. (2000). *The tipping point: How little things can make a big difference.* Little, Brown and Company.

Gladwell, M. (2008). *Outliers.* Back Bay Books.

Hambrick, D. Z., & Oswald, F. L. (2005). Does domain knowledge moderate involvement of working-memory capacity in higher-level cognition? A meta-analysis. *Journal of Applied Psychology, 90*(2), 306–321.

Kahneman, D. (2011). *Thinking, fast and slow.* Farrar, Straus and Giroux.

Klein, G. (1999). *Sources of power: How people make decisions.* MIT Press.

Miller, G. A. (1965). The magical number seven, plus or minus two: Some limits on our capacity for processing information. *Psychological Review, 63*(2), 81–97.

Murdock, B. B. (1962). The serial position effect of free recall. *Journal of Experimental Psychology, 64*(5), 482–488.

How Do We Learn?

The Role of Cognitive Science?

Cognitive science is the study of how the mind works—it brings together research from psychology, neuroscience, linguistics, and related fields to understand how people learn. In education, it helps us understand the mental processes involved in learning so we can design more effective teaching strategies. The use of cognitive science to identify effective teaching techniques has grown significantly in UK education over the past decade. As teachers have developed a better understanding of how learning happens, their focus has shifted towards strategies that maximise the chances of learning taking place. This has led to a greater emphasis on capturing students' attention and increasing their participation in the classroom.

One subtle but significant shift in classroom practice has been the increased use of *cold calling*—a strategy in which the teacher poses a question, pauses, and then names the student who will respond. This approach encourages all students to engage with the question during the pause, knowing they could be selected. In contrast, when a teacher names a student before asking the question, others may disengage, assuming they won't be called upon.

Why has this approach become so popular? As Daniel Willingham (2009) puts it, "Memory is the residue of thought." We know that students are more likely to remember something if they have spent time thinking about it. By placing the student's name at the end of the question, teachers can encourage more students to engage, increasing the likelihood that they will retain the information.

This book does not aim to revisit cognitive science as a way of identifying effective teaching strategies—many excellent books already do this. Instead, I want to take a different approach.

Cold calling undoubtedly encourages students to think more deeply and strengthens their understanding of a subject. However, if we return to the scenarios in the introduction, we must ask: does it help create expert learners?

After all, in a university lecture, no one will be cold calling. A supervisor overseeing an apprentice plumber may not have a deep understanding of cognitive science to guide their learning.

If we want children to thrive beyond school, we need to bring them along on the journey of understanding how they learn best.

First, I want to start with the premise that learning is really hard. In the introduction, I defined learning as the process of acquiring knowledge or skills through study, experience, or instruction. However, there is a caveat to this—when I say acquire knowledge, I mean being able to recall it later by creating memories.

My seven-year-old daughter is currently learning about rocks in school. She came home and excitedly told me that some rocks are impermeable, meaning water cannot travel through them. She was delighted to use the word impermeable. However, being able to recall this a few hours after hearing it does not necessarily mean she has created a lasting memory that she will be able to use at a future point in time.

Educators have worked hard to address this challenge through carefully planned curricula that revisit key ideas, giving students opportunities to transfer knowledge to their long-term memory (LTM). They also use teaching techniques that encourage thinking, such as cold calling, whole class response, and retrieval practice.

Despite these efforts, ultimately a proportion of the success is down to the decisions that students make both in lessons and when completing homework or revising outside of school. There are many examples of poor decision-making; below are a few.

- A student deciding to copy either from the person next to them in class or copying statements for homework that they were asked to retrieve.
- A student giving up on their work in class because they find it too difficult.
- A student staring out the window when a teacher is introducing new knowledge.
- A student revising by creating flashy posters with lots of colour and fancy font.

If we want children to make better decisions, the first thing we need to do is help them understand why certain decisions are poor ones. To achieve this, the first step is to teach them about cognitive science.

So, where do we begin? I want to start with a quote I've already referenced: "Memory is the residue of thought." When reading Daniel Willingham's work, this phrase sparked a eureka moment for me, one that I hope students who directly or indirectly engage in this book will experience as well. To create lasting memories, we need to encourage students to engage deeply with what they are learning. The key takeaway here is that we want students to think, but what does that look like in practice? In the next chapter, we'll delve into this in more detail, but first, I want to step back and address an important point.

Before we establish a framework for teaching students how to think, we need to first convince them that thinking is a worthwhile endeavour. After all, we are asking students to think so they can create memories. In today's world, where AI is on the rise, it's more important than ever to emphasise that creating memories and retaining knowledge are valuable pursuits in their own right. The rest of this chapter will be dedicated to making this case.

Working Memory Is Limited

George Miller (1956) published a seminal paper in *Psychological Review* titled The Magical Number Seven, Plus or Minus Two: Some Limits on Our Capacity for Processing Information, in which he investigated the limited capacity of working memory (WM). Miller was captivated by what he called the "magical number 7," as evidenced by the striking opening lines of his paper:

> My problem is that I have been persecuted by an integer. For seven years this number has followed me around, has intruded in my most private data, and has assaulted me from the pages of our most public journals. This number assumes a variety of disguises, being sometimes a little larger and sometimes a little smaller than usual, but never changing so much as to be unrecognizable. The persistence with which this number plagues me is far more than a random accident. There is, to quote a famous senator, a design behind it, some pattern governing its appearances. Either there really is something unusual about the number or else I am suffering from delusions of persecution.
> (Miller, 1956, p. 81)

In his study, Miller investigated working memory capacity: how much information a person can remember before becoming overloaded. To do this, he gradually increased the number of letters presented to participants.

For example, participants were shown sequences like:

- A, J, R, M, B (five letters)
- T, F, S, C, Q, Z (six letters)
- P, R, S, W, B, L, X (seven letters)

The task was to repeat the letters back in the correct order before moving on to longer sequences. Miller found that the "magic number" for our brain's capacity in STM is about seven, plus or minus two. In other words, most people can manage between five and nine pieces of information, but anything beyond that starts to overwhelm WM.

I first encountered Miller's experiment during a presentation by Daisy Christodoulou. She asked everyone in the audience to try and remember a sequence of letters from her PowerPoint.

A, F, G, H, K, U, T, S, W, P, I, R, T, E, G

As expected, most participants remembered around the seven-letter range, though a few claimed to have remembered all 15.

Next, Daisy repeated the task, but this time she chunked the letters into three-letter words:

C, A, T   D, O, G   C, A, R   P, E, N   H, A, T

To no one's surprise, everyone remembered the full 15 letters. This is a great starting point to introduce students to the concept of the limits of working memory. However, I would modify the task slightly—not just to emphasise the limitations of working memory, but also to show that the more prior knowledge you have, the easier it becomes to retain new information.

Consider this set of acronyms:

B, R, B   L, O, L   F, Y, I   B, F, F   O, M, G

You could share this with a class of students or with your child as a parent reading this book ask them a follow-up question:

How Would Your Grandparents Do on This Test?

This question encourages students to think about the importance of prior knowledge. While students might recognise the acronyms as meaningful chunks, their grandparents may still see them as 15 random letters and struggle to remember them. Some grandparents might recognise a few acronyms, but overall, students with more familiarity would likely perform better. This task can be redesigned several ways to ensure it is age-appropriate.

MOB   ORE   TIN   ARC   NET   DIM

Would be much easier to recall by a student who likes the game Minecraft.

It's important to note that this doesn't mean students are "cleverer" than their grandparents. I use the term "clever" intentionally, as one of the goals of teaching cognitive science to students is to challenge preconceived notions. The point I want students to understand is that in this specific task, they perform better simply because they have more prior knowledge.

Why Do We Need to Remember?

In 2005, David Hambrick and Frederick Oswald carried out a study looking at baseball knowledge and working memory capacity. They wanted to find out how much knowing about a topic helps people understand new information. To do this, they first had to conduct a test to compare the working memory of the participants by measuring their working memory capacity (Hambrick & Oswald, 2005).

If you've read about the test before, you may have seen a simplification stating that they compared participants' reading age. The actual experiment used a test measuring reading span, which, although related to student comprehension, is more focused on working memory. The acronym task is a good starting point with students to help them understand that working memory is limited but can be expanded with prior knowledge. The reading span test is a more scientific approach that students could undertake to strengthen their belief in the limitations of working memory.

Below is an example of a trial that can be carried out by students either in class or at home.

Instructions for the Participant

In this task, you will read a series of sentences aloud. After each sentence, you will see a single word that you must remember. At the end of a set of sentences, I will ask you to recall all the words in the correct order. The number of sentences in each set will vary, so try your best to remember the words while also focusing on reading the sentences carefully.

Trial Example (Three-Sentence Set)

Step 1: Read Each Sentence Aloud

Sentence 1: "The boy kicked the ball across the field before running to his friend."
Remember this word: **Apple**
Sentence 2: "She was excited to see her grandparents, who had travelled from another country."
Remember this word: **Table**
Sentence 3: "The teacher asked the students to solve the difficult math problem on the board."
Remember this word: **Lamp**

Step 2: Recall the Words

"Now, tell me the words you just saw, in the correct order."
Correct Answer: Apple, Table, Lamp

Increasing Difficulty

The next set might contain four sentences (with four words to remember), and so on. The test continues until the participant can no longer reliably recall the words in order. The largest number of words they successfully remember in order gives their working memory capacity score.

Students will score lower in this test compared to the magic number seven referred to earlier in George Miller's experiment, but this provides a good discussion point with students.

Why is it that students can remember seven or eight random letters, but in the reading span test, they can only remember three or four? The answer lies in cognitive overload, a theory developed by John Sweller in the late 1980s. Sweller's Cognitive Load Theory (CLT) states that our working memory has limited capacity, and when it is overloaded with too much information, learning becomes less effective

In Miller's test, participants are asked to remember random digits, a task that primarily tests intrinsic load, or the inherent complexity of the material itself. The task demands a limited amount of cognitive resources, as the information is simple and familiar. However, in the reading span test, participants are required to process and store information simultaneously. This introduces extraneous load, as the need to understand the sentences while remembering unrelated words places additional demands on working memory. The sentences take up cognitive resources, leaving less capacity for the words.

To measure working memory capacity David Hambrick and Frederick Oswald also measured operation span. Below is an example of the test:

Trial Example (Three-Problem Set)

Step 1: Solve Each Math Problem and See a Word

Math Problem:
$(3 \times 2) + 1 = ?$
(Participant solves: 7)
Remember this word: **Dog**
Math Problem:
$(8 \div 2) + 3 = ?$
(Participant solves: 7)
Remember this word: **Chair**
Math Problem:
$(5 \times 2) - 4 = ?$
(Participant solves: 6)
Remember this word: **Apple**

Step 2: Recall the Words

"Now, tell me the words you just saw, in the correct order."
Correct Answer: Dog, Chair, Apple

Increasing Difficulty

The next set might contain four math problems (with four words to remember), and so on. The test continues until the participant can no longer reliably recall the words in order. The largest set they successfully recall in order determines their O-Span score.

After measuring working memory capacity, David Hambrick and Frederick Oswald had participants listen to a fake baseball match. The broadcast was designed to include lots of domain-specific terms, such as.

WHIP, Pitcher's Mound, Double Play, Pickoff, Bullpen, Sacrifice Bunt

The results were clear: they showed that knowledge of specific baseball terminology was more important than the measured working memory capacity of the participants. In simple terms, participants with high baseball knowledge and low working memory capacity outperformed those with higher working memory capacity but little to no knowledge of baseball.

Why Is This Important?

This study is an important building block for teaching students about cognitive science. Many students say that school feels hard or that they struggle to learn, but these findings can help challenge that belief. Research shows that working memory has a limited capacity, and when it comes to memorising random words or numbers, most people perform similarly. In other words, students start from a fairly equal baseline. So why do some perform better in school than others? The difference isn't in how much they can remember in the moment, but in how well they can retain and build on that knowledge over time. Once students begin to develop memory in a particular area, it becomes easier to learn more in that domain—prior knowledge makes new learning stick more effectively. For example, if you taught a lesson next week on football tactics or the history of dance, students who already play football or dance would likely remember more. Their existing knowledge makes it easier to absorb and connect new information.

Why Is Remembering So Hard?

Once it has been established with students that working memory is limited, we can introduce the idea of LTM. Understanding the complexity of LTM gives them the foundation they need to make better decisions and, over time, to develop more effective learning habits. Some key questions that will need to be addressed are:

- If working memory is limited, where do we store information?
- Why do I sometimes forget things I've tried to remember?
- What can we do to ensure information is retained?

If working memory is limited, where do we store information?

14 Learning Habits

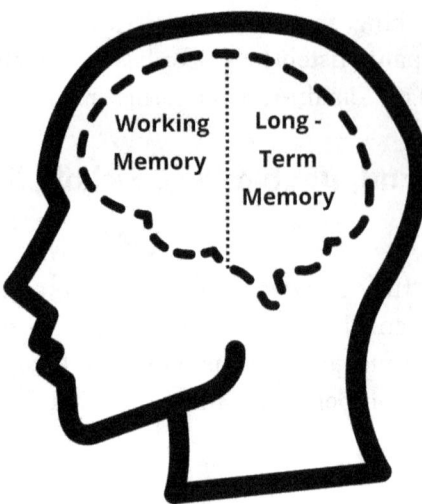

Figure 1.1 Working memory and long-term memory have different functions in the brain

In 1962, Murdoch's free recall experiment provided key insights into the idea that there are two distinct memory systems (Murdock, 1962) (Figure 1.1).

Building on George Miller's work, Murdoch's experiment focused on recalling a series of words. However, instead of simply counting how many words were remembered, Murdoch wanted to understand which words were more likely to be recalled.

Participants were shown a list of 15 words, one by one, at a rate of about one word per second. For example:

List of Words

Cat
House
Lamp
Ball
Flower
Car
Book
Dog
Tree
Pen
Chair
Bird
Shirt
Table
Phone

Task: After the list was shown, participants were asked to recall the words in any order.

> **Results**
>
> - Participants were most likely to recall words presented at the beginning of the list.
> - Words at the end of the list were also more likely to be remembered.
> - Words in the middle of the list were the least likely to be recalled.

Given how similar this experiment is to George Miller's work (Miller, 1956), running it with students might feel tedious. Instead, you could have them hypothesise why the results turned out the way they did. This task might be challenging for beginners with little understanding of cognitive science, but providing some guiding questions can help them make connections.

Guiding Questions Could Include

- What makes the first word easier to remember after repeating it over time?
- Why is the last word more likely to be remembered after practicing?

If we focus on the last word first, this can be explained by the *recency effect*—because the last word is the most recent one seen, it is more likely to still be in working memory. The first word, however, is remembered for a different reason. Knowing that working memory has a limited capacity (around seven items; Miller, 1956), why is it that the first word is remembered, even though it was likely read out before 14 others? This happens because of *rehearsal*. As participants rehearse the list, the first word gets repeated more often, strengthening its presence in memory. A likely pattern is that they rehearse in chunks, such as:

Cat
Cat, House
Cat, House, Lamp
And so on…

Murdoch's work laid the groundwork for further developments by Atkinson and Shiffrin (1968), who proposed the concept of STM and LTM:

- **Short-term memory** has limited capacity and duration.

- **Long-term memory** stores information for much longer periods of time.

Atkinson and Shiffrin's model suggested that rehearsal helps transfer information from STM to LTM.

An important follow-up study by Glanzer and Cunitz (1966) explored interference and delay, demonstrating the disappearance of the recency effect. They modified Murdoch's free recall experiment by introducing a delay before participants after they had seen all of the words. In one version of the experiment, participants had to count backward for 30 seconds after recalling the words. As a result, they were no longer able to remember the last few words.

This demonstrated that information in STM is temporary and fragile—if not rehearsed, it fades within 15–30 seconds. However, participants were still able to recall the earlier words, highlighting the important role of rehearsal in transferring information to LTM.

> Why do you sometimes forget things i have tried to remember?

I can remember that the Battle of Hastings took place in 1066—something I must have learned in a history lesson over 25 years ago. Yet beyond that, my memories of studying history are vague, except for recollecting that we covered the Tudors for some time—though even those details have faded.

In contrast, I can recall the entire starting lineup of my favourite football team, Cardiff City, from their promotion into England's second division in 1993. I can also recite the lyrics to countless songs spanning the last four decades. But despite being reminded every year, I'm ashamed to admit that I don't know my mother's birthday and would struggle to remember what I had for breakfast on any given day two weeks ago.

This kind of forgetfulness is familiar to every student. Everyone has at some point had an experience where we felt completely engaged in something, only to struggle to recall key details later. I use "engaged" deliberately, as students often interpret this word in different ways.

After exploring the experiments discussed so far in this book, students should begin to form two key principles about how we learn and remember:

1. Prior knowledge helps us learn new information more easily.

2. Rehearsal strengthens memory and boosts long-term retention.

In the short term, these insights might encourage students to practise revision strategies like retrieval practice (strategy that involves actively recalling information from memory) more frequently outside of lessons, helping them become more effective learners. However, in later chapters, I'll explore why motivation alone isn't enough—and discuss strategies to help students sustain their motivation and develop better learning habits.

For now, the focus is on what it truly means to be engaged in the process of learning.

A common reason we forget things is that we simply weren't thinking about them in the first place. To illustrate this, consider how easy it is to misplace a mobile phone. If your goal of reading this book is to support younger primary students, you might swap this example for a favourite toy, but the principle remains the same.

> Sarah walked into her house while listening to a voice note from a friend. The message was a helpful reminder that tomorrow was a non-uniform day—useful information, but not something she had been thinking about at that moment. Her mind was already busy with the pile of homework waiting for her that evening.
>
> As she walked into the kitchen to grab a drink, Sarah put her phone down on the counter without really noticing. Then she headed upstairs. She had planned to get started on her homework right away, but instead, she got distracted by thinking about what to wear for non-uniform day. Half an hour later, after finally choosing an outfit, she reached for her phone to check her homework—but realised she had no idea where she'd left it.
>
> Trying to remember, she looked around her room. A cup on her desk reminded her that she'd been in the kitchen earlier. So she retraced her steps and found her phone on the kitchen counter.
>
> Now, think about what was happening in Sarah's mind during all of this. At first, she was listening to her friend's message while also thinking about homework. Then, without much conscious thought, she grabbed a drink. Her attention shifted again—this time to planning her outfit—and only later returned to the idea of doing homework.
>
> But there was one thing she never thought about at all: her phone.

"Memory is the residue of thought." I'll keep returning to this idea because it's fundamental in helping students make better decisions about learning.

Since Sarah never consciously thought about where she put her phone, her brain treated it as unimportant. To most students, this seems absurd—their phone is one of their most prized possessions. How could they forget it? But in that moment, it wasn't a priority. Because Sarah never paid attention to where she placed it, her brain didn't store that information.

Notice that when retracing steps, I suggested the cup left on the desk served as a reminder of going to the kitchen. In the scenario, I deliberately wrote, "without really thinking about it, Sarah grabbed a drink." This was a conscious choice to emphasise that the action wasn't actively considered at the time.

A surefire way to forget something is to not think about it at all. However, thinking is hard work. Just like lifting weights at the gym, constantly thinking about things can be exhausting. To compensate for this, our brain operates using two separate systems—System 1 and System 2. This idea was popularised by Daniel (Kahneman 2011), who described these systems as fast thinking and slow thinking.

Fast thinking is a mental shortcut that allows us to process information quickly and efficiently. It is necessary to prevent us from becoming mentally exhausted by every small decision.

To illustrate this, consider the experience of driving home from work. On a normal commute, there are times when you arrive home and barely remember the journey at all. This is the work of fast thinking—familiar cues allow your brain to take mental shortcuts, guiding you home with little conscious effort.

Now compare this to a time when roadworks forced you to take a detour. Suddenly, you are more alert, watching the road ahead, checking for speed signs, and scanning for potential hazards from side streets. This is slow thinking—you are actively processing each step of the journey. Unlike your normal commute, the detour is a journey you are likely to remember, probably even recalling specific turns and landmarks.

Why is this?

During fast thinking, you are not using your working memory at all. And if you're not engaging working memory, you cannot transfer information to LTM.

In the earlier example, getting a drink from the kitchen may have been an instance of fast thinking. Perhaps there was a cue—a dry throat, for example—that prompted them to get a drink. But the thought "I am thirsty" never even entered their mind. Instead, fast thinking created a mental shortcut, leading them to grab a drink without actively considering the action.

Fast thinking doesn't just make it harder to remember things later—it also plays a critical role in learning because it is prone to biases that can lead to poor decision-making. This is a crucial point. I will discuss in more detail in the next chapter. I will explore the impact of fast thinking on decision-making and how we can overcome the challenges it presents.

One of the most compelling demonstrations to share with students—showing that *how hard you think about something* impacts the likelihood of remembering it—comes from Craik and Tulving (1975), whose research on levels of processing provides clear evidence that the depth of thinking determines memory retention.

In their study, participants were shown a series of words and asked different types of questions, each requiring a different level of cognitive processing:

- **Shallow Processing**
  - **Question:** Is the word in capital letters?
  - **Example Word:** "TABLE"
  - **Answer:** "Yes"

- **Intermediate Processing**
  - **Question:** Does the word rhyme with "cat"?
  - **Example Word:** "HAT"
  - **Answer:** "Yes"

- **Deep Processing**
  - **Question:** Does the word fit into this sentence: "The ____ is a type of fruit"?
  - **Example Word:** "APPLE"
  - **Answer:** "Yes"

After this phase, participants were given a surprise memory test to assess how many words they could recall. The results revealed that the deeper the level of processing—particularly when words were linked to meaning—the better the recall. This highlights that memory is strengthened through meaningful engagement rather than passive exposure.

Another key factor influencing memory is the focus of our attention during learning. The classic study by Anderson and Pichert (1978) demonstrates how our perspective shapes what we remember. Participants recalled different details from the same story depending on the role or perspective they had been assigned (e.g., homebuyer vs. burglar). This is an experiment that students can experience firsthand, making it a powerful and memorable demonstration that what we think about determines what we remember.

Part 1: The Story

Students are presented with the following story:

A couple of teenagers decide to explore an old house that is rumored to be haunted. The house has a large garden with a crumbling stone wall and a rusty iron gate. They notice an old oak tree with a tire swing hanging from one of its branches. As they enter, they first observe a large living room with an old-fashioned fireplace and dusty furniture. In one corner, there's a grand piano that looks like it hasn't been played in years.

As they move through the house, they find broken windows and peeling wallpaper. Eventually, they discover a hidden staircase leading to the attic. Inside, there are boxes of old books, a collection of antique clocks, and some forgotten family portraits. In one corner, they spot a dusty old chest with a locked lid. Just as they decide to leave, they catch a glimpse of a shadowy figure in the window.

Part 2: Assigning Perspectives

Students are divided into two groups, each given a specific perspective:

- Burglar Perspective—This group focuses on details useful to a burglar, such as valuables, access points, and hiding spots. They might note:
  - Valuable items (e.g., the grand piano, antique clocks, family portraits).
  - Entry points (e.g., broken windows, hidden staircase, rusty gate).
- Homebuyer Perspective—This group considers the house's condition and features relevant to a buyer. They might focus on:
  - The state of the house (e.g., broken windows, peeling wallpaper).
  - Features that affect value (e.g., the old fireplace, attic, large garden, grand piano).

> **Part 3: First Retrieval Quiz**
>
> After reading the story, students recall as many details as possible from their assigned perspective. Their memories will align with what was most relevant to their viewpoint:
>
> - Burglar group recalls valuables and access points ("There was a piano," "The attic had old clocks," "There was a broken window").
> - Homebuyer group recalls structural details ("The wallpaper was peeling," "The house had a big garden," "The fireplace was old and dusty").
>
> **Part 4: Shifting Perspectives**
>
> Next, students switch perspectives:
>
> - The burglar group now adopts the homebuyer perspective.
> - The homebuyer group now adopts the burglar perspective.
>
> They then attempt to recall the details of the house again, but from their new perspective.
>
> **Part 5: Second Retrieval Quiz**
>
> Students will notice that they now recall different details, ones that they hadn't focused on during the first quiz. This shift highlights a crucial lesson:
>
> > What we think about determines what we remember.

Key Takeaways

This experiment illustrates that memory is not just about exposure to information but about what we actively think about at the time of learning. Students should understand:

1. Thinking carefully about important information is essential—To remember something later, they need to process it deeply at the time of learning.
2. Focusing on meaningful details enhances recall—By directing attention to key elements, they can improve what they remember over time.
3. They haven't "learned" anything yet—The information isn't stored in LTM just because they were exposed to it. This would be evident if you asked students to recall elements of the story in a week.

Why Students Forget—And What We Can Do About It?

Even when students think hard about something, there's no guarantee they'll remember it forever. One of the most influential insights into how memory works comes from Hermann Ebbinghaus (Ebbinghaus, 1913), a pioneering psychologist who was the first to systematically study forgetting. His research gave us the concept of the *Forgetting Curve*—a visual representation of how quickly information fades from memory if it's not revisited.

Ebbinghaus found that shortly after we learn something, our ability to recall it drops sharply. Within just 24 hours, a significant portion can be lost. After about a week, people typically remember only 20%–30% of what they initially learned. Without review or reinforcement, most of what we learn is forgotten.

This has clear implications for learning in school. If we want students to retain important knowledge, we must help them actively counteract the natural decline of memory. Research shows that students are far more likely to use effective learning strategies when they understand *why* those strategies matter and how they support memory and learning (Bjork et al., 2013). Understanding begins with explicitly teaching students how memory works—and showing them that learning is not a one-off event but a process that strengthens through deliberate practice and revisiting over time.

Strengthening Memory

When we learn something new, the brain forms fresh neural connections. These connections are fragile at first—easily broken and easily forgotten. But every time we recall that information, the connections are reactivated and strengthened.

Think of it like walking a path through a field. The first time you walk it, the grass is tall and the route is unclear. But the more often you walk the same path, the more defined it becomes. Over time, it turns into a well-worn track. Memory works the same way: the more we revisit information, the stronger and more permanent it becomes.

Crucially, the real benefits come not from reviewing material immediately after learning it, but from revisiting it after some time has passed. When the brain has to work to retrieve a memory, that effort helps it stick. Repetition, then, isn't just about doing something again—it's about training the brain to *remember.*

This is why many schools now use the term *retrieval practice* to describe the process of consolidating knowledge. The aim is to strengthen memory by repeatedly pulling information from long-term storage and making it accessible when needed.

Schemas

British psychologist Frederic Bartlett introduced the concept of schemas to explain how people make sense of new information based on what they already know. He believed that memory is not a perfect recording of events but a process of reconstruction influenced by our existing knowledge, experiences, and cultural background. When we encounter something unfamiliar, we unconsciously use schemas—mental frameworks built from past experiences—to interpret and remember it. Bartlett's experiments, such as the *War of the Ghosts* study, demonstrated how memory is not a perfect record of events but rather a reconstructive process influenced by our existing knowledge and beliefs. In this study, participants were asked to read a Native American folk tale filled with unfamiliar cultural elements and then recall the story after various intervals. Bartlett found that people often changed or distorted details in the story to make it more familiar or logical to their own experiences and cultural background. For example, they might omit strange or confusing parts, simplify complex details, or alter events to better fit their expectations. This revealed the powerful role that schemas—mental frameworks built from prior knowledge—play in shaping how we remember and understand new information (Bartlett, 1932).

Below is a story similar in style to the *War of the Ghosts* study, in that it contains information that may be unfamiliar to many students.

The Crystal Feather

One evening, a traveller wandered into the mountain village of Eridu. The people there warned him not to stay past sunset, for that was when the Sky Birds returned to the cliffs with their crystal feathers.

But the traveller was curious and stayed. As night fell, he saw glowing birds descend from the sky, their feathers shining like glass. One of the birds dropped a crystal feather near him, and he picked it up.

Suddenly, his vision blurred. He saw distant cities made of wind, voices calling his name, and rivers flowing uphill. The villagers found him the next morning, lying quietly by the cliffs, the feather gone.

He never spoke again, but sometimes he pointed to the sky and smiled.

Instructions

The instructions below are for groups of students, but it could also be completed by one student in a mentoring session in school or at home.

1. Place the students into small groups.
2. Give the story to one student to read silently.
3. Have that student then retell the story to another student in their own words.
4. Keep passing the story along to each member of the group.
5. Have the final student write down the story.
6. Compare the final version with the original.

> **Discussion**
> 1. What details were added, changed, or removed?
> 2. How did the students' own knowledge or culture influence the changes?
> 3. What does this tell us about how memory works?

Some Examples of What Might Be Different and Why

Unfamiliar Elements Simplified or Replaced

- "Sky Birds" might become more familiar creatures like owls, eagles, or simply "birds."
- "Crystal feathers" might turn into shiny feathers, magic feathers, or glowing feathers—depending on what the child associates with crystals (e.g., fairy tales or cartoons).
- "Cities made of wind" might be omitted, misunderstood, or transformed into something more concrete, like castles in the clouds or invisible cities.

Ambiguity Made Logical

- Participants might add explanations that were not in the original story:
  - Why did the birds come at night? ("They were magical" or "They protected something.")
  - Why did he go silent? ("He was cursed" or "He saw something scary.")
- Children tend to seek cause and effect, adding motives or outcomes to make the story more coherent.

Modern or Familiar Vocabulary Substituted or Removed

- "Traveller" might become man, boy, explorer, or even tourist.
- "Mountain village of Eridu" might be shortened simply to "village."

Simplification of Structure

- The story often becomes shorter and more streamlined.
- Minor details, like warnings or villagers, may be dropped.
- The structure may shift to a more familiar narrative arc with a clear beginning, middle, and end.

Cultural Insertions or Personal References

- For example, the man might be described as dreaming instead of having a vision—something more relatable to the listener's own experience.

The Importance of Schemas

Schemas play a central role in learning because they help students organise, interpret, and store new information. Think of schemas as mental "filing systems" that learners use to make sense of the world. They allow students to connect new knowledge to what they already know. If a student is learning about volcanoes and already has a schema for "mountains," they can use that prior understanding to grasp the idea of a volcanic eruption. Revisiting the baseball study, the more knowledge you have, the easier it is to learn new knowledge, a child without knowledge of mountains, or has never seen one before would have greater difficulty understanding what a volcano is. But the connection between new and preexisting knowledge strengths the understanding of both mountains and volcanoes (Figure 1.2).

This bridging of the known and unknown makes learning smoother. Learning isn't just about adding facts—it's about restructuring and expanding schemas. As students encounter more examples or deeper explanations, their schemas become more detailed and flexible. For example, a young child's schema for "animal" might start with just "dog" or "cat," but over time it grows to include mammals, reptiles, classifications, and ecosystems (Figure 1.3).

Another psychologist Piaget suggested that schemas develop through two key processes: assimilation and accommodation. When Piaget first began studying how children think, he had a unique advantage: his own children. Piaget didn't just write about theories from a distance—he observed firsthand how his children grew and learned. His home became his laboratory, and his children, Lucienne, Jacqueline, and Laurent, were his "case studies" (Piaget, 1952).

One of the most striking things Piaget noticed was how his children learned to make sense of the world around them, starting from a very young age. For example,

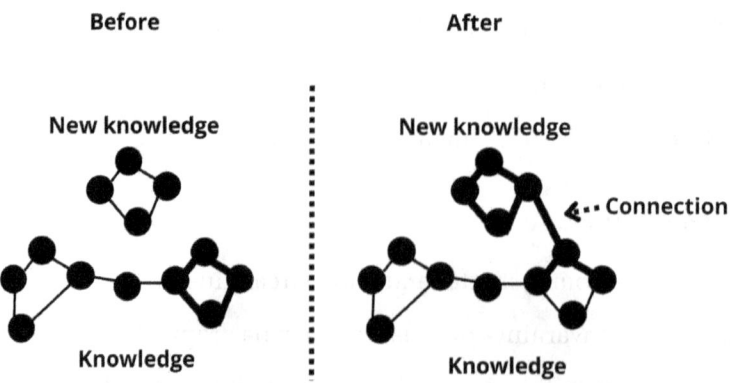

Figure 1.2 A model of a schema illustrating how new knowledge links to prior knowledge

Evolving Schema

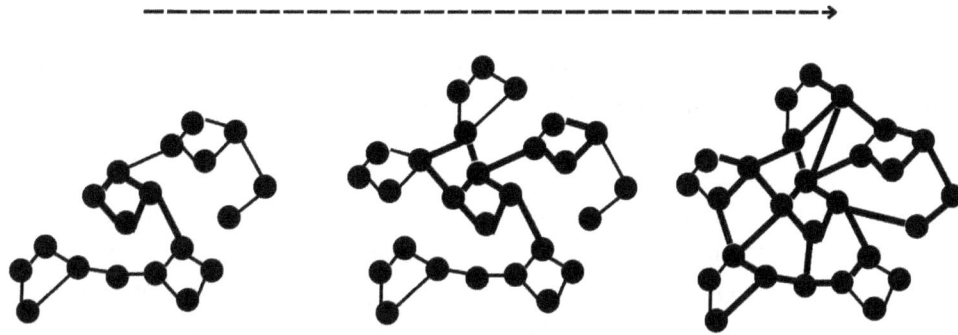

Figure 1.3 A model showing how a schema can develop and expand over time

when his infant daughter, Lucienne, first discovered a toy, she reached out to grab it with her tiny hands. This simple action marked the beginning of a process that Piaget would later call assimilation—fitting new experiences into the mental frameworks (schemas) she already had.

At first, Lucienne tried to squeeze the toy, as if it were a soft object she was used to holding. But when the toy didn't give in the way she expected, she was faced with a problem. Instead of giving up, Lucienne adjusted her approach. She started banging the toy on the floor, discovering that it made a noise. Through this change in behaviour, Piaget saw accommodation in action: Lucienne had altered her existing schema (a soft, squeezable toy) to incorporate this new object into her understanding of the world (a hard, noise-making object).

As Lucienne grew, Piaget observed her interactions with other objects. Each new toy or challenge led her to either assimilate it into what she already knew or accommodate her thinking when it didn't fit. This process of balancing the two—assimilation and accommodation—was Piaget's key to understanding how children's minds develop, and he called this process equilibration.

In conclusion

Assimilation

- When we encounter something new, we try to fit it into an existing schema.
- Example: A child sees a zebra for the first time and calls it a "horse"—they are assimilating it into their schema for "horse."

Accommodation

- When the new information doesn't quite fit, we adjust or create a new schema.
- Example: The child learns that a zebra has stripes and isn't the same as a horse. They adjust their schema to accommodate this new animal.

Equilibration

- This is the process of balancing assimilation and accommodation to create stable understanding. Piaget believed learning happens best when we're slightly "off balance" (in cognitive conflict) and then reorganise our thinking.

As evidence-informed practice has developed in the United Kingdom, educators have adjusted their curriculums to ensure that the idea of schemas is incorporated with the goal of making it easier for students to assimilate and accommodate new information. However, the explicit teaching of schemas to students has a key benefit to help students have a better understanding of how to organise their ideas.

In order to support students with their schemas it is common for schools to have some kind of advanced organiser, first introduced by David Ausubel in the 1960s. It is used before new learning begins to help students connect new information to their existing knowledge. The advance organiser provides a framework or overview of key concepts, terms, and ideas that will be explored in a lesson. By offering this structure upfront, advance organisers help activate prior knowledge, reduce cognitive load, and make it easier for students to integrate new material meaningfully (Ausubel, 1960).

In the 1980s, Joseph Novak developed the idea of concept mapping as a way for learners to organise their ideas after learning has taken place. His approach was strongly influenced by David Ausubel's theory of meaningful learning and his use of advance organisers (Novak & Gowin, 1984). In a concept map, ideas are placed in nodes—usually boxes or circles—and connected by lines with linking phrases that describe the relationship between them. This visual layout helps learners clarify their understanding by showing how different concepts relate to one another.

What is important to note, however, is that not all concept maps are created equal, and this is where an understanding of schemas is important. In order to make sense of new knowledge you must place it within an existing schema. What the image shows (Figure 1.4) is that these connections are not all straight lines. In order to increase the chances of retrieving this new information at some point in the future, you need to organise it in the easiest way possible.

A simple analogy would be a supermarket owner deciding to move bananas and apricots from the fruit and veg aisle and swap them with chicken from the meat section. Your chances of finding the bananas initially are reduced, as they're no longer where you expected them to be. Then, if you return to the supermarket four weeks later, your chances of locating them again are not much higher compared to if they had just remained in the fruit and veg aisle all along.

I've experienced this kind of frustration myself. My youngest daughter is a fussy eater, but one of the few snacks she enjoys—and that isn't as unhealthy as many of her other preferences—is rice cakes. The problem is that supermarkets can't seem to agree on where rice cakes belong. We don't always shop at the same store, so depending on what we're doing that day, we might end up in several different

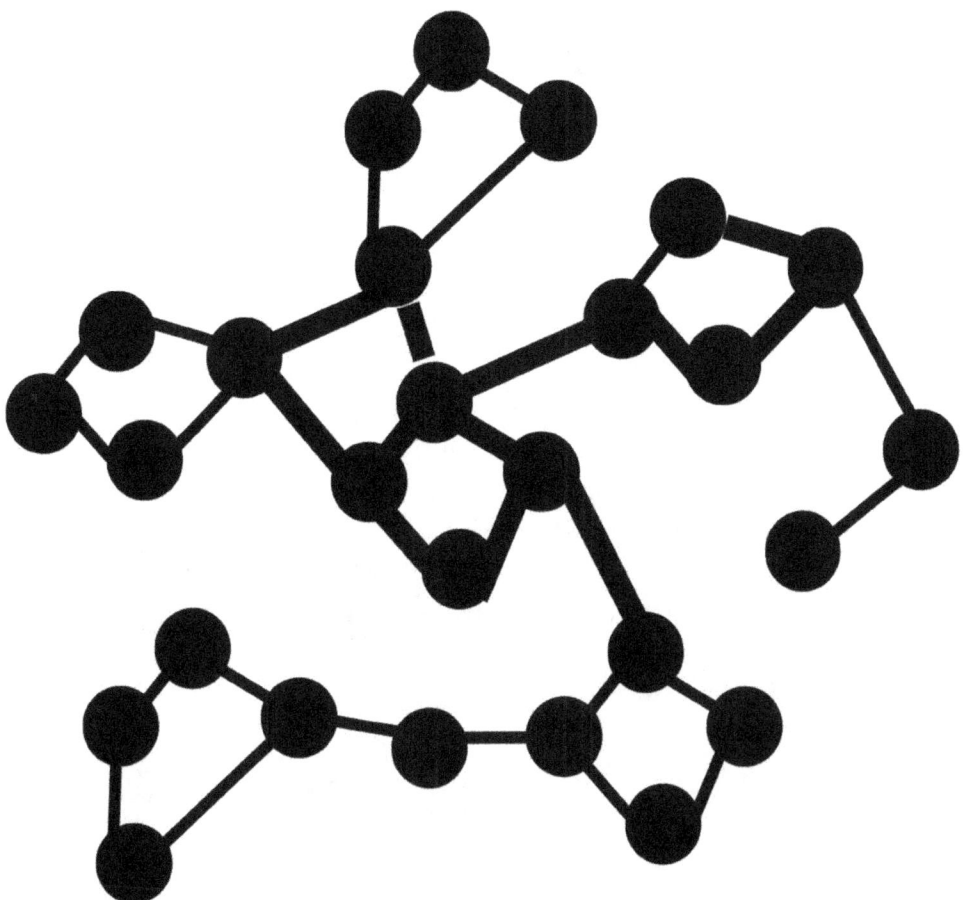

Figure 1.4 Model of a complex schema

ones. And in each, the rice cakes are often placed in completely different sections. Some put them with the cereal, others with the crisps, and some even with the chocolate snacks. Even when I return to the same supermarket, weeks may have passed—I rarely remember where they were last time.

So, when students are creating concept maps, they must consider the easiest way to both help it connect to new knowledge and be able to retrieve it later.

If students are studying the history of events in World War II, creating a timeline is often more effective than using a mind map, as it clearly shows events in chronological order (Figure 1.5).

However, when dealing with concepts that have a clear hierarchical structure, such as the three ideas in my book—learning, thinking, and habits—a tree diagram is a better option than a mind map (Figure 1.6).

For comparisons, like the characteristics of the Capulets and Montagues in *Romeo and Juliet*, a Venn diagram would be more suitable, as it helps illustrate the overlapping traits of the two families (Figure 1.7).

28 Learning Habits

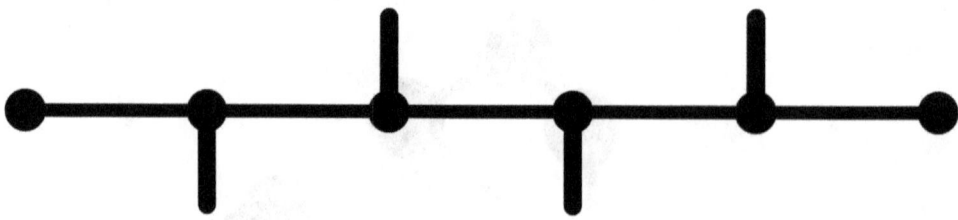

Figure 1.5 Timeline

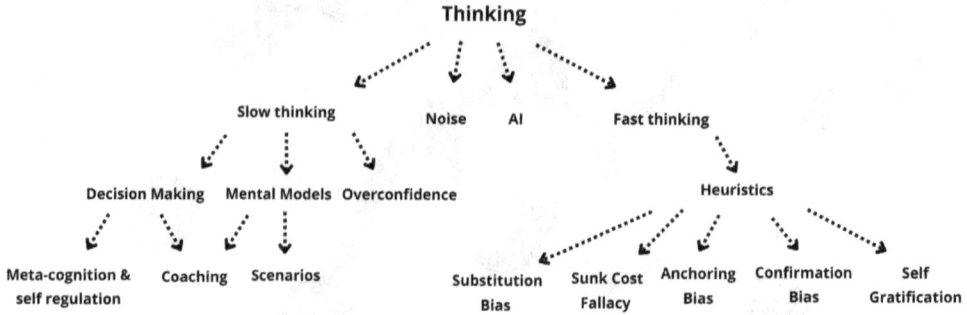

Figure 1.6 Tree diagram

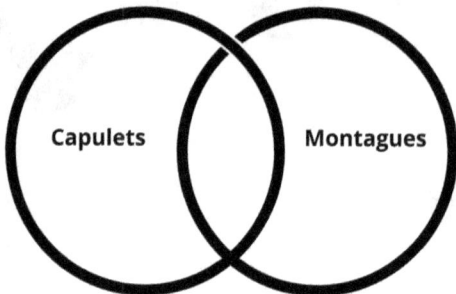

Figure 1.7 Venn diagram

A study that solidifies the importance of schema is an experiment by psychologists Ericsson et al. (1993) on expertise and memory, involving chess players. In the study, grandmasters (highly skilled chess players) were shown a chessboard with pieces arranged in a realistic game position (i.e., positions that could naturally occur during an actual game). The grandmasters were able to recall the positions of the pieces much better than novice players or intermediate players. They were able to remember and recreate the board with impressive accuracy.

However, when the pieces were randomly placed on the board (in a non-playable style), the grandmasters' performance significantly dropped. They struggled to remember where each piece was, and their recall was no better than that of intermediate or novice players.

Just as the chess grandmasters couldn't recall random chess pieces effectively, students who create concept maps with disjointed information may find it harder to make connections between ideas, because their mental map lacks structure and coherence.

A simple way to show the importance of schema to students is to get them to complete the following task:

Procedure

1. Split the class into two groups (Group A and Group B). If working on their own a student can complete both stories starting with story B.

2. Give Group A the version with the schema (Story A), and Group B the ambiguous version (Story B).

Story A—With Schema (Title: "Escape from Dunkirk")

In May 1940, thousands of British and Allied troops were trapped on the beaches of Dunkirk, surrounded by German forces. With their backs to the sea and nowhere to retreat, a massive evacuation was launched. Naval ships and hundreds of civilian boats crossed the English Channel under fire to rescue the stranded soldiers. Despite constant attacks from the air and sea, around 338,000 troops were brought back to Britain in what became known as the "Miracle of Dunkirk."

Story B—Without Schema (No Title, No Proper Nouns, No Historical Cues)

For several days, large groups of people waited on a long stretch of sand, unable to move forward and surrounded by danger. Some sat, some stood, all exposed to threats from above and around. Eventually, vessels of all kinds began arriving—large and small—risking everything to carry people away across the water. Explosions sounded in the distance, and the skies were rarely clear, but many made it out. The memory of that escape would be spoken of for years to come.

1. Ask them to read the story once, then immediately write down everything they remember about it (no re-reading).

2. After five to seven minutes, discuss:

   a. What do you think the story was about?

   b. How easy was it to remember the events?

   c. Were there any parts that were confusing?

Students could then create two versions of a concept map from the two stories.

Desirable Difficulties Dilemma

We often assume that students avoid difficulty, but that's not quite accurate. People regularly choose to engage with mentally demanding tasks—not because they're easy, but because they offer the right kind of challenge. Take Sudoku, for example. It starts with a few numbers on a grid and asks you to use logic and deduction to complete the puzzle. There's no shortcut. You must think carefully, test ideas, revise your approach, and hold multiple possibilities in your mind. And yet millions of people play it daily—not for a prize, but for the satisfaction of working something out. The enjoyment doesn't come from speed or ease; it comes from the moment of insight when a tough puzzle finally clicks into place. That small victory feels earned, and the struggle leading up to it only makes the reward sweeter. This same pattern shows up when someone finishes a tricky jigsaw, beats a difficult video game level, or cracks a riddle that's been bothering them all day. These tasks are enjoyable not despite the difficulty, but because of it—if the person feels the challenge is achievable. We crave that feeling of progress after effort. The struggle is motivating when it leads somewhere and when we feel we're growing because of it.

But here's the paradox: the very things that help students remember information in the long term—deep thinking, effortful processing, and sustained attention—are often the things they instinctively resist. Why? Because they're hard, and the benefits are not immediately visible. This brings us to a powerful idea from the work of Robert Bjork: desirable difficulty.

Bjork (1994) coined this term to describe the kinds of learning challenges that feel effortful in the moment but ultimately lead to stronger, more durable memory traces. Strategies such as retrieving information from memory, spacing out practice, or interleaving different types of problems all introduce a degree of struggle. They make learning feel slower, less fluent, and more mentally taxing. But crucially, these difficulties enhance long-term retention and transfer—they work precisely *because* they're challenging.

This runs counter to how students often judge their own learning. When something feels easy—like re-reading notes or watching a teacher explain something clearly—they assume they've learned it. When it feels difficult—like trying to recall something without prompts or applying knowledge in a new context—they assume they're failing. The struggle is a sign that their brain is working harder to encode and retrieve the information, which makes it more likely to stick.

The problem is that desirable difficulties don't feel desirable at all—at least not in the moment. Students may avoid them because they associate ease with progress and effort with failure. Even teachers can be tempted to smooth over these challenges to keep learners comfortable. But comfort doesn't lead to growth. If we want students to remember and apply what they learn, we must help them embrace the productive struggle that comes with real learning.

A relatable example for students is the story of Jessie Diggins.

The following story is a narrative interpretation inspired by the public experiences of Jessie Diggins, the most decorated cross-country skier in U.S. history. While the details are adapted for illustrative purposes, they reflect the challenges and growth she has spoken about in interviews. Her journey aligns with what psychologists describe as *desirable difficulty*—the idea that long-term learning is often best supported by strategies that feel harder in the short term (Bjork, 1994).

Jessie Diggins: The Power of Struggling to Grow

Jessie Diggins, the most decorated cross-country skier in U.S. history, has always believed that real success comes from the process, not the performance. The shiny medals and photo finishes came later. What built her into a world champion were the invisible choices—the ones that demanded patience, discomfort, and long-term thinking.

In her early training, Jessie often fell into the same trap many students do: the urge to *look good* now. When learning a new skiing technique or preparing a race strategy, it was tempting to run through it again and again in one intense session—until it *felt* smooth. Her movements looked sharp. Her pace was consistent. It gave the impression that she'd mastered it.

But the next day? It was as if that progress had vanished. Timing was off. Transitions felt clunky. Her skis didn't glide like they had the day before. The hours she'd poured in hadn't stuck.

Her coach saw the problem: she was cramming. Just like students who rewrite notes or re-read textbooks thinking they're learning—she was going through the motions, not building deep memory or reliable technique. It looked like learning, but it was only performance.

So, they changed approach. Instead of rehearsing the whole routine in one go, Jessie began breaking it into small chunks, practiced deliberately over time. She revisited technique drills she'd done as a teenager. She would slow things down, walk through each phase mentally, and challenge herself to recall the right movements cold—without a warm-up or repetition leading into it. It felt harder. Slower. Less satisfying in the moment.

But that difficulty was the point.

Over time, those small, effortful steps laid a foundation that stuck. Her skiing became more automatic under pressure. Her recovery time shrank.

This shift mirrored a deeper transformation happening in her life. Jessie has spoken openly about her battle with bulimia, and how for a long time, she sought control and immediate results—just like she once did in training. But it was only through sustained effort, through building small, healthy habits over time, that she truly began to heal. Quick fixes never lasted. Deep, sometimes painful work did.

Jessie's journey shows what psychologists call desirable difficulty—the idea that learning and growth often feel harder in the moment but result in longer-lasting

> progress. Whether in sports or study, what feels easy often doesn't stick. What challenges you is what shapes you.
>
> Her story is a reminder: looking polished today doesn't mean you'll be ready tomorrow. But if you're willing to slow down, embrace the struggle, and do the hard things now, the results will come—and they'll last.

Reflective Questions

1. Can you think of a time you gave up on something—even though you knew it would be useful if you stuck with it?

2. Some strategies, like cramming, re-reading, or copying notes, might *feel* helpful—but they often don't lead to real learning. What harder, more effective strategies could you try instead?

Encouraging students to embrace desirable difficulty needs to start early—well before the summative years of their education. By that point, poor habits are often already in place, and changing them requires significant effort and motivation.

This matters because when learning feels hard, the brain's instinct is to avoid it. In Chapter 3, we'll explore why ineffective habits are often more appealing, and what we can do to overcome them. But prevention is always better than cure. If we want students to revise effectively later, we need to help them build strong habits before the poor ones take hold.

The following table outlines strategies that introduce desirable difficulty. The goal of this book isn't to persuade you of their effectiveness—that has already been well established in research. Instead, the aim is to present them in a way that helps students understand *why* they matter and how they can support long-term learning.

Strategy	How It Works	Why Is It Effective
Spaced Repetition—is the practice of reviewing information at increasing intervals over time, rather than cramming it all at once.	Instead of studying a topic once and moving on, students revisit it: • Shortly after first learning it (e.g., same day) • Then again a day or two later • Then a few days or a week after that • Then again at longer intervals (e.g., two weeks, a month)	Each time the brain has to retrieve the information, it works a little harder—which strengthens the memory. Repeated effortful recall at spaced intervals turns weak, short-term memories into durable, long-term ones.

(Continued)

Strategy	How It Works	Why Is It Effective

Retrieval Practice—involves actively recalling information from memory—*without* looking at notes or textbooks. It's about testing what you know, not reviewing what you've already seen.	Flashcards
	1. Start with Box 1: All cards begin here.
	2. Quiz yourself:
	   a. If you get a card right, move it to Box 2.
	   b. If you get it wrong, it stays in Box 1.
	3. Review at intervals:
	   a. Box 1: every day
	   b. Box 2: every two days
	   c. Box 3: every four days, and so on
	4. If a card in a higher box is answered incorrectly, it returns to Box 1.
	5. Repeat: Over time, correct answers move further apart, while weaker material gets more frequent practice.
	
	Blurting
	1. After studying a topic, students try to "blurt out" everything they remember—by writing or saying it aloud.
	2. They do this quickly, without worrying about mistakes, to force their brain to actively retrieve.
	3. Then they check their notes and identify gaps or inaccuracies.
		It mirrors real-life situations like exams, where knowledge must be retrieved under pressure.
		It interrupts forgetting and helps move knowledge from short-term to long-term memory.

Interleaving—means mixing up topics within the same subject during study sessions, instead of covering one topic at a time (known as blocked practice).	Biology Example
	1. **Diffusion, Osmosis and Active Transport** (ten minutes)
	   a. Compare the three processes with diagrams.
	   b. Apply them to root hair cells or gas exchange in lungs.
	2. **Enzymes and Temperature/pH Effects** (ten minutes)
	   a. Review lock-and-key theory.
	   b. Connect enzyme activity to the transport of substances.
		Helps students make connections across topics—like how temperature or concentration affect different processes. Encourages more effortful thinking, as students must constantly shift and compare concepts.

(Continued)

Strategy	How It Works	Why Is It Effective
	3. **Photosynthesis** (ten minutes) a. Link enzymes in chloroplasts to the rate of photosynthesis and limiting factors.	Disrupts autopilot learning. When students are forced to think more carefully, they're more likely to remember the material later.
Organising information visually—using timelines, mind maps, or tree diagrams—helps students structure their thinking and make connections between concepts.	Instead of revising content as isolated facts, students arrange ideas in meaningful ways: • **Timelines** show events in chronological order, helping with topics like history or processes that unfold over time. • **Mind maps** allow students to place a central idea in the middle and connect related ideas around it, showing relationships between concepts. • **Tree diagrams** are useful for showing hierarchical structures, such as causes and effects, or main ideas and subpoints.	Organising information helps students form schemas—mental frameworks that group related ideas. When students can "see" how ideas are connected, it's easier to understand them, recall them later, and apply them in different contexts.

Conclusion

This brings me back to the work of David Ausubel, whose theory of *meaningful learning* remains highly relevant. One of his most enduring insights was the distinction between rote learning—memorising without understanding—and meaningful learning, where new information is connected to existing knowledge. His thinking is captured in a quote that underpins much of what this book has explored so far:

> The most important single factor influencing learning is what the learner already knows. Ascertain this and teach accordingly.
>
> (Ausubel, 1968, p. vi)

I've previously discussed how students benefit from organising their ideas *after* learning—through strategies such as concept mapping, for example. But what about *during* the process of acquiring new knowledge? In my experience, this is actually harder to get right than what happens before or after a learning episode.

During revision, we can direct students to use retrieval practice and consolidate their understanding with visual tools. But supporting meaningful learning *as it happens* relies far more heavily on the teacher and their in-the-moment decisions.

Over the last decade, classroom teaching has evolved significantly, informed by research into how learning works. In my own practice, four strategies have become foundational:

- **Cold Calling**
- **Mini Whiteboards**
- **Choral Response**
- **Pair Talk**

Rather than getting caught up in the specific terminology—*cold calling*, for example, a term popularised by Doug Lemov in *Teach Like a Champion* to describe the practice of calling on students regardless of whether they raise their hands—the focus here is on why these strategies have become so widely adopted in classrooms across the country.

Broadly speaking, these techniques help address two persistent challenges in teaching:

1. Increasing **student participation**
2. Increasing **student thinking**

At a recent researchED event in New York, I had the pleasure of watching Zach Groshell lead a session that exemplified these principles in action. His delivery was a masterclass in how to promote both engagement and depth. At one point, he asked us to imagine a typical classroom of 30 students. After just five minutes of acting out the role of a teacher, he posed a question: *How many questions do you think were asked of those 30 students?* The answer? In the hundreds.

These techniques are powerful. They get more students involved. They encourage active thought. They create a buzz in the room. But while they're highly effective, I believe they only tell part of the story.

To truly support meaningful learning, we also need to help students make better decisions during the lesson itself. So what does that look like?

When students are engaging with new content—whether reading a textbook or listening to teacher instruction—two cognitively active strategies can significantly enhance both understanding and retention: elaborative interrogation and self-explanation.

- **Elaborative interrogation** involves asking, *"How does this relate to what I already know?"* or *"Why is this important?"* This encourages students to make deliberate links between new content and existing knowledge—essentially activating and expanding their schemas.

- **Self-explanation** prompts students to pause and articulate their understanding: *"How does this idea fit with what I already know?"* or *"Why does this make sense?"* This metacognitive pause strengthens comprehension and helps secure LTM.

Both techniques are supported by a strong evidence base (e.g., Pressley et al., 1987; Wong, 1985) and align closely with Ausubel's theory: meaningful learning happens when we connect the new to the known.

At the beginning of this book, I introduced two very different learners: one sitting in a university lecture and the other working as an apprentice plumber. Despite the contrast in setting, both face a common challenge—they cannot rely on classroom-based strategies like cold calling or mini whiteboards to support their learning. These techniques are effective in structured environments, but they are not designed to carry over into the real world where independent learning is essential.

The subtitle of this book is *How to Develop Successful and Independent Learners*. While classroom strategies play a valuable role in supporting short-term academic performance, they do not always equip students with the tools needed to continue learning once that external support is removed. If we are serious about preparing students for life beyond the classroom, we must go further.

John Sweller, the originator of Cognitive Load Theory, underscores the importance of designing learning experiences that align with how the human brain processes information. CLT is based on the understanding that our working memory—the part of the brain responsible for holding and manipulating information in the moment—is extremely limited. When too much information is presented at once, or when it's not structured effectively, learners can become overwhelmed. This overload prevents new knowledge from being processed and transferred into long-term memory, where it can be retained and built upon. Sweller argues that *"without knowledge of human cognitive processes, instructional design is blind"* (Sweller, 1994, p. 295). In other words, if we don't consider how the brain handles information, teaching risks becoming inefficient or even counterproductive.

The same principle applies to learners themselves:

Without knowledge of how learning happens, students' ability to develop effective learning habits is limited.

Chapter Summary

- Working memory is limited.
- Prior knowledge makes learning new information easier.
- Rehearsal strengthens memory and improves retention of knowledge.

- To remember something, you must think really hard about it.
- Schemas play an important role in what new knowledge we remember.
- Connecting new knowledge with existing knowledge will help you to remember it.
- Learning requires struggle.

References

Anderson, R. C., & Pichert, J. W. (1978). Recall of previously unrecallable information following a shift in perspective. *Journal of Verbal Learning and Verbal Behavior, 17*(1), 1–12. https://doi.org/10.1016/S0022-5371(78)90485-1

Atkinson, R. C., & Shiffrin, R. M. (1968). Human memory: A proposed system and its control processes. In K. W. Spence & J. T. Spence (Eds.), *The psychology of learning and motivation: Advances in research and theory* (Vol. 2, pp. 89–195). Academic Press. https://doi.org/10.1016/S0079-7421(08)60422-3

Ausubel, D. P. (1960). The use of advance organizers in the learning and retention of meaningful verbal material. *Journal of Educational Psychology, 51*(5), 267–272. https://doi.org/10.1037/h0046669

Ausubel, D. P. (1968). *Educational psychology: A cognitive view*. Holt, Rinehart and Winston.

Bartlett, F. C. (1932). *Remembering: A study in experimental and social psychology*. Cambridge University Press.

Bjork, R. A. (1994). Memory and metamemory considerations in the training of human beings. In J. Metcalfe & A. P. Shimamura (Eds.), *Metacognition: Knowing about knowing* (pp. 185–205). MIT Press.

Bjork, R. A., Dunlosky, J., & Kornell, N. (2013). Self-regulated learning: Beliefs, techniques, and illusions. *Annual Review of Psychology, 64*, 417–444. https://doi.org/10.1146/annurev-psych-113011-143823

Craik, F. I. M., & Tulving, E. (1975). Depth of processing and the retention of words in episodic memory. *Journal of Experimental Psychology: General, 104*(3), 268–294. https://doi.org/10.1037/0096-3445.104.3.268

Ebbinghaus, H. (1913). *Memory: A contribution to experimental psychology* (H. A. Ruger & C. E. Bussenius, Trans.). Teachers College, Columbia University (Original work published 1885). https://doi.org/10.1037/10011-000

Ericsson, K. A., Krampe, R. T., & Tesch-Römer, C. (1993). The role of deliberate practice in the acquisition of expert performance. *Psychological Review, 100*(3), 363-406. https://doi.org/10.1037/0033-295X.100.3.363

Glanzer, M., & Cunitz, A. R. (1966). Two storage mechanisms in free recall. *Journal of Verbal Learning and Verbal Behavior, 5*(4), 351–360. https://doi.org/10.1016/S0022-5371(66)80044-0

Hambrick, D. Z., & Oswald, F. L. (2005). Does domain knowledge moderate involvement of working memory capacity in higher-level cognition? A test of three models. *Journal of Memory and Language, 52*(3), 377–397. https://doi.org/10.1016/j.jml.2005.01.004

Kahneman, D. (2011). *Thinking, fast and slow*. Farrar, Straus and Giroux.

Miller, G. A. (1956). The magical number seven, plus or minus two: Some limits on our capacity for processing information. *Psychological Review, 63*(2), 81–97. https://doi.org/10.1037/h0043158

Murdock, B. B. (1962). The serial position effect of free recall. *Journal of Experimental Psychology, 64*(5), 482–488. https://doi.org/10.1037/h0045106

Novak, J. D., & Gowin, D. B. (1984). *Learning how to learn*. Cambridge University Press.

Piaget, J. (1952). *The origins of intelligence in children* (M. Cook, Trans.). International Universities Press (Original work published 1936).

Pressley, M., McDaniel, M. A., Turnure, J. E., Wood, E., & Ahmad, M. (1987). Elaborative interrogation facilitates acquisition of facts. *Journal of Educational Psychology, 79*(3), 189–194.

Sweller, J. (1994). Cognitive load theory, learning difficulty, and instructional design. *Learning and Instruction, 4*(4), 295–312.

Willingham, D. T. (2009). *Why don't students like school? A cognitive scientist answers questions about how the mind works and what it means for the classroom*. Jossey-Bass.

Wong, B. Y. L. (1985). Self-questioning instructional research: A review. *Review of Educational Research, 55*(2), 227–268.

2 The Challenges with Thinking

The Role of Bias in Learning

In the previous chapter in the mobile phone scenario, I introduced the idea of two types of thinking: System 1 and System 2 (Figure 2.1).

Once students are focused on the importance of thinking, the next step is to explore how we engage in different types of thinking and how this effects our ability to make good decisions. So why are the concepts of System 1 and System 2 so important when it comes to learning?

System 1 is fast and automatic and operates without conscious effort. However, many of its characteristics can work against students who are trying to learn through deliberate thought. Because it is effortless and requires little mental strain, it relies on mental shortcuts, known as heuristics, rather than logical

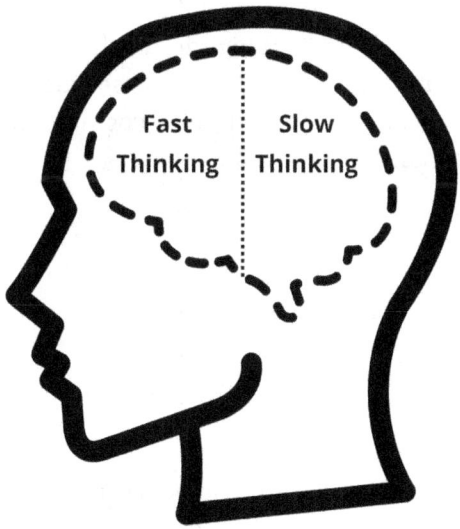

Figure 2.1 Fast thinking and slow thinking serve different functions in the brain

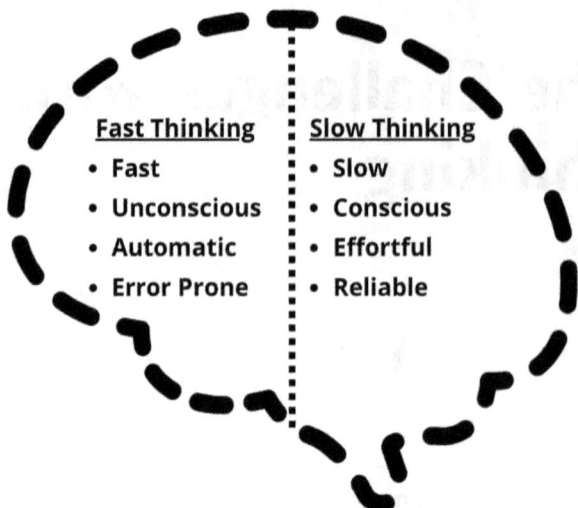

Figure 2.2 The distinct characteristics of fast (System 1) and slow (System 2) thinking

analysis. This dependence on heuristics can lead to biased or flawed thinking, which is a challenge we need to address if we want students to develop better learning habits.

System 1 is also heavily influenced by emotions. When people talk about having a *gut feeling*, it is often the result of this type of thinking. Even when students become aware of their reliance on System 1, it can be difficult to shift away from it, as it is naturally resistant to change (Figure 2.2).

However, there is a way to turn this to our advantage. System 1 is particularly effective at handling routine tasks. As discussed in the previous chapter's example of driving a familiar route, once a task becomes automatic, it requires little conscious effort. This is why the final big idea of this book focuses on habits. By establishing effective learning habits that become second nature, students can not only improve decision-making but also reduce cognitive load, freeing up mental resources for deeper thinking (Figure 2.3).

Substitution Bias

A well-known example that demonstrates the difference between intuitive and analytical thinking comes from the Cognitive Reflection Test (CRT), developed by Shane Frederick (2005). The test includes a deceptively simple math problem:

> A bat and a ball together cost £1.10. The bat costs £1.00 more than the ball. How much does the ball cost?

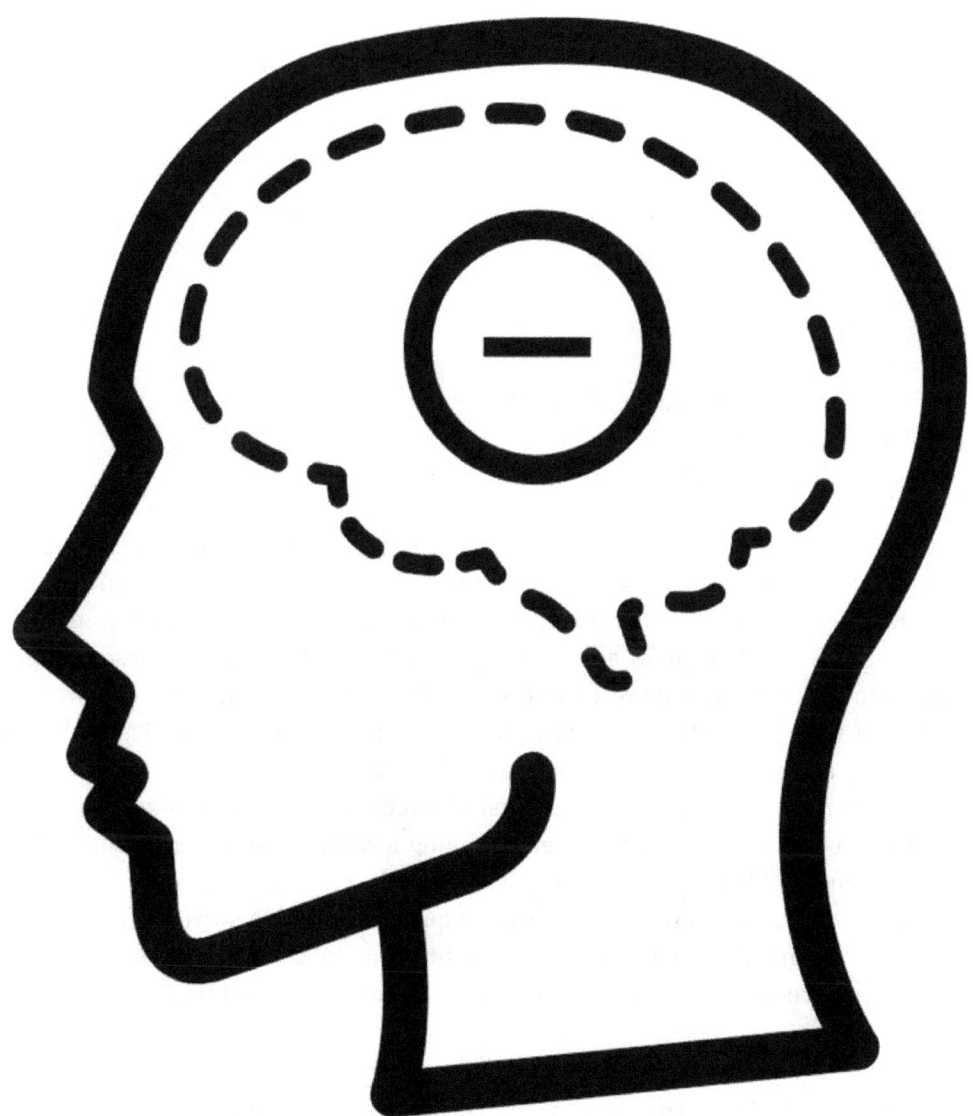

Figure 2.3 Substitution bias occurs when we unconsciously replace a difficult question with an easier one and answer that instead, often without realising it

Most people instinctively respond with "10 pence." This answer feels correct and is arrived at quickly. However, it's incorrect. A more careful approach reveals the actual cost of the ball is 5 cents.

Let's break it down:

Set up the equation:

- X = ball
- Y = bat

The total cost is £1.10, so:
X + Y = 1.1
Also, we know the bat costs £1.00 more than the ball:
Y = X + 1
Now, plug the equation for Y into the total cost equation:
X + (X + 1) = 1.1
Solve for X:
2X = 0.1
X = 0.05
Now, substitute the value of X into the second equation to find Y:
Y = 0.05 + 1 = 1.05
So, the ball costs £0.05 and the bat costs £1.05.

Frederick designed the test to show how people often default to an intuitive, quick response rather than slowing down to engage in more deliberate reasoning. His work highlights the ease with which our thinking can be misled by initial impressions, especially when tasks appear simple on the surface. In this case, people unconsciously replace a more complex problem with a simpler one—a process known as the substitution heuristic. Rather than solving the precise question asked, they answer an easier version that *feels* right.

This example shows how such mental shortcuts can lead to systematic errors and underscores the importance of encouraging learners to slow down and reflect when solving problems.

You can test students with the following questions, which serve as further evidence of System 1 thinking. While they might get a few correct, even a handful of incorrect answers shows that they are relying on intuitive reasoning.

1. A lily pad doubles in size every day. On day 48, it covers half the pond. On which day will it cover the entire pond?

   Answer: Day 49.

   (Many students will guess Day 24, assuming the growth follows a simple, linear progression. They'll divide the 48 days by 2, which is an intuitive but incorrect approach.)

> 2. A mother and daughter are 50 years old in total. The mother is 20 years older than the daughter. How old is the daughter?
>   Answer: 15.
>   (A quick response might be 30 years old, because people see that adding 20 to 30 gives 50, without considering the proper relationship between their ages.)
>
> 3. A farmer had 17 sheep. All but 9 died. How many sheep does the farmer have left?
>   Answer: 9.
>   (When people hear "All but 9 died," they often focus on the numbers "17" and "died" and quickly subtract 9 from 17, arriving at an incorrect answer of 8.)

The substitution heuristic is one of many shortcuts that System 1 uses to provide quick responses. While it's deeply flawed in the context of solving math problems—where simplifying questions can lead to errors—it does have its advantages in other areas. It's important to highlight these merits to students. For example:

Imagine you're interacting with someone briefly—perhaps a friend or even a stranger—and you're trying to gauge their emotional state or mood. Rather than over-analysing every detail of their body language, tone of voice, or other subtle cues, you might rely on a simpler shortcut. This is where the substitution heuristic comes in.

Instead of asking the complex question, *How is this person feeling right now? What factors are affecting their mood? Is it stress, fatigue, or something else?* you substitute that with a simpler question: *Is this person smiling or frowning?*

This shortcut allows for a quick judgement. A smile or frown offers a clear, visible cue that we often associate with positive or negative emotional states. By recognising this cue early on, you can respond quickly and avoid potential negative interactions that might otherwise escalate if unnoticed.

The understanding of heuristics goes beyond decision-making when trying to learn new knowledge but into wider decision-making that effects students success in school. They can help explain a student making poor choices, such as copying in lessons. In this case, the student may have learned through previous experiences that copying is a quick way to avoid perceived failure, gain praise, or escape discomfort, especially if the act of copying has been reinforced over time. This response becomes automatic and is part of the student's learned behaviour. Essentially, the student may not think deeply about the consequences of copying in the moment, relying instead on an automatic, learned behaviour that seeks immediate gratification or relief from stress. This is not to say we should not hold students accountable for their actions, but it is fair to say in some cases when challenging a student on why they carried out a particular action like copying their response of "I wasn't thinking" may actually be the truth.

In this chapter we will look at several strategies students can use to reduce their reliance on System 1 thinking; however, the first is awareness of the biases that System 1 brings.

Anchoring Bias

Another common heuristic is anchoring bias, in which people rely too heavily on the first piece of information they encounter (the "anchor") when making decisions or judgements (Figure 2.4). This initial information serves as a reference point, and subsequent judgements are made by adjusting away from that anchor, often insufficiently. As a result, people's decisions can be skewed towards that initial piece of information, even if it is irrelevant or arbitrary.

Anchoring Bias Experiment—Kahneman and Tversky's

1. **Task:** You will be estimating the number of countries in Africa. However, before making your guess, you'll first be given a number to consider.

Group 1

a. Question: Is the number of countries in Africa greater or less than 65?

b. After considering this, estimate how many countries are in Africa.

Group 2

a. Question: Is the number of countries in Africa greater or less than 25?

b. After considering this, estimate how many countries are in Africa.

1. Write down your estimate on a piece of paper.

2. After completing the task, we will compare the estimates and discuss how the initial number affected your guesses.

Results

- Participants given the higher anchor (65) estimated the number of countries in Africa to be much higher, with their guesses averaging around 45 countries.

- Participants given the lower anchor (25) estimated the number of countries in Africa to be much lower, with their guesses averaging around 30 countries.

- Despite the actual number of countries in Africa being approximately 54, participants' estimates were heavily influenced by the initial anchor number, illustrating the anchoring bias. The findings showed that people tend to rely too much on the first piece of information (the anchor), which skews their judgements and decision-making.

Figure 2.4 Anchoring bias is the tendency to rely too heavily on the first piece of information (the "anchor") when making decisions or judgements, even if it is irrelevant

The experiment demonstrated that even arbitrary or irrelevant anchors can significantly affect how people make estimates or judgements.

A practical example of this could be in a science lesson on the boiling point of water; the teacher might tell the class, "Water boils at 100°C." This number becomes the anchor for the students' understanding of water's boiling point. However, when teaching about different conditions (like pressure, altitude, or impurities), some students might fail to adjust their understanding due to the anchor they were given.

Ask yourself the question, how many times may similar conversations like the one below have taken place in classrooms.

A group of high school students are working together on a project about the Great Depression. They are discussing the impact of unemployment during that period. One student, John, begins the conversation by confidently saying, "The unemployment rate during the Great Depression was 50%. It was so high that half the country was out of work."

The rest of the group, unsure but influenced by John's certainty, starts to adopt this figure. Sarah nods and adds, "Yeah, I remember hearing that the Great Depression was really severe, and 50% unemployment is shocking." Mark, another student, mentions, "That makes sense because it was the worst economic crisis in U.S. history."

As the discussion continues, the group keeps referring to the 50% unemployment rate, and the conversation is framed around this number. Even though the actual rate was 25%, no one challenges the initial claim.

The deeper we explore the role of System 1, the wider the effect we can see it may have on students' decision-making, in terms of anchoring bias. In terms of motivation and confidence, if a student performs poorly in a particular subject early on, they may anchor that experience and believe that they are "bad" at the subject, which could influence their effort in future lessons.

Sunk Cost Fallacy

A significant barrier to students' thinking is the sunk cost fallacy, a cognitive bias that causes people to continue investing in a decision simply because they have already spent time, money, or resources on it—even when the current costs outweigh the benefits (Figure 2.5). Instead of making a rational choice based on future outcomes, people allow past investments to dictate their decisions.

This is one of the key reasons why a teacher's or parent's request for change—such as asking students to alter their study habits—is often not enough. Over the years, I've taught hundreds of students who spend excessive time making their notes look aesthetically pleasing. A quick search on YouTube will reveal countless "study with me" videos showing students doing exactly the same thing. There is good reason for this, as it provides a form of self-gratification—a concept I'll explore in more detail later in this book, given its significant role in decision-making.

Figure 2.5 The sunk cost fallacy is the tendency to continue with a decision or action because of the time, money, or effort already invested, even when it no longer makes sense to do so

When students face the choice between using flashcards or copying out notes in an aesthetically pleasing way, the latter often feels better. It provides a sense of accomplishment, whereas flashcards, though more challenging, often don't feel like a "success" in the moment. Telling a 16-year-old, "Stop making aesthetically pleasing notes; instead, use flashcards," may not be effective—especially when the student has already invested heavily in what they consider to be an effective strategy. This is particularly true if they've felt that strategy has worked for them in the past.

To help students understand this, we can turn to the work of Richard Thaler. Thaler (1980) expanded on the concept of the sunk cost fallacy by linking it to his theory of mental accounting—the idea that people categorise money and resources into different "mental accounts" instead of treating them as interchangeable.

A practical example can be drawn from a study by Arkes and Blumer (1985).

> **Scenario**
>
> You've purchased a £100 ticket to a concert of an artist you like. Two months later, a friend invites you to another concert of an artist you prefer—one that was sold out when you tried to buy a ticket. They have a spare ticket because someone let them down, and they're only charging you £20. You agree to buy the ticket, but a few days later, you realise both concerts are scheduled at the same time.
>
> You've now spent £120 in total, and there are no refunds. What do you do?
>
> a. Go to the £100 concert
>
> b. Go to the £20 concert
>
> **Answer**
>
> You should choose the £20 concert, as it offers the better experience, regardless of cost. The £100 spent on the original concert is a sunk cost—it's already gone and shouldn't influence your decision.
>
> In the original study, 46% of participants chose the £100 concert simply because it cost more. Despite the fact that they would enjoy the £20 concert more, they didn't want to feel as if they "wasted" the extra £100. When conducting this study with students, you may see similar results, but ideally, 100% of students would choose the better experience. Unfortunately, this is often not the case.

This phenomenon is a clear example of mental accounting—where people categorise money emotionally rather than logically, leading them to make suboptimal choices.

This bias isn't limited to money; it also applies to time and effort. A simple example would be spending three seasons watching a TV show, only for the fourth season to be terrible. Despite this, people often keep watching because they've "already spent so much time" on it.

In addition to mental accounting, another challenge at play is loss aversion—the tendency for the pain of losing something, such as £100, to feel stronger than the pleasure of an equivalent gain. Kahneman and Tversky's (1979) prospect theory explains that people often overreact to potential losses and undervalue potential gains, rather than weighing probabilities logically. This phenomenon was demonstrated by Kahneman et al. (1990) in their study on the endowment effect. In this experiment, participants who were given mugs valued them more highly when asked to sell than when asked how much they would pay to buy the same mugs. This suggests that ownership increases perceived value because giving up an item feels like a loss, illustrating loss aversion in action.

To help students understand this concept, consider offering them a retest of a recent exam, but with the stipulation that whatever score they achieve will be reported to their parents. Most students will likely decline the opportunity, fearing that receiving a lower score will outweigh the potential gain of achieving a higher score.

In conclusion, students often overvalue the time they've already invested in previous study habits and undervalue the potential gains they could make by adopting new strategies, such as using flashcards.

At the end of this chapter, I will discuss general strategies to reduce the cognitive biases we've covered. However, research suggests that there is a particularly effective strategy to address the sunk cost fallacy: framing decisions in terms of future gains or losses.

(Arkes & Blumer, 1985). When decisions are framed with a past-oriented focus—for example, "I've already put in so much time or money, so I should keep going"—individuals are more likely to continue even when it is irrational to do so. Conversely, framing decisions with a future-oriented perspective encourages more rational decision-making. For instance, focusing on potential future benefits and costs ("If I continue, what might I gain or lose?") helps individuals to disengage from sunk costs and make choices based on current and future value (Arkes & Blumer, 1985; Hsee & Hastie, 2006).

A practical example for students might be:

- **Past-Oriented Framing:** "I've already spent two hours meticulously copying up my notes, so I should keep going"

- **Future-Oriented Framing:** "Instead of spending more time copying notes, I could use my time testing myself on the material, which will help me transfer knowledge to my long-term memory in the future."

This approach of framing decisions with a focus on the future, rather than past investments, can help students make better choices, encouraging them to focus on the potential benefits of their actions rather than the time and effort they've already spent.

Confirmation Bias

Confirmation bias is a cognitive bias that refers to the tendency for individuals to search for, interpret, favour, and recall information in a way that confirms their preexisting beliefs or hypotheses, while giving less consideration to alternative viewpoints or contradictory evidence. In essence, people are more inclined to focus on information that supports what they already believe and ignore or dismiss anything that challenges it (Figure 2.6).

Figure 2.6 Confirmation bias is the tendency to seek out, interpret, and remember information in a way that supports our existing beliefs or opinions, while ignoring evidence that contradicts them

This bias can significantly affect decision-making and reasoning across various contexts, from personal beliefs to scientific research. It often leads to poor judgements or decisions, as it limits one's exposure to a balanced view of the situation.

> **When Evidence Isn't Enough: A Story of Confirmation Bias**
>
> In the mid-19th century, a Hungarian doctor named Ignaz Semmelweis made a discovery that could have saved thousands of lives. But instead of being celebrated, he was ignored, ridiculed—and eventually ruined.
>
> Semmelweis worked at the Vienna General Hospital, where he noticed a horrifying pattern: women who gave birth in the hospital's doctors' ward were dying at a much higher rate than those in the midwives' ward. Death from what was called "childbed fever" was so common that many women feared going to the hospital at all.
>
> Determined to find the cause, Semmelweis examined everything the doctors did differently. Then he noticed something crucial: medical students and doctors often moved straight from dissecting dead bodies to delivering babies, without washing their hands. Midwives, on the other hand, did not work with corpses.
>
> Semmelweis proposed a radical idea: something invisible—what we now know as germs—might be carried on the doctors' hands from the dead bodies to the living mothers. He introduced a strict handwashing policy using a chlorinated lime solution.
>
> The results were immediate. Mortality rates on the doctors' ward plummeted.
>
> Yet instead of gratitude, Semmelweis faced outrage. Many doctors were offended by the suggestion that they—educated men, respected professionals—could be responsible for the deaths of their patients. Accepting Semmelweis's evidence would have meant admitting they had caused unimaginable harm.
>
> So they rejected him.
>
> This is a classic example of confirmation bias: when people have a deeply held belief—like "doctors are healers, not killers"—they tend to ignore or twist new evidence to protect that belief. Even overwhelming proof can be dismissed if it threatens their view of themselves or the world.
>
> Semmelweis died in disgrace, his ideas mocked and dismissed. It was only decades later, with the rise of germ theory through scientists like Louis Pasteur and Joseph Lister, that the medical community finally recognised the truth.
>
> By then, countless lives had been lost—not because the knowledge wasn't there, but because human thinking got in the way.
>
> Confirmation bias isn't just something that happened to doctors 150 years ago—it affects how we think every day. For example, a student who believes they are "bad at maths" might notice every mistake they make and ignore the times they succeed. Another student might decide that a teacher "doesn't like them" and focus only on

> criticisms, missing the moments of encouragement. Even in friendships, confirmation bias can appear: we might believe a close friend is always right and overlook evidence when they are wrong. In all these cases, our existing beliefs shape what we see, hear, and remember—sometimes leading us away from the truth.

Recently, during a visit to a researchED conference in New York, I attended a presentation by Holly Korbey, a freelance writer who has spent 15 years covering education. She discussed the challenges educators face when sharing research on the science of learning. Research from the Pew Research Center (2023) indicates that only 57% of Americans believe science has had a positive effect on society. Statistics like this show why it is so important to give students the opportunity to learn from the studies I have presented in this book. By allowing students to see first-hand how their brain works even those who are sceptical of the science of learning may be persuaded to challenge their preconceived biases.

Many students have the belief some subjects are harder than others. For example, they may think maths is inherently more difficult than subjects like geography. This belief often stems from focusing on past experiences where they struggled with maths, using these instances as evidence that they are bad at the subject. They may ignore moments when they performed well or felt confident, reinforcing their belief that they struggle with maths. As a result, they may avoid extra practice or revision, convinced that maths is too difficult for them. This lack of effort and focus on negative experiences leads to poorer results, further strengthening their belief that maths is difficult.

A discussion around confirmation bias is a perfect opportunity to revisit earlier themes in this book and encourage students to consider whether maths is truly harder than other subjects. This discussion can naturally lead to a conversation about the role of working memory and long-term memory and that the more knowledge you have, the easier it is to learn new information.

One of the earliest studies on confirmation bias was conducted by Peter Wason (1966). In this experiment, participants were given a set of cards and asked to test the rule: "If there is a vowel on one side, there must be an even number on the other." The cards presented were a vowel, a consonant, an even number, and an odd number.

Findings: Most participants flipped over the cards that would confirm the rule (vowel and even number), but few flipped over the odd-numbered card, which could potentially disprove the rule. This demonstrated confirmation bias, as people tended to seek information that confirmed their hypothesis, while ignoring information that could contradict it.

This task can be carried out with students.

Objective

In this task, your goal is to determine whether a given rule is true or false by selecting the appropriate cards to turn over.

Scenario

You are given four cards. Each card has a number on one side and a letter on the other. The rule is as follows:

> If there is a vowel on one side of the card, then there must be an even number on the other side.

Method

You will see four cards placed in front of you. Each card shows one of the following:

- A vowel (A, E, I, O, U)
- A consonant (B, C, D, etc.)
- An even number (2, 4, 6, etc.)
- An odd number (1, 3, 5, etc.)

You need to choose which cards you should flip over in order to test if the rule is true. Remember, the rule is: "If there is a vowel on one side, there must be an even number on the other."

Record Your Results

Card Flipped	Other Side

Reflection

This task is a great example of how confirmation bias can shape our thinking.
Here's what we learned:

When testing a rule or hypothesis, we often seek out information that supports our beliefs and ignore information that might challenge them. In this task, many of you likely flipped over cards that confirmed the rule (vowel and even number) but might have missed the cards that could disprove the rule (odd number).

Confirmation bias can be subtle because it makes us feel more confident in our choices, even when we're not testing the rule thoroughly. It's essential to challenge our thinking and actively seek evidence that may contradict our beliefs, especially when making important decisions.

Although confirmation bias influences students' decision-making, it has a much broader impact in society. This experiment presents an opportunity to work with students to create a set of guidelines to help reduce the role confirmation bias plays in their lives.

A suggested set of guidelines

Strategies to Reduce Confirmation Bias

Principle	Strategy	Example
Seek out contradictory information	Actively look for information or viewpoints that challenge students' beliefs. This encourages balanced judgement and critical thinking.	If a student believes a particular study technique works well, ask them to explore research or opinions about alternative methods.
Question your assumptions	Encourage students to ask, "What evidence supports this belief?" and "What evidence contradicts it?" to uncover potential biases.	Before sticking with a study method, reflect on whether you've only focused on when it worked and ignored times it didn't.
Diversify your sources	Avoid relying on a single source, especially one that reinforces existing views. Explore a variety of perspectives and disciplines.	When researching for an assignment, include articles from different disciplines or authors with diverse viewpoints.
Be open to feedback	Seek input from others with different experiences or expertise. Constructive criticism helps reveal blind spots in thinking.	Ask a teacher or peer to review your revision plan and highlight overlooked or less effective areas.
Play the "Devil's advocate"	Challenge your own beliefs by arguing against them to test their strength and uncover weaknesses.	Critically argue against your preferred study strategy to uncover possible flaws or better alternatives.

(Continued)

Principle	Strategy	Example
Check your emotions	Recognise how emotions may affect decision-making. We often favour beliefs that feel comfortable rather than those that are accurate.	If you feel defensive about a study method, pause and ask whether your attachment is emotional or evidence based.
Focus on data and evidence	Prioritise objective data over personal stories or opinions. Evidence-based thinking leads to better, less biased decisions.	If you think something is correct works well, compare your outcomes with those of others or refer to research on its effectiveness.

Overcoming Bias

One of the most effective things we can do as educators to tackle cognitive bias is simple: teach students that these biases exist. Just raising awareness can have a powerful impact. This approach has been highly successful in the field of medicine.

Professor Pat Croskerry, an expert in emergency medicine, has dedicated much of his work to exploring how cognitive biases affect medical decision-making. He found that these biases often lead to serious errors, including misdiagnoses and delayed treatment (Croskerry, 2003).

Croskerry explained that doctors—like all of us—are influenced by heuristics and biases, especially in fast-paced environments. In fact, it's widely accepted that people spend around 95% of their time relying on "System 1" thinking, which is quick, intuitive, and often unconscious. While this mode of thinking helps us function efficiently, it also leaves us vulnerable to error.

Through his research, Croskerry identified several key cognitive biases that commonly affect medical professionals some of which I have already discussed.

Bias	Description
Anchoring Bias	Placing too much weight on the first piece of information received (e.g., an initial diagnosis) and failing to adjust as new evidence emerges.
Availability Bias	Making decisions based on easily recalled or recent examples, which may be rare or not representative of the current situation.
Confirmation Bias	Paying attention only to information that supports an initial belief or diagnosis, while ignoring evidence that contradicts it.
Premature Closure	Jumping to a conclusion too quickly without gathering sufficient evidence or considering alternative explanations.

Building Mental Models in the Classroom

In later chapters, we'll explore how using scenarios can help students develop expert-like thinking. In the example below, the aim is to support students in recognising how heuristics and biases can influence their own thought processes—and to encourage reflection on strategies that can lead to better decision-making.

Scenario: "The Case of the Misleading Symptoms"

Characters

- **Dr. Sam Taylor**—A young, confident emergency room doctor
- **Nurse Jenna**—Experienced and observant
- **Mr. Daniels**—A 50-year-old patient with chest pain

Scene 1: Emergency Room—Early Morning

Dr. Taylor enters the ER, scanning Mr. Daniels' chart. Nurse Jenna stands by the bedside.

DR. TAYLOR: What do we have here? Mr. Daniels, 50, came in with chest pain after dinner?

NURSE JENNA: That's right. He describes it as a burning pain that started about an hour ago, right after he ate.

DR. TAYLOR: Classic heartburn. I've seen two cases just like this this week. Must be something in the chili around here.

NURSE JENNA: He looks a little pale though, and his pulse is elevated.

DR. TAYLOR: Probably just from the discomfort. Let's give him an antacid and keep an eye on him.

Dr. Taylor writes his notes and leaves the room.

Scene 2: 30 Minutes Later

Dr. Taylor is taking a break when Nurse Jenna approaches, concerned.

NURSE JENNA: Mr. Daniels says the pain's getting worse. He's also short of breath now.

DR. TAYLOR: Still sounds like acid reflux. Remember Mr. Hayes last week? Same symptoms, and it turned out to be nothing.

NURSE JENNA: Maybe… but this feels different.

DR. TAYLOR: We'll keep monitoring. If things don't improve, we'll reevaluate.

Scene 3: Back in the Patient Room

Mr. Daniels is now sweating and breathing heavily.

DR. TAYLOR: Still feeling the burning?

MR. DANIELS: Yeah… and now it's spreading to my left shoulder.

DR. TAYLOR: Spicy food really can do a number on your system. I'm still leaning toward heartburn.

NURSE JENNA: His blood pressure has dropped again.

DR. TAYLOR: Probably just anxiety. Let's stay the course.

Scene 4: Emergency Response

Suddenly, alarms sound. Mr. Daniels has gone into cardiac arrest.

NURSE JENNA: He's coding! We need the crash cart now!

Dr. Taylor rushes in as the team begins CPR.

Scene 5: Later, in the Break Room

Dr. Taylor sits alone, stunned.

DR. TAYLOR: It was a heart attack all along… I didn't even run an ECG. I was so sure it was just heartburn.

Nurse Jenna quietly joins him.

NURSE JENNA: You're a good doctor, Sam. But sometimes we get too sure of ourselves. Moments like this are how we learn.

They sit together, the gravity of the situation sinking in.
End Scene

Some points to discuss with students after reading the scenario

Bias	Example
Anchoring Bias	Dr. Taylor made an early decision (heartburn) and stuck with it, even when symptoms changed.
Availability Bias	He relied on recent cases of heartburn to guide his diagnosis, even though this case had important differences.

(Continued)

Bias	Example
Confirmation Bias	He focused on the symptoms that matched his theory and ignored others that didn't.
Premature Closure	He made a decision too quickly, without running basic diagnostic tests like an ECG.

Croskerry's research showed that simply being aware of cognitive biases—especially anchoring—can reduce their power. While we can't eliminate bias completely, we can learn to spot it, slow down, and reflect before acting.

Croskerry also recommended some other practical strategies to help healthcare professionals make better decisions, including:

- **Structured Decision-Making**
Using checklists, algorithms, and diagnostic tools to slow thinking and ensure all possibilities are considered.

- **Reflection and Feedback**
Encouraging doctors to reflect on past decisions and learn from errors.

Teachers will be familiar with these strategies as they are a part of everyday practice and are used to providing step-by-step models to students; an example of this being applied to solving linear equations in maths can be found below.

Step	What to Do
1. Understand the Problem	Check what you're being asked. Underline key parts of the question. Is it asking for the value of x or to prove something is always true?
2. Plan Your Approach	Identify the type of equation (e.g., one-step, two-step, with brackets, or fractions). Decide what to do first and why.
3. Solve Step-by-Step	*Show each step clearly.* Don't skip steps—even if they seem obvious.
4. Reflect and Check	Substitute your answer back into the original equation. Does it work? If not, revisit your plan and correct any errors.

It's not that all the steps above aren't important—but one step that will frustrate maths teachers of all age groups: *show every line clearly.* However, after teaching students about fast thinking and the role of heuristics, educators can reframe this feedback in a way that helps students recognise the importance of following instructions.

Take the following maths example:

$$\frac{3}{8} - \frac{1}{8}$$

I noticed on your whiteboard that several students gave an answer of 4/8. This is incorrect; I imagine some of you were fast thinking through this question. Discuss in pairs for 15 seconds what heuristics may have impacted your decision-making? Follow-up question: what could these students have done to correct these biases?

The Psychology behind Our Statistical Blind Spots

One of the things humans struggle with when thinking quickly is understanding statistics.

A simple way to demonstrate this to students would be asking them which scenario feels scarier—a plane landing or flying through a lightning storm?

You'll likely get a range of answers. Some students might say the storm sounds more frightening, while others might worry about landing. But the statistics tell a different story:

You are over 1,000 times more likely to be involved in an accident while landing than during a thunderstorm in flight.

So technically, anyone scared of thunderstorms should be *even more* scared of landing. But our brains don't always work that way—and that's the point.

Our instincts often ignore the facts when a story or image feels more powerful.

This scenario is adapted from a classic study by Kahneman and Tversky (1983), which revealed how our intuitions can lead us to make flawed probability judgements.

The case of Emma

Emma is 12 years old. She's cheerful, loves reading books, and is always the first to help others in class. She enjoys looking after the school garden and often volunteers to tidy up the library.

Now ask students:

Which of the following is more likely?

A. Emma is in Year 7.

B. Emma is in Year 7 **and** the class prefect.

Most people instinctively choose **B** because it feels more detailed and paints a clearer picture. It sounds more specific and plausible.

> However, **A is statistically more likely**.
> Why?
> Because **B is a subset of A**. In other words, **every person who fits B also fits A**, but not everyone in A fits B.
> Think of it like this:
>
> - All class prefects in Year 7 are, of course, in Year 7.
>
> - But not all Year 7 students are class prefects.
>
> So the group described in **A** (all Year 7 students) is larger than the group described in **B** (Year 7 students who are class prefects).
> And since larger groups are more likely to include any random individual, **A must be more probable than B**, even if B sounds more specific.
> This thinking mistake is known as the conjunction fallacy—when we believe that specific, detailed scenarios are more probable than simple, general ones, just because they sound more accurate or vivid.

Reflective questions:

- Why do you think so many people pick B?
- How did the description of Emma influence your thinking?
- Should we always trust our gut feeling about people or situations?
- Can being aware of this mistake help us make better decisions?

How can this flawed logical effect students' learning habits?

Laila has an English homework assignment due tomorrow. It's to write the first page of a story. She's feeling tired and is tempted to leave it for the morning. She thinks to herself:

> I'm tired, and I probably won't come up with any good ideas tonight. I'll just do it in the morning when I'm fresh. Plus, I do better work under pressure anyway.

Laila is using a story about herself—a vivid mental image that feels true:

> "I'm a creative person *under pressure*," and "I don't work well when I'm tired."

Because of this vivid belief, she makes a specific prediction (that she'll do *better work* in the morning) feel more likely than the general one (that doing it now might be more sensible and avoid stress). Statistically she is incorrect; she's treating a specific, idealised story as more likely than a more general, reliable truth (that doing it early is usually better).

A study by Gerd Gigerenzer (2002) in the field of medicine showed that teaching statistics, especially through natural frequencies instead of percentages or probabilities, significantly improves understanding and decision-making—even among professionals like doctors.

Gigerenzer is a strong advocate for the teaching of statistics, particularly medical statistics, because he found that statistical illiteracy can have serious consequences for health. In the context of this book's broader goal—to help students develop learning habits that support better decision-making—his work suggests that the purpose of teaching statistical reasoning goes far beyond what is needed to pass exams. It is, in fact, essential for life. He argues that statistical literacy is a necessary foundation for an educated citizenry in a technological society.

Understanding risks and learning to ask critical questions can also shape the emotional climate of a society, helping people become less vulnerable to manipulation and more capable of developing an informed, calm attitude towards their health and wellbeing.

Some may argue that we already teach statistics as part of the mathematics curriculum. However, Gigerenzer makes the case for introducing children early to the concept of probability, and for focusing on statistical literacy as a practical tool for solving real-world problems—not just a subject taught through formulaic exercises involving coins and dice.

He recommends using:

- **Frequency statements** instead of single-event probabilities,

- **Absolute risks** instead of relative risks,

- **Mortality rates** instead of survival rates, and

- **Natural frequencies** instead of conditional probabilities.

Use This	Instead of This	Why It Matters
Frequency statements	Single-event probabilities	Saying "30 out of 1,000" is easier to understand than "a 3% chance." It grounds risk in real numbers.
Absolute risk	Relative risk	Saying "risk increases from 2 in 10,000 to 4 in 10,000" is more meaningful than "your risk doubles."
Mortality rates	Survival rates	Mortality rates provide a more realistic picture, whereas survival rates can sound overly optimistic.
Natural frequencies	Conditional probabilities	Using counts like "9 out of 98 test positives actually have cancer" avoids confusion from complex probabilities.

An Example

Imagine a disease that affects 1 in 1,000 people. This is called the base rate.
There's a test for the disease that is 99% accurate:

- If a person has the disease, the test correctly identifies it 99% of the time.

Now suppose someone tests positive. What are the chances they have the disease?
Most people would say, "The test is 99% accurate, so there's a 99% chance the person has the disease." But that's incorrect, because it ignores the base rate.
Understanding natural frequencies:
Out of 1,000 people:

- One person has the disease and is likely to test positive.

- Of the 999 people without the disease, about ten will still test positive by mistake (this is because if one person does not have the disease, the test incorrectly comes back positive 1% of the time as it is only 99% accurate).

This means:

- Eleven people test positive in total.

- But only one of them actually has the disease.

So, the actual chance that the person has the disease is 1 in 11—roughly 9%.
This simple example shows how easy it is to overestimate risk when the base rate is ignored.

The Pill Scare

Although this example is hypothetical, a very similar misunderstanding occurred during the 1995 Pill Scare in the United Kingdom.
In October 1995, the UK's Committee on Safety of Medicines warned that third-generation oral contraceptives might double the risk of blood clots (deep vein thrombosis, or DVT).
This announcement triggered widespread panic. Many women stopped taking the pill, leading to a sharp rise in unintended pregnancies—estimated to have caused more than 13,000 additional abortions the following year.
However, the base rate tells a more complete story:

Group	Chance of Blood Clot (DVT) per Year
Women not on the pill	1 in 10,000
Women on older pills	2 in 10,000
Women on third-generation pills	4 in 10,000

While it's true that the risk doubled from 2 in 10,000 to 4 in 10,000, the actual increase was very small—just two extra cases per 10,000 women per year.

What was not widely communicated was that pregnancy itself carries a much higher risk of blood clots: around 10–20 per 10,000 pregnancies.

So, in trying to avoid a very small increase in the risk of clots from taking the pill, many women ended up facing a significantly greater risk due to pregnancy. As well as greater risk of blot clots the increase in birth rates as well as subsequent abortion rates cost the NHS an estimated £46 Million.

What is striking about Gerd Gigerenzer's research is that even trained physicians often struggle to interpret medical statistics correctly. In one study, only 21% of doctors could accurately estimate the likelihood that a woman who tested positive in a mammogram actually had breast cancer. However, after being taught to use natural frequencies, that accuracy rose to 76%. This simple shift in presentation dramatically improved understanding and decision-making. If readers of this book take away one change to have a meaningful impact on students, it would be to ensure they have an understanding of natural frequencies through real-world problems.

Nudge Theory

One way to minimise the impact of fast thinking on students' decision-making is through the concept of nudge theory (Figure 2.7). Developed by Richard Thaler and Cass Sunstein (2008), this idea comes from behavioural economics and suggests that subtle changes in how choices are presented can significantly influence people's behaviour—without taking away their freedom to choose. A "nudge" is essentially a small environmental tweak or cue that gently steers individuals towards a more beneficial decision, while still preserving their autonomy. Nudge theory is grounded in the idea that people rely on fast thinking—particularly when they're distracted, tired, or overwhelmed—which can lead to poor choices. Nudges work by making the better choice easier, more visible, and more appealing, without forcing a particular decision.

Nudges work by applying the following principles.

- **Making the better choice easier or more visible**: A study by Hanks et al. (2012) demonstrated the effectiveness of nudging in promoting healthier food choices in a school cafeteria. By placing healthier food options at eye level, making them more visually appealing, and providing nutrition labels, schools were able to increase the consumption of healthy foods without restricting students' freedom to choose. This study showed that subtle environmental changes can lead to better choices.
- **Tapping into social norms**: A study conducted by Schultz et al. (2007) examined the use of social norms to reduce energy consumption. In this study, participants received feedback about their energy consumption compared to their neighbours. Those who consumed more energy than average were given messages

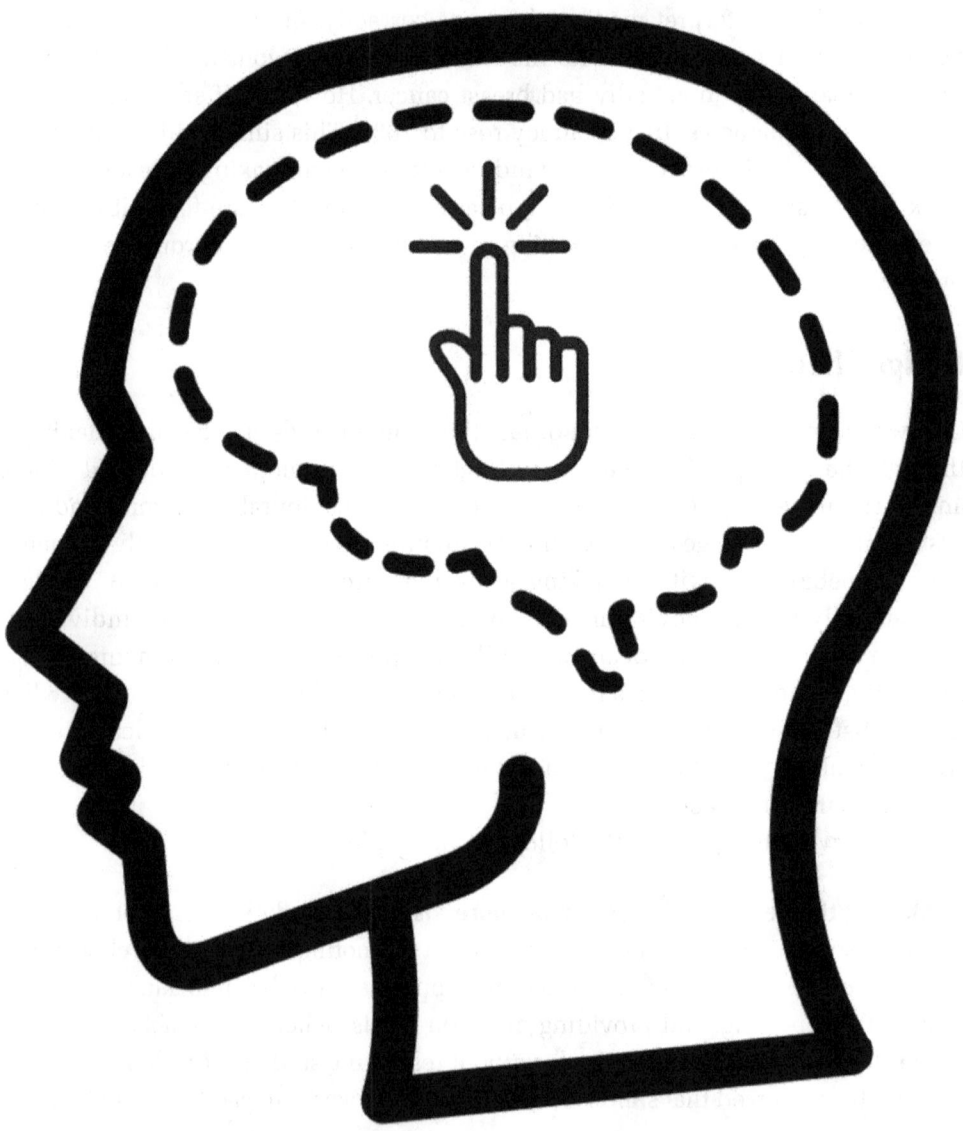

Figure 2.7 Nudge theory is the idea that subtle changes in how choices are presented can influence people's behaviour without restricting their freedom of choice

stating that most of their neighbours used less energy. This social nudge led to a significant reduction in energy use, proving that people are influenced by the behaviour of others.

- **Framing information in a more motivating or accessible way**: Fitness apps often use progress bars or achievement badges to motivate users. This makes the goal feel more attainable by framing it as a series of small wins. A study by Tversky and Kahneman (1981) explored how the framing of health information affects decision-making. In their experiment, participants were given the same health scenario but with different frames. When a choice was framed in terms of lives saved, people were more likely to opt for a programme that promoted saving lives compared to when the same choice was framed in terms of lives lost (even though the statistical outcomes were identical).

  - **Example**: A message like "90% of people who stop smoking reduce their risk of lung cancer" is more motivating than "10% of people who continue smoking develop lung cancer." The positive frame focuses on benefits and makes the action seem more achievable.

- **Helping people pre-commit to future actions**: Websites like booking platforms or travel apps often encourage users to commit to a purchase with limited-time offers or countdowns, making it harder for them to delay their decision and increasing the likelihood they'll follow through. One of the most cited pieces of evidence for nudge theory comes from the example of organ donation. Research by Thaler and Sunstein, the creators of nudge theory, shows that countries with an "opt-out" system for organ donation (where individuals are automatically enrolled and must choose to opt out) have significantly higher organ donation rates compared to countries with an "opt-in" system. This demonstrates the power of a default choice in influencing behaviour without limiting freedom. And finally in a study on pre-commitment and reminders in an educational setting, (Himmler et al., 2019) found that students who received regular reminders about deadlines and were asked to commit to a study schedule were more likely to turn in homework on time and perform better on tests.

Behavioural Insights Team (also known as the Nudge Unit) is a UK-based organisation that uses insights from behavioural science to design public policies that encourage better decision-making. Founded in 2010, the team applies nudge theory to improve outcomes in areas like health, education, and finance, by subtly guiding people towards beneficial choices without restricting their freedom. Their work has gained global recognition, with partnerships across governments, private sectors, and international organisations. In the education sector they improved attendance at career advice appointments. By sending simple, motivational messages like *"No one is born with a perfect career. Time and effort can boost your skills & CV,"* Behavioural Insights Team (BIT) increased attendance by 24%, making it easier for students to engage with the support available to them. Similarly, BIT worked to improve the uptake of Tax-Free Childcare by simplifying the application process into a clear, easy-to-follow checklist. This nudge led to a 13% increase in applications, demonstrating how simplifying complex tasks can encourage positive habits and decisions.

They simplified nudge theory into a practical framework called EAST—which stands for Easy, Attractive, Social, and Timely. This framework condenses the core principles of nudge theory into a simple, actionable guide for designing effective nudges.

- **Easy**—Remove friction.
- **Attractive**—Use visual cues, rewards, or social proof.
- **Timely**—Intervene when it matters most (e.g., before habits set in).
- **Social**—Show what others are doing (e.g., "90% of students handed in homework on time").

In 2010, BIT partnered with Her Majesty's Revenue and Customs (HMRC) to address the challenge of tax non-compliance. The goal was simple: increase the number of people paying their taxes on time, without resorting to punitive measures or heavy-handed enforcement.

The team applied their key principles to redesign the communication sent to taxpayers. Instead of the usual, formal, and impersonal tax letters, BIT experimented with different approaches that incorporated behavioural science insights. The revised letters included:

- **Personalisation:** Addressing taxpayers by name to create a sense of individual relevance.
- **Social Norms:** Highlighting that most people in the recipient's local area were paying their taxes on time, creating a sense of social pressure to conform.
- **Reciprocity:** Emphasising the positive impact of tax contributions on public services, fostering a sense of community responsibility.

The results were striking. After sending out the new letters, tax payments increased by **15%** compared to the previous standard communications. This modest shift in messaging led to an additional £1.2 million in tax payments within the first month. By subtly nudging taxpayers towards the desired behaviour—without restricting their freedom or resorting to fines—the BIT successfully demonstrated the power of behavioural insights in driving more effective public policy. The idea of nudging students may appear contradictory to the wider aim of this book—to develop independent, self-regulated learners. However, as we have already seen, students' choices are often shaped by powerful cognitive biases such as the sunk cost fallacy and confirmation bias. These biases make it genuinely difficult for them to shift away from familiar but ineffective habits, even when they know those habits are not helping them learn. In this context, nudges are not about controlling students or making decisions for them; they are about creating small, supportive adjustments to the environment that make better choices easier to begin with. Students often need gentle guidance to get started on the path toward independence, particularly when they are trying to replace long-established routines with more demanding but more effective ones. Crucially, these nudges are temporary supports. Once positive learning habits become established and normalised, these structures can be steadily withdrawn, allowing students to take full ownership of their learning.

I have used this framework myself to increase homework completion. After becoming frustrated with students missing homework, we initially sent texts home stating how many pieces of homework per week their child was missing. The only impact this had was that parents called to tell us it was, in fact, three pieces missing, not four. We then changed our approach. We texted the parents of students with missing homework the following message:

> 92% of students have completed all their homework this week. Jason unfortunately had some missing, completing his homework will increase his chances of success in the future. To monitor next week's homework please check firefly (the homework platform we used).

This shift in messaging led to a noticeable change in response—rather than disputing the number of missing pieces, parents became more engaged and were calling to seek advice.

An example of this in action is in an English lesson where a teacher wants to ensure students slow down and follow a clear structure when answering essay questions. The teacher might provide a step-by-step guide, such as first, plan your introduction, then state your argument clearly in the first paragraph, and follow with supporting evidence in the next paragraphs.

- **Easy—Remove friction**: To make it easier for students to follow a set procedure, the teacher could provide a simple, step-by-step checklist or flowchart on the desk or whiteboard. This removes the cognitive load of remembering the process and helps them focus on following the steps.

- **Attractive—Use visual cues or rewards**: Place up on the board a visual cue on the board with the words "slow thinking." Rewarding students with the school's behaviour system when they complete the steps correctly can reinforce the desired behaviour.

- **Timely—Intervene when it matters most**: After a teacher has modelled what they expect from students, it is always a good idea to design a task to check for understanding before students set off independently. This is the best time to intervene with any students who have not followed the slow-thinking procedure the teacher wanted. Circulating the room and giving a verbal or visual reminder of the "slow thinking" sign if you can see them rushing.

- **Social—Show what others are doing**: Sharing students' answers with the class that meet the criteria, and asking for a show of hands to see who followed this procedure, can help reinforce that it is a social norm.

Whether you're a parent reading this book directly or an educator working with families, you are in a powerful position to influence children's learning habits. By applying simple, evidence-based nudges at home, parents can help steer their children towards more focused, consistent, and productive revision routines.

Easy—Remove Friction

Make it as easy as possible for your child to begin revising. Rather than simply saying "Go revise," provide a clear and simple structure to guide them:

- Print out a revision timetable with short, manageable sessions (e.g., 20–30 minutes) and display it in their study space.
- Lay out the materials they'll need—such as flashcards, books, or notes—in advance, so getting started feels effortless.
- Use ready-made revision resources or familiar online platforms your child already enjoys, rather than expecting them to create everything from scratch.

Attractive—Use Visual Cues or Rewards

Use visual cues to reinforce positive revision behaviour:

- Create a revision tracker on the wall where your child can tick off sessions—seeing progress builds motivation.
- Offer small, agreed-upon rewards for completing chunks of revision (e.g., time on their phone, snacks, a break with a favourite show).
- Add visual reminders like a post-it on their desk that says, "*One session now = less stress later!*"

Social—Show What Others Are Doing

Help your child see that revision is something others are doing too:

- Casually mention how a friend's child is preparing for exams or how older siblings used a revision checklist and found it helpful.
- If they have a study group or friend revising for the same subjects, encourage short catch-ups to share what they've revised.

- If they're on social media, show examples of revision communities or videos of students sharing tips (e.g., "study with me" content on YouTube).

Timely—Intervene When It Matters Most

Step in with gentle prompts at key decision points:

- Ask at the start of their usual study time, "What's your plan for the next 30 minutes?" rather than after they've been distracted.
- If they look stuck or frustrated, guide them to take a short break or switch to a different revision method rather than pushing through unproductively.
- Praise immediately after a session ends—catching them right after success reinforces the habit.

Noise—Measuring Variability in Learning Habits

In *Noise: A Flaw in Human Judgment*, Daniel Kahneman et al. (2021) along with co-authors Olivier Sibony and Cass Sunstein, explores a hidden problem that undermines decision-making: the issue of "noise." Noise refers to the random variability and inconsistency in human judgements—the idea that two people, or even the same person at different times, can make very different decisions when faced with the same information (Figure 2.8).

Noise in Courtrooms

Imagine you're sitting in a courtroom, where people's lives can change forever depending on what happens. Judges are supposed to be fair and consistent, carefully weighing the facts of each case before making a decision. However, researchers have discovered that even in a setting where we expect the highest standards of fairness, decisions can vary dramatically—and not because of the facts of the case.

An example comes from a study by Danziger et al. (2011), which analysed over 1,000 parole rulings by Israeli judges. The study found that the likelihood of a prisoner being granted parole depended not on the legal merits of the case but on the time of day it was heard. Early in the day, or just after a food break, judges were significantly more lenient. As the day progressed and fatigue or hunger set in, they became much harsher. Identical cases could receive dramatically different outcomes based on something as trivial as whether the judge had recently eaten—a powerful illustration of how subtle, irrelevant factors can introduce "noise" into critical decisions.

Now, imagine how unsettling this is. A person's fate—their future—could depend not on the details of their case or the facts but on whether the judge had

Noise

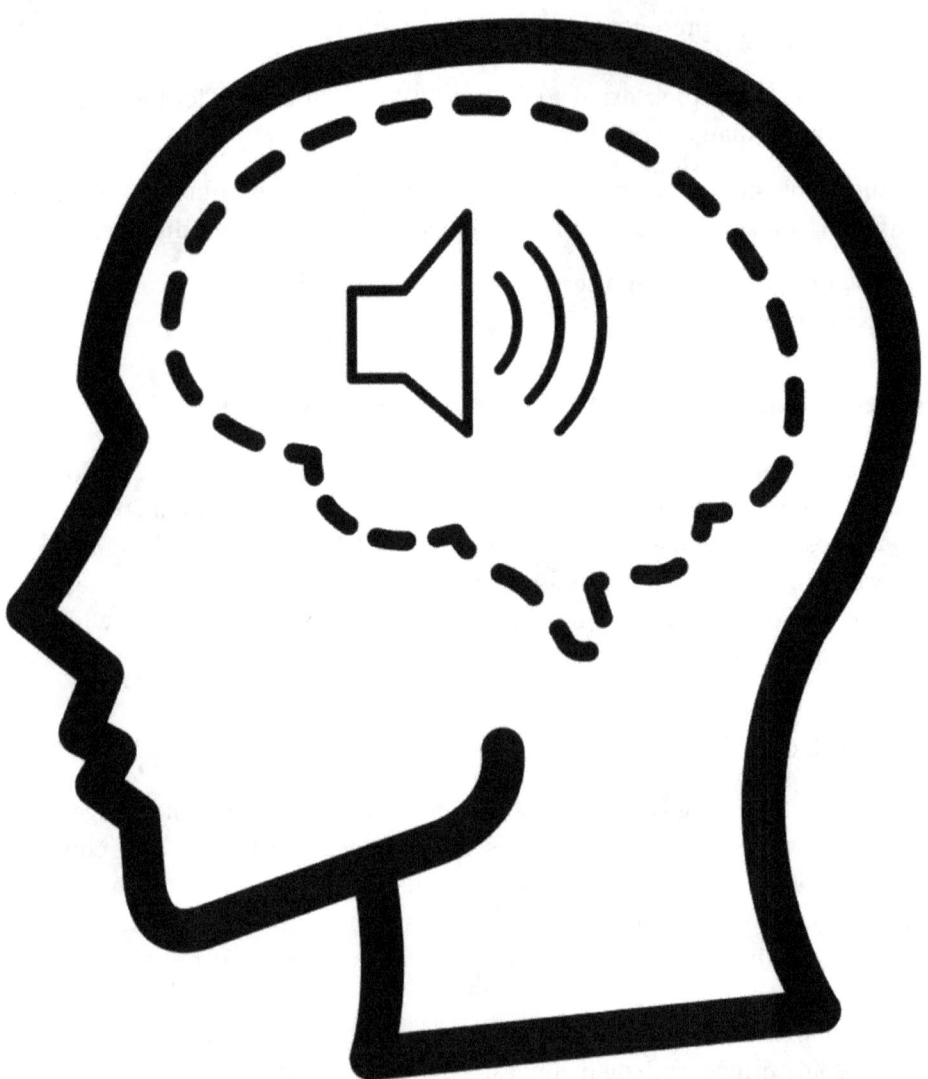

Figure 2.8 Noise is the random variability in human judgement that causes different decisions or assessments in similar situations, even when the same person is involved

recently had a sandwich. This randomness is what Daniel Kahneman and his colleagues call "noise." It's the unpredictable variability in human decisions, and it can lead to unfair and inconsistent outcomes.

This story serves as a powerful reminder that human judgement is not only influenced by biases but also by the chaotic, unseen force of noise. Even in high-stakes situations, like a courtroom, noise can cause decisions to vary without any logical reason. It's a hidden factor that affects us all, even when we least expect it, and it's something that we often overlook.

In this way, the study of noise helps us understand why even in places where we expect fairness and consistency, randomness can still play a big role in shaping outcomes.

This idea has important implications for how people develop learning habits. Decisions about when or how to study can vary significantly depending on seemingly unrelated factors like fatigue, mood, or time pressure. Even when working with the same material, choices around learning strategies can feel inconsistent or reactive. Just as the judges' rulings shifted with irrelevant influences like hunger or time of day, students' decisions can be shaped by factors that shouldn't matter. Recognising how "noise" can creep into these decisions is a key step towards building more consistent, purposeful learning habits that align with actual goals and evidence-based practice.

Reading about this study reminded me of my own experience taking a driving test. My instructor recommended that I book a test first thing in the morning, as in his experience, clients were far more likely to pass at that time of day. He suggested it might be related to quotas, but if his hunch of increased chance of passing in the morning is correct, it's also possible that noise played a role. Similar to the judges, it's plausible that decision-making in like-for-like scenarios could be different in the late afternoon, when instructors are more tired or potentially more agitated.

Let's look at a more detailed example of how this can play out with students. Imagine a student named Sarah who is preparing for a crucial exam. She knows that her classmates, including some who are doing well, have used a variety of study methods—some have used flashcards, others have worked through past papers, and some prefer summarising their notes. Sarah is unsure of which strategy to adopt and makes different choices on different days based on random factors like mood, energy levels, or the time of day.

How noise affects Sarah's decision-making:

1. **Mood Variability**: One day, Sarah feels confident and positive, so she decides to use flashcards, as she knows they will be challenging but is up for the challenge. On another day, she might feel stressed or tired and, because of that mood, opt for watching videos on YouTube, which feels like a more comforting and low-energy option. Her decision-making is influenced by her emotional state, not by an objective evaluation of which method is more effective for her learning.

2. **Time of Day**: Sarah may have had a late-night study session one day and is feeling tired the next morning. Her decision to study might be influenced by how alert or fatigued she feels. In the morning, she might decide to read over her

notes as she doesn't have the energy for a longer session. Later in the evening, she has gained some energy back and so opts for past papers. This inconsistency in approach introduces noise into her decision-making process.

3. **External Distractions**: One day, Sarah is studying in a quiet library, so she feels focused and makes a decision to tackle a challenging topic she's been avoiding. On another day, however, she's studying at home, where there are many distractions (e.g., noise, family members, or even her phone). Feeling distracted and overwhelmed, she decides to stick with easier material or re-read old notes instead of engaging with more complex content. The environmental noise leads her to make a different choice, which affects her learning outcome.

4. **Peer Influence**: One week, Sarah overhears a group of friends talking about how they're using a specific app to help with revision, and she decides to try it out, thinking it's the best approach. The next week, another group talks about how summarising notes is the key to understanding the material, so she shifts her focus and spends hours doing summaries, even though she hasn't tested whether that's the best method for her. Her decisions are influenced by what others are doing at the time, without her critically evaluating what works best for her.

5. **Fatigue and Cognitive Load**: After a full day of school, Sarah might be exhausted, and because of this fatigue, she opts to revise science a subject she knows she is really good at instead of tackling French which she knows is challenging. The physical and mental fatigue introduces noise into her study decisions, making them less effective, despite knowing what a better approach might be.

Impact of Noise on Sarah's Learning

- **Inconsistent results**: Sarah may find that some days she feels like she's making progress and other days she doesn't, simply because she chose different study strategies based on random factors. This inconsistency can lead to confusion about what works best for her.

- **Frustration and confusion**: Because her decisions are based on factors like mood, environment, or the influence of peers rather than objective analysis of study methods, Sarah might struggle to identify the best strategies for her learning. She may start doubting her ability to study effectively, as the noise in her decision-making clouds her judgement.

- **Wasted time**: Due to the randomness in Sarah's choices, she may spend time on less effective study methods, leading to poor performance on her exams. If she keeps switching study methods based on random factors (such as mood or peer influence), she might not fully develop or refine the strategies that work best for her.

Creating a Survey to Measure Noise in Students' Learning Habits

Creating a survey to measure noise in students' learning habits provides valuable insights into the variability of their study decisions. By identifying the factors that contribute to inconsistent choices or random fluctuations in how students approach their studies, educators and parents can provide support to promote consistent and purposeful learning habits.

Step-by-Step Guide

Create scenarios involving specific study decisions that reflect real-life situations. By creating realistic, relatable questions, you can understand the choices students make when studying and the level of variability in their decision-making.

Scenario 1: *"You have a Science test in two days. How will you spend the next hour studying?"*

Possible options could include:

- Reviewing practice problems
- Watching a video
- Engaging in retrieval practice
- Summarising notes from class
- Re-reading the textbook

Scenario 2: *"You feel tired but need to study for an upcoming history exam. What's your plan?"*

Possible options could include:

- Take a short nap and then study
- Power through and study anyway
- Start with the easiest material to feel accomplished
- Study later in the evening when feeling more awake

Scenario 3: *"Your friend suggests using flashcards to study for the test. You are familiar with this method but have never tried it. Do you try it?"*

Possible options could include:

- Yes, I'll give it a try
- No, I prefer my usual method
- Maybe, but only if I see it working for others
- Not sure, I'm sceptical

Using a Likert Scale to Measure Noise

Another way to measure noise in students' study habits is through a Likert scale. This method allows students to rate their agreement with specific statements, helping quantify variability in their responses. By asking about their habits and tendencies using structured response options, parents and educators can gain insight into how noise may influence their decision-making (Boone & Boone, 2012; Likert, 1932).

For example, on a scale of 1–5, ask students to rate how strongly they agree or disagree with the following statements:

- "I always stick to the same study routine before exams."
- "I feel more motivated to study in the morning than in the evening."
- "When I'm tired, I choose easier study tasks instead of harder ones."
- "I select what subjects to revise based on how I am feeling."
- "I often change my study strategy depending on my mood."

Interpreting the Results

The next step is to interpret the findings:

- Substantial variability in how students choose their study strategies indicates noise—meaning their decisions are influenced by random factors like mood, time of day, or external distractions.
- The greater the variability in responses to identical or similar scenarios, the more random the students' decision-making process appears to be.

Identifying Noise and Bias

These surveys not only allow you to identify noise across a large group of students but also help uncover any biases that may exist within the school community or an individual. After identifying noise—random variation in responses—it's important to focus on any consistent patterns across different students. For example, if a significant portion of students repeatedly choose the same study method (such as reviewing notes), despite evidence suggesting that a different method (like retrieval practice) might be more effective, this could point to a bias in the cohort's study habits.

Tracking Progress over Time

All of the strategies introduced in this chapter aimed at improving students' thinking and decision-making are aimed at reducing both biases and noise. If you plan to implement some of the strategies discussed in this book within your classroom or school, a good place to start is by surveying students at various stages of their learning journey. This gives you a baseline to measure the effectiveness of the changes you implement. Success would be evident when you reduce both the random variation in students' decision-making and shift more students towards decisions that align with the science of learning. The same can be done by an individual parent by tracking the changes in the responses of your child over time.

Chapter Summary

- There are two systems of thinking: fast thinking and slow thinking.
- Fast thinking, while quick, is more prone to errors.
- To reduce the impact of fast thinking, we can:
  - Teach students about heuristics and cognitive biases.
  - Develop structured decision-making routines to guide their thinking.
  - Help students build statistical literacy to better understand data and probabilities.
  - Provide nudges to encourage more thoughtful, deliberate choices.
- Noise is the random variability and inconsistency in human judgements or decisions, where different outcomes occur even under the same conditions, often influenced by irrelevant factors like mood, time of day, or distractions.
- Both noise and bias can be measured using survey results considering surveys are used to measure the impact of any changes you might make.

References

Arkes, H. R., & Blumer, C. (1985). The psychology of sunk cost. *Organizational Behavior and Human Decision Processes, 35*(1), 124–140. https://doi.org/10.1016/0749-5978(85)90049-4

Boone, H. N., & Boone, D. A. (2012). Analyzing Likert data. *Journal of Extension, 50*(2), Article 2TOT2. https://tigerprints.clemson.edu/joe/vol50/iss2/2/

Croskerry, P. (2003). Cognitive forcing strategies in clinical decision making. *Annals of Emergency Medicine, 41*(1), 110–120. https://doi.org/10.1067/mem.2003.22

Danziger, S., Levav, J., & Avnaim-Pesso, L. (2011). Extraneous factors in judicial decisions. *Proceedings of the National Academy of Sciences, 108*(17), 6889–6892. https://doi.org/10.1073/pnas.1018033108

Frederick, S. (2005). Cognitive reflection and decision making. *Journal of Economic Perspectives, 19*(4), 25–42. https://doi.org/10.1257/089533005775196732

Gigerenzer, G. (2002). *Calculated risks: How to know when numbers deceive you.* Simon & Schuster.

Hanks, A. S., Just, D. R., & Wansink, B. (2012). Smarter lunchrooms can address new school lunchroom guidelines and childhood obesity. *Journal of Pediatrics, 162*(4), 867–869. https://doi.org/10.1016/j.jpeds.2012.12.031

Himmler, O., Jäckle, S., & Weinschenk, P. (2019). Soft commitments, reminders, and academic performance. *American Economic Journal: Applied Economics, 11*(2), 114–142. https://doi.org/10.1257/app.20170273

Hsee, C. K., & Hastie, R. (2006). Decision and experience: Why don't we choose what makes us happy? *Trends in Cognitive Sciences, 10*(1), 31–37. https://doi.org/10.1016/j.tics.2005.11.007

Kahneman, D., Knetsch, J. L., & Thaler, R. H. (1990). Experimental tests of the endowment effect and the Coase theorem. *Journal of Political Economy, 98*(6), 1325–1348. https://doi.org/10.1086/261737

Kahneman, D., Sibony, O., & Sunstein, C. R. (2021). *Noise: A flaw in human judgment*. Little, Brown Spark.

Kahneman, D., & Tversky, A. (1979). Prospect theory: An analysis of decision under risk. *Econometrica, 47*(2), 263–291. https://doi.org/10.2307/1914185

Kahneman, D., & Tversky, A. (1983). Extensional versus intuitive reasoning: The conjunction fallacy in probability judgment. *Psychological Review, 90*(4), 293–315. https://doi.org/10.1037/0033-295X.90.4.293

Tversky, A., & Kahneman, D. (1981). The framing of decisions and the psychology of choice. *Science, 211*(4481), 453-458

Likert, R. (1932). A technique for the measurement of attitudes. *Archives of Psychology, 22*(140), 1–55.

Pew Research Center. (2023). *Public views on science and society*. https://www.pewresearch.org/science/2023/

Schultz, P. W., Nolan, J. M., Cialdini, R. B., Goldstein, N. J., & Griskevicius, V. (2007). The constructive, destructive, and reconstructive power of social norms. *Psychological Science, 18*(5), 429–434.

Thaler, R. H. (1980). Toward a positive theory of consumer choice. *Journal of Economic Behavior & Organization, 1*(1), 39–60. https://doi.org/10.1016/0167-2681(80)90051-7

Thaler, R. H., & Sunstein, C. R. (2008). *Nudge: Improving decisions about health, wealth, and happiness*. Yale University Press.

Wason, P. C. (1966). Reasoning. In B. M. Foss (Ed.), *New horizons in psychology* (pp. 135–151). Penguin.

3 The Challenge of Change

The Curse of Self-Gratification

I have dedicated a chapter to the role of self-gratification, as it is fundamental not only in the way students think but also in its role in hindering habit formation (Figure 3.1).

While self-gratification itself is not a heuristic, it is influenced by several key heuristics.

Bias	Definition	Example
Present Bias	The tendency to overvalue immediate rewards and undervalue future ones.	A student scrolling on their phone instead of studying for an exam in two weeks. The pleasure of watching TV is immediate, while the benefits of studying feel distant.
Affect Heuristic	Decisions are driven more by emotions than by rational analysis.	A student feels happy after copying notes, so they choose this over more effective study methods, even though the latter have a higher chance of success.
Availability Heuristic	Judging the likelihood of an event based on how easily examples come to mind.	After scoring poorly on a test, a student may give up revising for future exams because the failure is still fresh in their mind.
Optimism Bias	The belief that negative consequences are less likely to happen to oneself.	A student thinking, "I'll be fine. I always manage to pull it off in the end," even when unprepared.
Status quo Bias	The preference to stick with current habits rather than making a change.	A student procrastinates because their routine of gaming after school feels "normal," even though they know studying would be better in the long run.

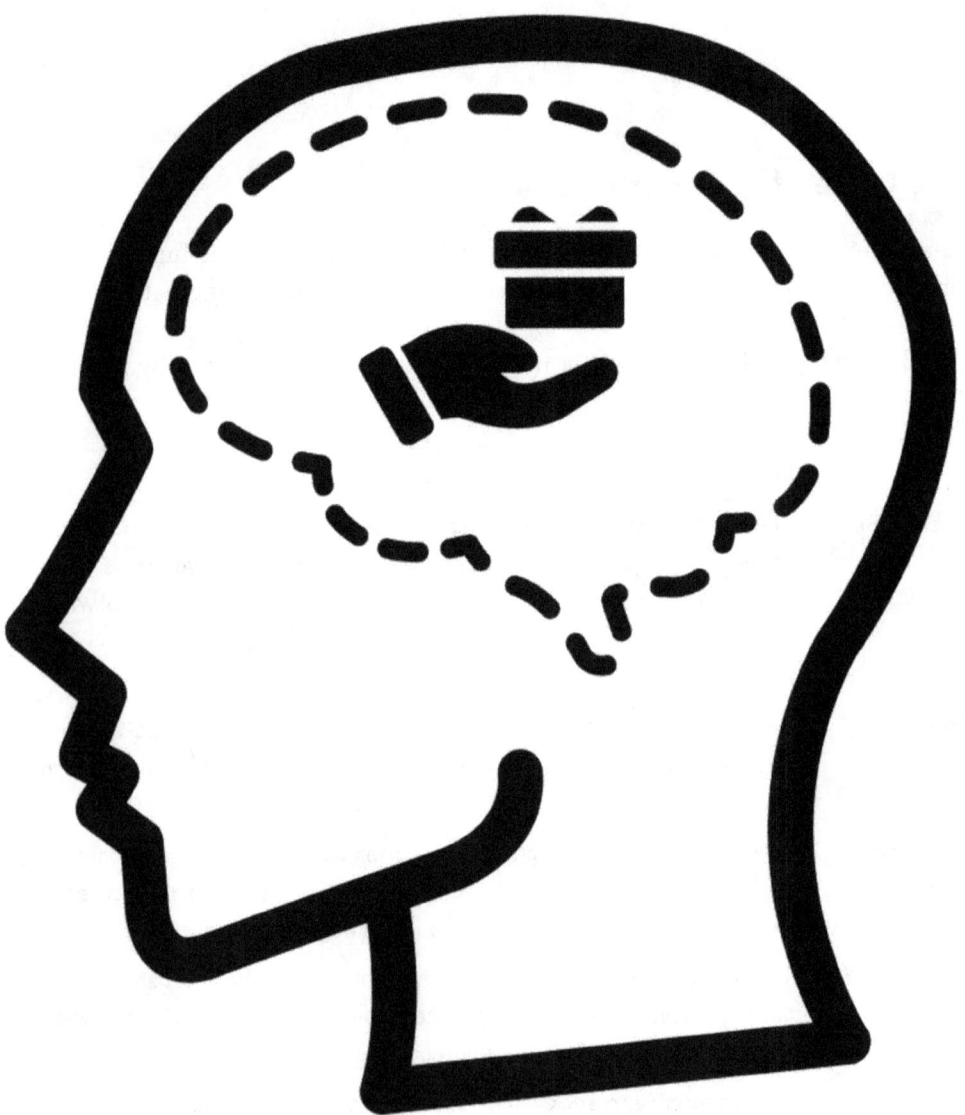

Figure 3.1 Self-gratification is the act of satisfying one's own desires or needs, often for immediate pleasure or comfort, without considering long-term consequences

Together, these heuristics create a monumental challenge for students, especially given the society they are growing up in. Every now and then, a conversation might come up with friends or family about the "good old days" when you had to walk to Blockbuster to rent a video, or listen to the Top 40 on the radio and hit record when your favourite song came on. Back then, if you wanted to listen to it again, you had to rewind the tape and stop it at just the right place. These experiences taught the value of delayed gratification. Today, however, everything is instant—music and video streaming have made things quick and easy, leaving students with few examples of the benefits of waiting for a reward.

An important experiment illustrating the role of gratification is the Harvard Marshmallow Experiment, conducted by Walter Mischel in 1972 with four- to five-year-olds. This experiment may ring a bell after a recent trend on social media replicated the findings of the study (Mischel et al., 1972).

Method

Each child was placed in a room with a table, a chair, and a single marshmallow in front of them.

They were given two options: one treat now, or two treats if they could wait. Most chose the option for two treats.

The experimenter explained they had to leave the room, but if the child could wait, they would get the second treat. If the child couldn't wait, they were allowed to ring a bell and call the experimenter back—but they would only get one treat.

The time the child waited before ringing the bell was measured in seconds, with any times exceeding 15 minutes being truncated.

This experiment was followed up 14 years later, and parents were surveyed on a range of questions, such as:

- How likely is your child to be sidetracked by minor setbacks?

- How likely is your child to exhibit self-control in frustrating situations?

- How able is your child to pursue their goals when motivated?

They also compared SAT scores of the participants, revealing some striking results:
There was a positive correlation between delayed gratification and:

- Higher SAT scores

- Better social skills and stress management

- Higher frustration tolerance and self-control

There are some ideas in this book that readers may feel are more relevant for older students; however, the study shows that gaps in children's ability to cope with self-gratification challenges appear as early as the age of 4. These gaps could indicate future difficulties students may face as they grow older.

A 2018 study by Watts et al. examined how socioeconomic factors impact children's ability to delay gratification. The study found that children from wealthier, more stable environments were more likely to wait for the second marshmallow, while children from lower-income backgrounds were more likely to take the marshmallow immediately. This suggests that a child's environment plays a significant role in their ability to delay gratification.

Variable	Children of Nondegreed Mothers (n = 552)	Children of Degreed Mothers (n = 366)
Delay of gratification (minutes waited)	3.99	5.38

They concluded the discrepancy is likely because children in lower-income households often grow up in unpredictable environments where resources—such as food, money, or even parental attention—are not guaranteed. In these circumstances:

- Waiting does not always lead to better rewards. Delaying gratification may not be a rational choice if past experiences have shown that the reward could be taken away or never materialise.
- For children who have faced scarcity, taking an immediate reward may seem like the logical option. Certainty over uncertainty feels safer.

In contrast, children in higher-income families are more likely to grow up in environments where:

- Delaying gratification is consistently rewarded (e.g., savings accounts grow over time, education leads to good jobs, promises are kept).
- They have the security to wait—there is no fear that the reward will disappear.

However, after controlling for these socioeconomic differences, the correlation identified by Mischel between delayed gratification and SAT scores was found to be weaker than initially expected. Nonetheless, the correlation remains significant, and knowing that the gap is wider for the most deprived students reinforces the importance of prioritising time spent with students in developing good learning habits and decision-making skills.

The original study demonstrated that children who were trained to use strategies like distraction—such as turning away from the marshmallow, singing, or covering their eyes—were more successful at delaying gratification compared to those who weren't given these strategies. Therefore, it is possible that by teaching students effective strategies, we can reduce the impact of self-gratification and improve their learning habits.

In a seminal study, Samuelson and Zeckhauser (1988) demonstrated how humans tend to favour the comfort of the status quo, even when better alternatives are available. In their experiment, participants were asked to choose between different options for health insurance and retirement plans. They found that when presented with a default option—one that they were already familiar with—participants were much more likely to stick with it, even if other options would have provided better benefits. This study highlights a common behaviour in human decision-making: the desire to avoid the discomfort of change and stick to what is familiar. The experiment reveals that comfort can have a powerful influence on our choices, leading us to stick with the status quo, even when it's not in our best interest.

In essence, the human tendency to choose the path of least resistance can sometimes prevent us from making decisions that would lead to greater long-term gains.

Comfort versus Courage: Lessons from Blockbuster and Bill Gates

We can see this desire for comfort playing out in a real-life scenario, at the peak of its success, Blockbuster was the undisputed giant of the movie rental industry. With thousands of stores across the globe, it was the place where families went to pick out movies for the weekend, and the company seemed unstoppable. But somewhere along the way, Blockbuster became too comfortable with its well-established business model. The company thrived on the traditional formula: physical rental stores, late fees, and a system that had worked for years. However, when the internet began to transform entertainment consumption, Blockbuster's leadership resisted the discomfort of change.

Even as Netflix, a small startup, began to offer a new way of renting movies—without late fees and with the convenience of home delivery—Blockbuster stuck to its comfort zone. Despite seeing the signs that digital streaming and online rentals were the future, the company's executives clung to the familiar, choosing to ignore the growing wave of change. Blockbuster's failure to adapt wasn't because they lacked the resources; it was because they were unwilling to step out of their comfort zone. They feared the discomfort of disrupting their successful business, and as a result, Netflix capitalised on this hesitation. By the time Blockbuster realised the need to pivot, it was too late, and the company soon crumbled under the weight of its own complacency.

> In contrast, Bill Gates faced a very different but equally pivotal decision in his life, one that required him to step out of his own comfort zone. As a young man at Harvard University, Gates had the world at his feet. He was on a traditional path—one that promised security, a degree from a prestigious university, and the kind of stability that most people dream of. But Gates had a vision that extended beyond the comfortable life that Harvard and a conventional career could offer. He saw the future of computing, the rise of personal computers, and the potential to change the world. To pursue his dream, he would have to make a decision that pushed him far outside the comfort zone of academia and security.
>
> While many of his peers at Harvard were content with their education, Gates realised that in order to make his vision a reality, he would need to leave the comfort of Harvard's walls and take a risk by founding Microsoft. It wasn't an easy decision. Dropping out of Harvard meant leaving behind the safe, predictable path that so many people dreamed of. But Gates knew that staying in his comfort zone would mean giving up on his ambition. By choosing to face the discomfort of the unknown and leave the familiar world of academia, Gates stepped into a new reality full of uncertainty, risk, and opportunity. It wasn't just about creating a company; it was about stepping away from the comfort of what was expected and into the discomfort of innovation and risk-taking.
>
> Gates' willingness to embrace discomfort paid off. Microsoft grew from a small startup into one of the largest and most influential technology companies in the world, transforming the way people interacted with computers. His decision to step out of his comfort zone and face the challenges of building something new revolutionised technology and made him one of the richest men in the world.
>
> These two stories—Blockbuster's downfall and Gates' rise—serve as powerful reminders of the tension between comfort and growth. Blockbuster's decision to stay in its comfort zone, clinging to a business model that had worked for years, ultimately led to its demise. In contrast, Bill Gates' choice to leave the comfortable, predictable path and venture into the unknown led to incredible success and global change. The difference between the two is clear: while comfort can feel safe and secure, it can also trap you in a place where growth and innovation are impossible. Stepping outside of your comfort zone is difficult and often uncomfortable, but as these two stories show, it's the key to achieving extraordinary success and avoiding stagnation.

Comfort can be a real barrier to effective learning. Take the example of revision: although important, students can spend excessive time planning their study schedule, or organising their materials, rather than actually engaging in the revision itself. This tendency to plan extensively, while comforting in its structure, can act as a form of procrastination. The act of planning feels productive, but it's ultimately a way of avoiding the discomfort of actual learning—especially the risk of failure. The idea of failing to recall information during revision can be intimidating, so students retreat into planning because it feels safer.

The challenges students face support my belief in the importance of teaching students about the dangers of self-gratification and the role comfort can play in stifling learning. However, given the powerful influence that they can have on decision-making, simply educating students about it is not enough to resolve the issue. Instead, I will explore how they fit into a broader framework aimed at helping students form new, healthier habits.

The Misunderstand of Motivation

Everyone reading this book will have, at some point, set themselves a goal that they did not meet—perhaps to lose weight, quit smoking, or spend more time reading. Ultimately, these goals often fail due to an inability to form new habits.

What is a habit?

A habit is a routine or behaviour that is repeated regularly and tends to occur automatically and is an example of fast thinking. It develops through repetition and reinforcement—the more frequently a habit is performed, the more ingrained it becomes.

But committing to a new habit, such as exercising regularly or studying effectively, is difficult. This is because our brains are wired for instant gratification—seeking immediate rewards rather than long-term (Figure 3.2).

To develop new habits, students must not only challenge self-gratification but also break established routines and sustain long-term motivation. These three elements are like the legs of a stool—each one is essential, and without all of them, the cycle remains unbroken (Figure 3.2).

A good starting point for discussing habits with students is to explore a range of habits they may have and want to break. This allows them to draw on their preexisting knowledge of learning and revisit ideas they may have forgotten over time. Discussing why these are bad habits will encourage deeper thinking, helping them remember these concepts in the future and build their schemas associated with learning and thinking.

Habit Formation

Routines : Self Gratification : Motivation

Figure 3.2 To change habits effectively, consider the roles of routine, motivation, and the pull of instant gratification

Common Bad Habits That Hinder Learning

- **Copying from a classmate**—This requires no thinking. If a student is not thinking, they are not learning. An earlier example of this was the story about the house burglary/buyer and the misplaced mobile phone.

- **Skipping homework**—To retain knowledge over time, we need to revisit it. Homework is often an opportunity to reinforce learning. We also know that the more knowledge students have, the easier it is to learn new knowledge. An example discussed before was how students are more likely to remember letters than their grandparents if they are set up as acronyms like LOL or BRB that they are more familiar with. If students do not complete their homework, they will find it harder to learn in the future.

- **Drifting off during lessons**—If a student is not engaged while a teacher is explaining a new concept, they are unlikely to remember it later. Learning requires attention, and without it, information simply does not stick.

While these habits have clear, immediate consequences for learning, some ineffective study habits appear productive but ultimately lead to poor retention.

- **Highlighting key words in a text**—Simply marking words without processing their meaning does little to help remember it later. It would be better if students were linking this new information to knowledge they already have, to help organise these ideas into their preexisting schema making it more likely for them to remember it later.

- **Re-reading notes**—While this might feel like revision, it is a passive activity that does not engage memory retrieval.

Both strategies create the illusion of learning—they provide a sense of accomplishment and comfort in the moment but lead to disappointment when students struggle to recall information later.

One of the biggest barriers to building new habits is a common misunderstanding of how motivation actually works. Many people focus too much on setting goals, believing that motivation will naturally follow—but this often leads to giving up when progress feels slow or inconsistent.

While goals are helpful for setting a direction, it is systems that drive progress. I've lost count of how many times a student has said, "But they are cleverer than me," referring to the student with the top score. Often, students set goals to achieve a higher grade or percentage. But the focus should not be solely on the goal. What truly matters is the process—the daily habits and actions that lead to those results. If our goal is to develop independent, successful learners, then we should ask: Are students making the decisions that will help them retain knowledge long-term?

In every competition, there's a winner and a loser, yet they all begin with the same goal. I remember when I was a short-distance runner at school, and my goal was to run the 100 m faster than everyone else. Unfortunately, everyone else at the starting line had the same goal. It wasn't the goal that separated us at the finish line—it was the process, the actions we took leading up to the race, that made the difference.

My daughter is in Year 6, facing a big milestone in the English education system as she prepares for her SATs exams. It's an intense week of testing in English and maths, and she believes these exams define her six years at school. Her goal is to score "above average"—a goal she set herself, but one that I suspect is influenced by external pressures. The problem with such goals is that they're tied to a single moment in time. What happens if she hits the magical score of 34/40 on her maths test? Will she stop putting in the effort that got her this far? As the parent of someone writing a book on learning, I certainly hope not. I like to think of her as my main case study for implementing the ideas in this book.

Currently, she spends ten minutes a day practicing times tables using an app. This practice ensures that she's developing automaticity in basic arithmetic, allowing her to recall answers to 7 × 8—faster than I can. Applying cognitive load theory to working memory, this means that when she's tackling exam questions, she's not using any of her working memory on simple mental arithmetic. This frees up valuable space for more complex problem-solving. But if she were to stop this daily habit, her ability to recall her times tables could start to deteriorate, impacting her performance in future exams. Achieving a goal like scoring "above average" is only a momentary change, but is she aware of the systems she has in place that help her reach that goal?

Linked to this goal is my daughter's happiness. Each week, she comes home with a new practice test score. Two weeks in a row, she scored 31/40, and she was disappointed. It's easy to fall into the trap of believing that happiness depends solely on the goals we set for ourselves. It becomes a pass-or-fail mentality: you're either above average or not, with no room for growth in between. As James Clear puts it in *Atomic Habits*, "When you fall in love with the process rather than the product, you don't have to wait to give yourself permission to be happy. You can be satisfied anytime your system is running" (Clear, 2018, p. 28).

The final challenge with goals is that they can sometimes conflict with long-term progress. Teachers understand the complexities of becoming expert classroom practitioners. As Dylan Wiliam reminds us, "Every teacher needs to improve, not because they are not good enough, but because they can be even better" (Wiliam, 2012). Striving to become the best teacher possible is a continuous journey without a definitive endpoint. For instance, a teacher might set a goal to enhance student attention by incorporating new teaching techniques. However, after achieving this, they might discover that some students still struggle with key concepts, prompting a shift in focus to modelling or scaffolding. Teaching is an ongoing cycle of refinement and improvement. Ultimately, it's the commitment to the process, rather than a singular goal, that drives meaningful progress.

My daughter may not realise it yet, but she is developing excellent habits for becoming a successful learner, like her commitment to the retrieval of fundamental maths concepts. But when she moves on to high school, will she abandon these habits if she starts to underperform by some metric she's set for herself? Or will she push forward, looking for the next step in her learning journey? Will she sit in maths lessons, elaborating and interrogating when her teacher introduces a new concept, linking her understanding of basic arithmetic to rearranging equations to develop her schema?

To summarise, students who aspire to perform better in school don't necessarily rise to the level of their goals; rather, they fall to the level of their systems. This underscores the importance of helping students recognise that achieving academic success requires more than ambition—it requires an understanding of cognitive science. By understanding how learning works, students can design the right systems and routines to support their progress. In doing so, we equip them with the tools and habits necessary to build effective learning strategies that ultimately lead to lasting success.

So how do we begin to unpack this complex idea with students? After all, struggling to change habits isn't just a challenge for children. As I mentioned at the start of this chapter, every reader will likely recall a goal they've set but never achieved.

One way to explore this is through a simple analogy: the boiling kettle. Start by asking students, *What is the goal of a kettle?* Some might say it's to heat water, but with a bit of discussion, you'll likely agree that its goal is to boil water. Then ask: *How do we know when the kettle has reached its goal?* Students will usually mention the visible signs—steam, the whistle, or the rumbling noise.

Now pose this question: *If the water is currently at 40°C, is the kettle working?*

The instinctive response is uncertainty. There's no steam yet, no whistle, so it doesn't seem like progress is being made. But of course, it is. The water is heating, just not boiling *yet*. The progress is happening beneath the surface, silently and invisibly.

This is an important lesson for students: not all progress is immediately visible, and not all effort produces instant results. Measuring success solely by outcomes, especially quick ones, can be misleading and demotivating.

Not only is this progress invisible, but it's also non-linear, which often leads to frustration. James Clear (2018) popularised this idea through the concept of the *plateau of latent potential*, which describes how results can lag behind effort, creating the illusion that no progress is being made. In the context of learning, this can feel like a curse of invisible progress. Students may be working hard without seeing immediate results and begin to believe their efforts are futile, when in fact they are laying the foundations for a breakthrough that just hasn't arrived yet.

This closely links to students' expectations around instant gratification. Many believe that if they work hard, they'll see results straight away. When they don't, they feel discouraged. James Clear (2018) refers to this period as the *valley of disappointment*. In an educational context, I call it the *learning lag*: the frustrating

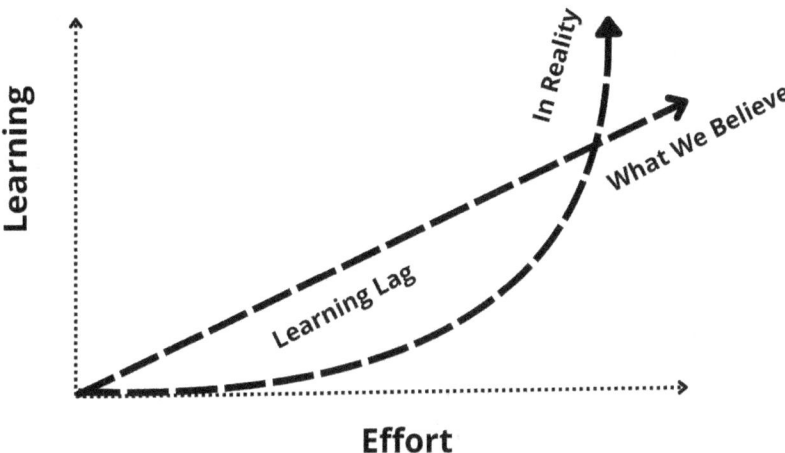

Figure 3.3 Graph illustrating the learning lag caused by the gap between students' perception of learning and their actual progress
Adapted from James Clear's *Atomic Habits* (2018)

gap between sustained effort and visible progress. This is often when students lose confidence, not because they're failing, but because the signs of success haven't surfaced. The learning is happening—just not in a way that can be seen or measured yet (Figure 3.3).

To make this more tangible, consider someone trying to lose weight by avoiding chocolate for a week, or someone hoping to build muscle after just a few visits to the gym. In both cases, progress is unlikely to be visible so soon, but that doesn't mean the effort is wasted. The same is true of learning: effort builds silently until it eventually shows itself.

Take language learning, for instance. No one expects a beginner to write a fluent paragraph in the first few weeks. Yet in their first language, that same task would feel routine. Progress in a new domain feels slower because it is; it's foundational, not fluent. A few words one week, some useful phrases the next. Eventually, with enough vocabulary and structure, students find themselves writing full paragraphs in entirely new contexts. That turning point only becomes possible because of the steady, unseen progress that came before it.

This concept can be used to prompt students to reflect on habits they've tried to form in school but abandoned when they didn't see benefits after a short time. Here are some examples:

- **Putting their hand up to ask for help**:
  For some, raising their hand to ask for help is a big step outside their comfort zone. Imagine the scenario where they raise their hand, receive help from their teacher, but then get stuck on another question just minutes later. Do they raise their hand again, or give up, frustrated that the first attempt didn't immediately solve all their problems?

- **Using flashcards to prepare for a test**:
  One of the biggest challenges in schools is encouraging students to engage in regular retrieval practice. Even when students commit to using flashcards for a couple of days, the benefits are often not immediately visible, leading to frustration and discouragement. This is a perfect example of the valley of disappointment—students expect immediate results, but the true benefits of retrieval practice take time to show.

Procrastination

A student who wants to improve their science scores may recognise that retrieval practice is a powerful strategy to help them achieve this goal. However, simply knowing this isn't enough—forming a habit requires overcoming obstacles, and one of the biggest barriers is procrastination.

Why do students procrastinate? The simple answer is that it makes them feel better. Playing video games or scrolling through social media provides instant gratification, whereas retrieval practice requires effort. Our brains are wired to prioritise immediate pleasure over future rewards, making it easy to put off hard work in favour of something more enjoyable in the moment.

A useful way to understand this is by comparing it to addiction. Imagine asking an alcoholic whether they would like a drink right now versus asking if they would like one in a week. The immediate temptation is far stronger than the abstract idea of drinking in the future, making it much harder to say no in the present moment.

The same principle applies to pain. At the time of writing this, I'm training for a charity cycle ride from London to Paris. The training is tough, and there have been moments when I've regretted signing up. But when I was asked six months ago if I wanted to take part, I said, "Yes, absolutely!" If they had instead asked, "Do you want to cycle to Paris tomorrow?", my response would have been something like, "Are you crazy?"

This helps explain why students procrastinate. They know that retrieval practice will help them reach their goals, but in the moment, it feels like a challenge they would rather avoid. In their minds, it might even feel as daunting as cycling 280 miles. The easiest way to deal with that discomfort? Put it off.

Overcoming procrastination isn't about willpower alone—it's about designing systems that make good habits easier to stick to.

One way to do this is by making a task more favourable. This might sound like an impossible task—if retrieval practice were more enjoyable, wouldn't students already be doing it? But we all have habits that we follow daily, even if they aren't particularly exciting.

Take brushing your teeth, for example. No one wakes up thrilled about brushing their teeth, but we do it automatically, without much thought. I never pause halfway through and think, *Should I switch hands and see if it feels different?* It's an ingrained habit that happens on autopilot.

The same applies to other unconscious routines. Think about how you shower—you likely wash your body in a set order, and that routine never changes. On some days, you might decide not to wash your hair, but before you realise it, you've done it anyway—because the habit has already taken over.

The goal, then, is to help students develop a system where retrieval practice becomes just as automatic. When a habit is truly embedded, procrastination is no longer an issue—because the decision to do the task disappears.

Counting What Counts: Motivation Through Measurement

Kamal's Turning Point: Tracking the Invisible Work

Kamal had always told himself he was "bad at revising." His desk was tidy, his books were highlighted in five different colours, and he'd even downloaded a study app—twice. But exam season was approaching fast, and the usual pattern was unfolding bursts of motivation followed by long stretches of avoidance.

Then, during a mentoring session, his teacher asked a simple question: *"How often are you actually revising, not just preparing to revise?"* Kamal didn't know. He *felt* like he was doing enough. But he couldn't prove it—to himself or anyone else.

That evening, Kamal created a revision tracker in the back of his notebook. He drew up a grid: days across the top, subjects down the side. Each time he completed a proper revision session—distraction-free, timed, and active—he coloured in a square. It was basic. But it gave him something he'd never had before: visibility.

At first, the tracker was more empty than full. But that discomfort became fuel. "I started to see the days I *thought* I was working... but wasn't," he said later. "The blank spaces told the truth."

As the days passed, his tracker became more colourful. More importantly, his confidence grew. He began setting small daily targets—two sessions a day, then three. He added a "reflection" box at the end of each week to note what was working and what wasn't. He even spotted patterns: his revision was most consistent when he did it straight after school, before dinner.

The tracker didn't make revision easier. But it made it *manageable*. It turned effort into evidence. When results day came, Kamal didn't say he was "bad at revising" anymore. He said, "I'm someone who can stick to a plan."

And that shift—from vague intentions to visible habits—changed everything.

Reflective Questions

1. *What habits or routines do I currently assume I'm doing "enough" of—without tracking them?*

2. *If I could see a visible record of my daily effort, what would it show me—and how might that change my approach?*

Research by Fishbach et al. (2006) provides valuable evidence that visual progress markers, like habit tracking, can significantly enhance motivation. Their study showed that when individuals could see their progress, even in small amounts, they felt more motivated to continue working towards their goal. This is because visible progress creates a sense of momentum—a feeling that the goal is attainable and that continued effort will lead to success. The researchers found that partial progress, such as completing a few tasks or hitting minor milestones, can be just as motivating as reaching the end goal. This aligns with how habit tracking helps individuals focus on the process rather than just the outcome, making the journey feel more manageable and rewarding. As a result, habit tracking doesn't just help people stay on task—it also fosters long-term commitment by providing a constant reminder of progress, even on difficult days.

Many learning apps are designed with this principle in mind. In his TED Talk, *How to Make Learning as Addictive as Social Media*, Luis von Ahn, co-founder of Duolingo, explained how the app maintains motivation by setting small, achievable goals that contribute to a larger sense of progress (von Ahn, 2023). Users complete short, gamified lessons and earn points towards daily XP targets, helping them maintain streaks and unlock rewards. These micro-goals—such as levelling up skills or climbing leaderboards—offer frequent feedback and a clear sense of momentum. By making each step feel manageable and meaningful, Duolingo turns language learning into a habit rather than a chore.

I recently experienced something similar during my training for the cycle ride to Paris. I was struggling to stay motivated and found it hard to spend long hours on the bike alone. So I installed Strava. Much like Duolingo, it boosted my motivation by breaking my training into incremental targets. Now, when I get back from a ride, I'm quick to check whether I've hit my subgoals—whether I've climbed faster at the 15 km mark or reached a new milestone. It's the small wins that keep me going.

However, for habit tracking to be effective, it's crucial to set the right kind of subgoals. Subgoals are the smaller steps or milestones along the way to achieving the larger, overarching goal. The key is that subgoals should complement the larger goal, not serve as a substitute. When subgoals are seen as partial accomplishments that bring the individual closer to their ultimate goal, they are highly motivating. For instance, a student tracking their daily revision for an exam is likely to feel encouraged by marking off each study session, seeing that these smaller efforts are building towards the final exam performance.

On the other hand, bad subgoals are those that lead to complacency. If the smaller goals are framed as the final achievements, students may mistakenly feel that completing them means they've reached the larger goal. For example, a student who tracks their revision by simply reading through notes or watching videos may feel as if they have now "learnt something." This can lead to a false sense of completion, where students feel they've accomplished enough and stop pursuing the deeper learning necessary for success in the exam.

In summary, a good subgoal is one that helps move a student forward, reinforcing their connection to the larger goal of deeper learning and exam preparation, and making it feel more achievable. A bad subgoal is one that makes them feel they've reached the goal prematurely, thus reducing further effort and commitment, further evidence that:

> Without knowledge of how learning happens, students' ability to develop effective learning habits is limited.

How Habits Are Born

Studies suggest that a significant portion of our daily actions are driven by automatic habits. Estimates vary, but it's generally accepted that around 40%–45% of our daily behaviour is automatic. That's a staggering thought—almost half of our day is shaped by decisions we didn't even realise we were making.

However, not all decisions are created equal. Some have a far greater impact on our lives than others. Take, for example, the routine we follow as a family. We try to sit together at the dining table for tea. Once that key event is over, there are only two remaining tasks for my wife and me before we can fully relax: putting the kids to bed and washing the dishes. My wife often struggles to put the girls to bed, and, as a result, she tends to take on the responsibility of washing the dishes while I handle bedtime. This struggle, in many ways, stems from the absence of clear routines and habits that have become automatic.

But this story isn't about the decision to choose one task over the other—it's about the pivotal moment when my wife decide when to wash the dishes. That moment, while seemingly small, is key. Most evenings, my wife will make a cup of tea after our meal, sit on the sofa to relax, and often scroll through her socials, telling herself she'll do the dishes later. This decision, though well-intentioned, often leads to procrastination, with the task stretching out for the rest of the evening. Given that my wife starts work later than I do, she knows there's always the option to do them in the morning—she believes she'll have more energy then, which is perfectly understandable. However, there's something interesting that happens on the rare occasion when she decides to do the dishes immediately after tea. Once she completes the task, she often feels a surge of energy and motivation to tackle other things. She might say, "I have lots of energy now; I'm going for a jog," or "I'm finally going to get that other job done that I've been putting off." That one decision—to do the dishes straight after tea—creates a ripple effect, making it easier for her to take on other tasks.

But if she decides to take that cup of tea to the sofa instead, those other decisions never happen. That one small choice—whether to tackle the dishes immediately or not—sets the tone for the rest of the evening. It's a great example of how one decision can lead to a series of others. If you want to start making better decisions, it's crucial to identify those key moments that influence the choices you make in the future.

Similarly, with students, one key decision occurs the moment they walk through the door after school. What's their next move? If they change into their comfy clothes, it's likely they'll follow that up by scrolling on their phone instead of getting started on their homework. However, if they delay changing into comfortable clothes and keep their uniform on, it might be the pivotal decision that leads to better choices later—such as sitting down and focusing on their studies. That small shift in mindset could be the key to fostering more productive habits in learning.

Edward Thorndike's early work on habits, conducted in 1898, unlocked a key insight into how behaviours are formed and reinforced (Thorndike, 1898).

Cracking the Habit Code: What a Cat in a Box Can Teach Us

In a small, dimly lit lab, Thorndike placed hungry cats inside what he called a "puzzle box." The box was a simple enclosure with a latch mechanism, a kind of mental challenge for the cats. Outside the box, he placed food—a tempting reward that motivated them to escape.

At first, the cats were confused. They scratched the walls, meowed, and pawed at the latch, but nothing worked. It was a chaotic display of trial and error, with each failed attempt offering no clear direction. However, eventually, one cat accidentally pressed a lever or pulled the right string, unlocking the box and gaining access to the food. Intrigued by this breakthrough, Thorndike watched as the cats, over time, grew more efficient. With each repeated attempt, they escaped faster, demonstrating a clear pattern of habit formation.

Thorndike observed that actions which led to satisfying outcomes—like escaping the box and getting the food—were more likely to be repeated. Conversely, behaviours that resulted in failure or discomfort, such as aimlessly scratching at the walls, gradually faded. This process of reinforcement and elimination of ineffective actions became the foundation of his law of effect. The idea—that behaviours leading to positive outcomes are more likely to recur—remains one of the most important principles in understanding learning and behaviour.

Humans, like Thorndike's cats, encounter new challenges regularly. When faced with unfamiliar situations, our brains instinctively seek the most effective course of action. This is why, just like the cats, we often stumble through trial and error until we discover a response that works. Over time, these repeated actions solidify into habits, shaping the way we react in similar circumstances.

Take, for instance, a student coming home from school after a long, exhausting day. Feeling drained, they instinctively reach for their phone, scrolling through social media to relax. It's a quick fix, providing immediate gratification with little effort. The next

> day, feeling tired again, the same impulse strikes—they grab their phone. Over time, this simple action—reaching for the phone—becomes an ingrained habit, repeated without even thinking about it. The satisfaction of the moment has reinforced the behaviour, turning it into an automatic routine, much like the cats learning to open the puzzle box.
>
> This story illustrates how habit loops are formed and reinforced through positive outcomes. Just as Thorndike's cats repeated behaviours that led to rewards, humans, too, form habits based on the satisfaction or gratification they receive from a particular action. Recognising how these habits form is the first step in understanding how we can change them for the better.

Reflective Questions

- **Understanding the Law of Effect:**

    1. In the experiment with the cats, why did certain behaviours (like pressing the lever) become more frequent, while others (like scratching the walls) faded away? How can you apply this principle to understand your own habits?

- **Real-Life Application:**

    2. Think of a habit you have, like checking your phone or organising your study materials. How did this habit likely develop? What rewards or satisfactions do you think reinforced this habit over time?

A similar process unfolds in the classroom. A student struggling with a difficult task may begin to feel anxious. To escape this discomfort, they start chatting with friends, a behaviour that provides an immediate distraction. If this response becomes routine, it can escalate—perhaps even resulting in them being sent out of the lesson. In this moment, the short-term relief from anxiety outweighs the long-term consequence of missing learning. This situation mirrors the example discussed earlier of the alcoholic struggling to turn down a drink in the present but able to resist it offered a drink in the future—our perception of the immediate moment is often more powerful than distant consequences.

I am not advocating for removing sanctions from students—consequences are essential in helping students understand the impact of their actions. However, it does explain why some students repeatedly make poor choices. To them, the behaviour does not feel like a mistake in the moment it was the more desirable option. If chatting with friends has become their default response to difficulty, simply enforcing punishments may not be enough to break the cycle. Instead, we must address the underlying habit and guide students towards more constructive responses—helping them replace unhelpful patterns with strategies that support learning and resilience.

My scenario may seem like an exaggeration, but take the striking example from an experiment conducted by researchers at the National Institute on Alcohol Abuse and Alcoholism (NIAAA), which illustrates just how ingrained behaviours can be, even when negative consequences are introduced.

In the experiment, the researchers trained mice to press a lever in response to a specific cue. In return for this action, they were rewarded with food. Over time, the mice learned to associate the lever press with a positive outcome—the food reward. This behaviour became ingrained, evolving into an automatic habit (Corbit & Janak, 2016).

But then, the researchers introduced a challenge: they made the food dangerous. In one case, the scientists poisoned the food, causing the mice to become violently ill after eating it. In another version, they electrified the floor, so the mice would receive a shock when they walked towards the reward.

Despite these painful and unpleasant consequences, the mice continued to press the lever and move towards the food. Even as they experienced discomfort—vomiting or jumping from the shocks—they could not stop themselves from following through on the habit they had learned. The habit was so automatic that it overrode their ability to make a rational choice, even when their brain knew the food was dangerous.

This experiment shows how powerful habit loops can be. Once a habit has been formed, even when it's clearly harmful, the brain's automatic systems take over. The cues (the lever press, the walk towards the food) trigger the learned response, and it can be nearly impossible to override that response without significant effort.

Chapter Summary

- Instant gratification is a major barrier to student success.
- Teaching students about delayed gratification is the first step in reducing its negative impact.
- Comfort can heavily influence decision-making, often steering students away from productive actions.
- Overcoming procrastination isn't about willpower alone—it's about designing systems that make good habits easier to sustain.
- While goals provide direction, it's systems that drive consistent progress.
- Habit tracking shifts the focus from outcomes to the process, helping students build momentum and stay motivated.
- According to the law of effect, behaviours that lead to positive outcomes are more likely to be repeated.
- Without an understanding of how learning happens, students struggle to develop effective learning habits.

References

Clear, J. (2018). *Atomic habits: An easy & proven way to build good habits & break bad ones.* Avery.

Corbit, L. H., & Janak, P. H. (2016). Habit formation and alcohol seeking: Emerging evidence and possible treatments. *Current Opinion in Behavioral Sciences, 13*, 34–39. https://doi.org/10.1016/j.cobeha.2016.05.002

Fishbach, A., Dhar, R., & Zhang, Y. (2006). Subgoals as substitutes or complements: The role of goal accessibility. *Journal of Personality and Social Psychology, 91*(2), 232–242. https://doi.org/10.1037/0022-3514.91.2.232

Mischel, W., Ebbesen, E. B., & Raskoff Zeiss, A. (1972). Cognitive and attentional mechanisms in delay of gratification. *Journal of Personality and Social Psychology, 21*(2), 204–218. https://doi.org/10.1037/h0032198

Samuelson, W., & Zeckhauser, R. (1988). Status quo bias in decision making. *Journal of Risk and Uncertainty, 1*(1), 7–59. https://doi.org/10.1007/BF00055564

Thorndike, E. L. (1898). Animal intelligence: An experimental study of the associative processes in animals. *Psychological Review, 2*(4), 289–316. https://doi.org/10.1037/h0070288

von Ahn, L. (2023, February). How to make learning as addictive as social media [Video]. *TED Conferences.* https://www.ted.com/talks/luis_von_ahn_how_to_make_learning_as_addictive_as_social_media

Watts, T. W., Duncan, G. J., & Quan, H. (2018). Revisiting the marshmallow test: A conceptual replication investigating links between early delay of gratification and later outcomes. *Psychological Science, 29*(11), 1748–1760. https://doi.org/10.1177/0956797618761661

Wiliam, D. (2012). Every teacher can improve [Video]. *YouTube.* https://www.youtube.com/watch?v=eqRcpA5rYTE

4 Creating Better Learning Habits

The Habit Loop

In the previous chapter, I introduced some of the key challenges students face when trying to make better decisions—highlighting the role of self-gratification as a significant barrier, the difficulty of maintaining motivation, and some simple strategies students can use to begin changing their habits. However, for many students, more comprehensive approaches may be necessary.

To truly understand how to change poor habits that have become ingrained over time, we need to delve deeper into the science of habit formation. In this chapter, I will break down the habit loop—the cycle of cue, craving, response, and reward—and explore practical ways to support students at each stage of this process.

By understanding and leveraging these habit loops, we can better equip students to replace unhelpful patterns with effective learning behaviours.

> **The Habit Loop: Uncovering the Science behind Our Behaviours**
>
> These stories have been moulded together to highlight the four critical stages of the habit loop: cue, craving, response, and reward.
>
> In a lab at MIT, a team of researchers led by Ann Graybiel placed a rat at the start of a T-shaped maze (Graybiel, 2008). At first, the rat was unsure—sniffing, pausing, turning the wrong way. Every step was deliberate, as its brain worked hard to figure out what to do. But something happened over time. Before each trial, the scientists played a clicking sound as the gate opened. Again and again, the rat heard the click, ran the maze, and found chocolate at the end.
>
> As the rat learned the routine, the researchers noticed a shift. Using brain scans, they saw that activity in the rat's brain, which had once fired constantly during the task, now spiked only twice—right at the click of the gate and again at the reward. The rest of the maze? The brain was almost silent. The behaviour had become automatic. The click, a simple cue, had come to signal, "Run the maze now." With just that sound, the rat

slipped into a habit. This experiment, led by Graybiel and colleagues, showed something powerful: habits don't start with the action, but with a cue. And once that cue is in place, the brain can take a back seat—letting the habit do the rest (Smith & Graybiel, 2013).

In a lab at the University of Michigan, neuroscientist Kent Berridge set out to answer a deceptively simple question: why do we keep doing the things we do? (Berridge, 2007) Is it because we enjoy them—or because we expect to enjoy them?

To explore this, Berridge and his team worked with lab rats. The setup was straightforward: press a lever, get a sugary treat, enjoy the taste. At first, that's exactly what happened. The rats pressed the lever, got the treat, and showed signs of pleasure. But then the researchers tweaked the experiment.

They stimulated the rats' dopamine systems—the part of the brain responsible not for pleasure, but for wanting. Suddenly, something strange happened. The rats began pressing the lever over and over, even when no treat came at all. Even when they did get the treat, but it had been altered to remove any enjoyable taste, they kept pressing. They weren't doing it because it felt good anymore. They were doing it because their brains expected it to feel good. They had developed a craving—not for the reward itself, but for the promise of the reward.

What Berridge discovered was powerful: it's not just the reward that drives habits, but the anticipation of it. The brain learns to predict pleasure, and that prediction alone can be enough to drive repeated behaviour. This is the engine behind many habits—our actions are often powered not by present satisfaction, but by the deep pull of craving what we think is coming next (Berridge & Robinson, 1998).

At Harvard in the 1940s, psychologist B.F. Skinner placed a pigeon inside a small chamber—what would later be known as the Skinner Box. On one wall was a small circular disc. Every time the pigeon pecked it, a food pellet dropped into a tray. At first, the pigeon wandered, flapped, turned in circles. Then, by chance, it pecked the disc—and food appeared.

The bird paused. Then it pecked again. More food. The connection clicked.

Over repeated trials, the pigeon learned that pecking the disc was the key to getting fed. Soon, the behaviour became automatic. Every time the light above the disc turned on (the cue), the pigeon immediately pecked (the response)—no hesitation, no trial and error. The response had become fast, reliable, and deeply ingrained.

Then Skinner did something subtle but revealing. He removed the food pellet. The pigeon still pecked. Again and again. Even though no reward followed, the response continued. This persistence showed how a behaviour, once reinforced enough times, can become automatic—decoupled from the original outcome. The pigeon wasn't thinking. It was just doing.

This experiment demonstrated a key part of the habit loop: the response is the action triggered by the cue and motivated by the craving—but once it becomes habitual, it can persist even when the reward disappears (Skinner, 1938).

In a lab at the University of Cambridge, neuroscientist Wolfram Schultz studied the brain's reward system in monkeys. His goal was to understand how animals (and humans) learn through reinforcement. To do this, Schultz set up a simple task: the monkeys had to press a lever to receive a juice reward. Initially, the monkeys received juice immediately after pressing the lever, and their brains reacted with a surge of dopamine, a neurotransmitter linked to pleasure and motivation.

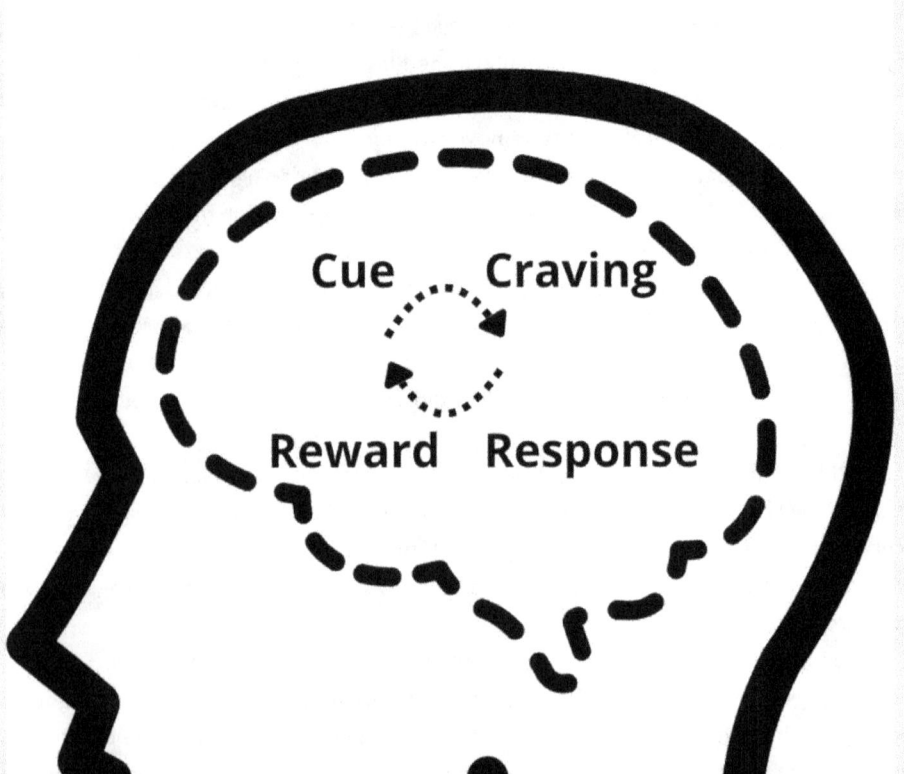

Figure 4.1 The habit loop

> But Schultz wasn't just interested in the juice itself—he was curious about what happened in the brain when the reward wasn't immediately available. So, he added a twist. He began giving the monkeys a cue, like a light flash, before they pressed the lever. Over time, the monkeys began to anticipate the juice. But here's the crucial finding: when the cue was presented, their brains released dopamine, even before they pressed the lever. The reward wasn't just the juice—it was the brain's expectation of it.
>
> Schultz's research revealed that dopamine release happened in response to the cue (the anticipation), not the actual reward. This shows that the brain is actively involved in reinforcing the behaviour long before the reward is received. The reward in the habit loop becomes a kind of signal that strengthens the habit. The anticipation and subsequent release of dopamine makes the monkey more likely to press the lever again when the cue appears (Schultz, 2016; Schultz et al., 1997) (Figure 4.1).

Reflective Questions

- In the first experiment with the rat and the T-shaped maze, what role did the cue (the clicking sound) play in shaping the rat's behaviour? How might this be similar to your own routines or habits?

- In the pigeon experiment by B.F. Skinner, what did the response (pecking the disc) become over time? Why do you think the pigeon continued the behaviour even when the food was removed?

- After reading these stories, how do you think habits, both good and bad, influence your daily routine and learning? Are there any habits that you'd like to change? If so, which part of the habit loop do you think needs the most attention (cue, craving, response, or reward)?

Making the Unconscious Conscious

We've already discussed the role of fast thinking in our decision-making. But it also plays a major part in the formation of habits. As habits form, our actions shift from conscious control to the direction of our automatic, non-conscious mind.

Take, for example, my wife. She bites her fingernails when she's anxious. The sound drives me mad, and when I point it out, she apologises and says she didn't even realise she was doing it. The nail-biting is triggered by a cue she can't even identify—her habit is already fully automated.

I'm guilty too. I often slip into my "teacher voice" when talking with friends. It's a necessary habit in my professional life, but I admit it must be annoying in social situations. These kinds of habits are deeply embedded and often operate outside of our awareness.

If our aim is to help children form better learning habits, we must first address the unhelpful ones they already have. The first step? Bringing those habits into consciousness.

> **The Hidden Cue: How a Film on Your Teeth Became a Habit**
>
> This story, originally detailed by Charles Duhigg (2012) in *The Power of Habit*, illustrates how marketers used the identification of a subtle cue—the sensation of a film on the teeth—to create a powerful habit loop that made brushing teeth a daily norm.
>
> To change a habit, we must first notice it. Often, the key to habit formation is identifying the subtle cues that trigger our behaviour. Let's look at a surprising example: toothpaste. There's no obvious craving when it comes to brushing your teeth—no hit of dopamine, no immediate gratification—but it's become an ingrained habit for most of us. So why is that?
>
> In the early 20th century, one of the most remarkable examples of habit formation through identifying cues came from the marketing of Pepsodent toothpaste. At the time, people didn't regularly use toothpaste, and the idea of brushing teeth wasn't yet widely ingrained. But Claude Hopkins, a clever marketing expert, identified a critical cue: the sensation of a film on the teeth.
>
> Hopkins noticed that most people didn't actively think about brushing their teeth. They didn't consciously think, "I should brush my teeth today." But what they did notice was a sticky, filmy layer that would slowly accumulate on their teeth over time—a sensation that many found unpleasant. Hopkins recognised that if he could get people to consciously identify this feeling, he could create the perfect cue for a new habit.
>
> His campaign was simple yet brilliant. He encouraged people to lick their teeth and notice that slightly gritty, film-like sensation. That feeling became the cue. From there, he connected the cue to a solution: brushing with Pepsodent. The film on the teeth signalled the need for action, and brushing became the response.
>
> Hopkins' real genius lay in linking this subtle sensation to a desirable outcome: cleaner, whiter teeth. By brushing with Pepsodent, people could immediately remove the invisible film on their teeth and enjoy a noticeable reward—whiter, smoother teeth. This sparked the formation of a powerful habit loop: the cue (the sensation of the film), the routine (brushing), and the reward (cleaner, more attractive teeth).
>
> But Hopkins didn't stop there. He added an extra layer to make the habit stick. He included ingredients that created a cool, tingling sensation, which people began to associate with cleanliness and freshness. This sensory feedback became a built-in reward, reinforcing the habit and helping Pepsodent become a massive success.
>
> What started as an invisible sensation—the film on the teeth—became the trigger for a daily routine that millions of people perform without even thinking about it. Hopkins demonstrated how identifying the right cue and pairing it with a rewarding outcome can transform an unfamiliar behaviour into a deeply ingrained habit.

Reflective Questions

- **Identifying Cues:**

    1. In the story, how did Claude Hopkins use the sensation of the film on teeth as a cue for a new habit? Can you think of any small cues in your daily routine that trigger certain behaviours?

- **Building New Habits:**

    2. Hopkins linked brushing teeth to the feeling of a film on the teeth and the reward of cleaner teeth. What habits do you think could be formed by identifying a similar "cue" in your own life? How could you make small changes to turn a routine into a habit?

By tapping into a simple, recognisable cue and offering an immediate reward, Hopkins made the act of brushing teeth something people wanted to do. His campaign didn't just sell a product—it built a habit. Today, brushing teeth is a global habit, demonstrating how spotting and emphasising a simple, often unnoticed cue can be used to create powerful, lasting routines.

We can teach children to identify cues through a strategy called "point and call." It's a method often used in high-stakes environments like train stations and factories, where workers physically point and verbalise their actions to stay focused and alert. The same approach can be adapted for learning environments.

A student is struggling in Spanish. They know they've fallen behind due to a lack of engagement. In class, they've developed a pattern: arriving late, slowly getting their book out, scanning the room, chatting, avoiding eye contact with the teacher. These have become habitual responses to the discomfort of not knowing the material.

They also know that the teacher begins every lesson with a retrieval task—an activity designed to get students thinking about what they learned last time. But instead of engaging, the student waits for their neighbour to finish and copies their answers. This habit continues, lesson after lesson. And even though they know that retrieval practice helps learning, they find themselves falling into the same behaviour every time.

The problem isn't knowledge—it's habit.

Creating a Habit Scorecard

To disrupt these patterns, students need a clear sense of their current behaviour. A habit scorecard helps them map out the first ten minutes of a lesson:

1. Enter the room on time

2. Chat with friends

3. Get class book and pencil case out

4. Open class book

5. Look around the room

6. Look at the board

7. Think carefully about the questions and try to answer

8. Copy from the person next to them

Next, they can assess each action as positive, negative, or neutral for learning:

Habit	Score
Enter the room on time	+
Chat with friends	–
Get class book and pencil case out	+
Open class book	+
Look around the room	–
Look at the board	+
Think carefully and try to answer	+
Copy from the person next to them	–

From here, they can create a personalised list of behaviours to focus on—what we want to keep and what we want to change.

Point and Call in Action

Once a student has this awareness, we move into the "point and call" phase. Here's how it works:

As the student enters the room, the first good habit they want to establish is getting out their pencil case and book. Once they stand behind their desk, they need to point at their bag and say, "Get out my pencil case and book." They then follow this up by pointing at the board as a reminder of the next step. This is the beginning of habit change—replacing old cues with new responses.

This may sound overly simplistic, but the "point and call" technique has been shown to work remarkably well in other fields, especially those where attention to detail and consistency are crucial.

For example, in the Japanese railway system, "pointing and calling" is a standard safety procedure used by operators and station staff to reduce mistakes. Workers physically point to gauges, signals, or operational steps and verbally confirm them aloud. This multisensory engagement reinforces attention and significantly reduces the likelihood of oversight. According to the Japan Industrial Safety and Health Association, this method has reduced operational errors by up to 85% (Japan Industrial Safety and Health Association [JISHA], 2009).

This technique is not limited to transport. In healthcare, researchers have applied a similar strategy to improve adherence to best-practice protocols. A study by Bauer and Beske-Janssen (2012) explored how verbalisation strategies can reduce error in medical environments. For instance, doctors and patients using simple verbal confirmations—such as stating out loud the dosage of a prescription or the steps in a procedure—showed improved accuracy and compliance. These verbal routines helped increase cognitive control, reduce memory lapses, and promote patient safety.

In both settings, the act of pointing and speaking serves to slow down the moment, engage more of the brain, and bring automatic behaviour into conscious awareness. When applied to the classroom, these strategies can help students solidify routines, become more intentional about their behaviour, and gradually internalise good habits.

Implementation Intention

Even with good intentions, students often struggle to maintain new habits. Many parents and educators try to supplement this process with encouragement:

> Good luck today!
> You've got this!

But does that really work?

A notable UK study examined the impact of *implementation intentions* on weight loss. Participants who were prompted to formulate specific plans—detailing *when*, *where*, and *how* they would exercise—demonstrated significantly higher adherence to their routines. This approach involves creating clear *if-then* plans that link situational cues with goal-directed actions, such as:

> **If** it is Monday morning, **then** I will go for a run in the park before work.

In this particular study, while just 35%–38% of participants in the control and motivational-only groups exercised at least once a week, an impressive 91% of those in the implementation intention group did so. The difference lay not in motivation, but in planning. By identifying precise moments for action, participants reduced the need for willpower in the moment and made the desired behaviour more automatic (Milne et al., 2002).

So, instead of relying on motivation alone, we should support children to form an implementation intention.

> When I get to Spanish, I'll use my habit scorecard.

This may sound tokenistic—but ask yourself: was "Have a good day" ever going to break a deeply ingrained habit?

Students can use implementation intentions as part of a daily habit-building routine. Whether in the morning, during tutor time, or after school, writing down learning intentions increases the chances of following through.

The structure is simple:

I Will [Behaviour] at [Time] in [Location]

Examples:

- I will complete flashcards at 8 a.m. on the bus to school.
- I will do my homework at 4 p.m. in my bedroom.
- I will complete my retrieval task in period 2 during Spanish.

Stacking New Habits

Children can build new habits by attaching them to routines they're already likely to follow—like taking their shoes off at the door. This takes advantage of the brain's natural tendency to link behaviours into sequences.

After [Current Habit], I Will [New Habit]

Examples:

- After I brush my teeth, I will write my habit plan.
- After I get my class book out, I will look at the board.
- After I take off my shoes, I will complete my homework.

Over time, these steps can be chained into larger learning routines:

> After I take off my shoes, I will do 20 minutes of flashcards, complete my homework, and pack my bag for the next day.

Design for Success: Start Small, Shape the Space

If you want students to start a new habit, one strategy is to make it as easy as possible to start. In 2009, the UK's National Health Service quietly launched a free programme called Couch to 5K. The idea was simple: take people who did no running at all—people who hadn't run since school, people who hated the very idea of it—and help them build up to running five kilometres without stopping. Not by shouting at them or demanding discipline, but by starting where they were. Week 1 asked for just 60 seconds of running at a time. Sixty seconds. Anyone could do that. The programme ran three times a week, gradually building up the running time in small steps. And those small steps mattered. The early wins, the feeling of "I can do this," were enough to keep people coming back. Over time, the walking gave way to running. People who once dreaded movement started to feel like runners. The shift wasn't just physical—it was psychological. It worked with human nature, not against it.

Even the name was clever. Couch to 5K begins by naming the very place that most people feel stuck: the couch. It's a word loaded with quiet comfort, easy distraction, and all the routines we turn to when we're avoiding effort—scrolling, bingeing, snoozing. By using the word "couch" upfront, the programme gently acknowledges those habits without judgement. It gives them a place in the story, but not the final word. You start on the couch, sure—but that's not where you stay.

By 2020, during the height of the pandemic, downloads of the Couch to 5K app had surged by 92%. More than five million people had taken part. A study by the University of Lincoln (2023) found that 87% completed the nine-week plan, and 80% reported improved mental health. But the most important number might be this: a year later, more than half were still running. That's the power of starting small and staying consistent. It wasn't willpower that got them through. It was a structure that made momentum feel inevitable. Comfort—the couch—wasn't confronted head-on. It was edged out, one minute at a time.

Imagine if students approached revision the way some approach Snapchat—regular, quick, and low-effort to start with, but consistent. Imagine a mindset called Snap to Grade 9. Not a programme or an app, but a new way of thinking about how progress is made. It starts with something familiar: the Snap streak. That daily ping, that tiny moment of connection—it's not much on its own, but it adds up. It creates momentum. It keeps the streak alive. Now imagine applying that same idea to revision.

Maybe it's one question a day. A ten-minute recap. A voice note summary. Small, quick actions that don't feel like a big deal at the time but compound over weeks. The beauty of Snap to Grade 9 is that it doesn't demand a total life overhaul. It meets students where they are—in short bursts, low pressure, but regular enough to build confidence and routine.

The goal isn't cramming or chasing perfection. It's forming a new identity: someone who revises, someone who shows up, even for ten minutes. And over time, just like those Snap streaks, it becomes second nature. No pressure. Just progress.

Snap to Grade 9: Start Where You Are, Not Where You Wish You Were

And here's the real magic: just starting is often enough to keep going. A runner tying their shoes and heading to the end of the street often finds themselves going a little further. Not because they planned to—but because the hardest part was getting out the door. Revision works the same way. Once a student sits down, opens their book, and answers just one past paper question, the momentum kicks in. One question turns into two. Ten minutes becomes 20. Consistency beats intensity.

As we've seen, one effective way to start a new habit is by making it easy. This principle aligns with the Couch to 5K approach, where the focus is on breaking down the overwhelming task of running a 5K into manageable, incremental steps. When something feels simple and achievable, people are more likely to take the first step, and from there, progress often follows naturally.

As well as making new habits easy to form, we can also approach behaviour change from the opposite direction—by making unhelpful habits harder to maintain. Earlier, I gave the example of a misbehaving student being removed from a lesson. In that scenario, I suggested that the student's behaviour may have become habitual, driven by an immediate reward that felt more powerful than the delayed consequence of a detention.

One common strategy schools use to address poor behaviour is the report card system. However, in my experience, the success of this approach is mixed. Ultimately, it hinges on whether the student sees the consequence of doing poorly on the report as more uncomfortable than the perceived reward of their negative behaviour. This is where parental support becomes crucial. Schools alone often lack the leverage to impose a consequence strong enough to break the habit.

Using a report card without involving parents is, in most cases, ineffective. I've seen students serve detention after detention, day after day—until even that becomes a routine. In some cases, students would show up automatically, assuming they were on the list, as detention had simply become part of their daily rhythm.

Occasionally, when issuing a low report score, I've seen students suddenly plead with urgency: "Please don't—my dad's going to take my phone off me!" But by then, it's too late. The behaviour that triggered the consequence has already happened. If a report card is going to be effective, it must function as a clear agreement between the school, the child, and the parents. Everyone involved needs to understand exactly what the expectations are and what the consequences will be if those expectations aren't met. This clarity should be communicated across all staff working with the student.

That's where the idea of a habit scorecard becomes so valuable. The child must understand the expectations, and those expectations should be framed around clear, simple, and achievable goals:

> When I get to my desk, I will take out my class book and pencil case straight away.
> When I get home, I will hand Mum my phone and start my homework.

Small habit changes like these, clearly defined and consistently reinforced, can play a powerful role in reshaping behaviour over time. And just as importantly, the consequence for not engaging with these new habits must be meaningful. For example, removing access to a games console or a mobile phone can be far more effective than repeated detentions, because it directly disrupts the immediate rewards that often reinforce the unwanted behaviour.

The Role of Environment

Just as we stack habits, we can also optimise our environment to support them. I'd always wanted to learn the piano. Over the years, I bought keyboards and tucked them away in different corners of the house. Unsurprisingly, I never stuck with it.

Then, two years ago, my daughter started piano lessons. Around the same time, a friend was giving away an upright piano. I accepted and placed it next to our dining table in our open-plan living space.

I created a simple implementation intention:

After dinner, before taking my plate to the kitchen, I play piano for 15 minutes.

That's it. And it worked.

Had the piano been upstairs, in a cupboard, or under a bed, I doubt I would have kept it up. The location was as important as the habit itself. The environment made it easier to act.

The power of altering the environment to disrupt poor learning habits is illustrated by the case of Eugene Pauly, studied by neuroscientist Dr. Larry Squire (Squire, 1992). Eugene suffered severe brain damage that left him unable to form new memories. Despite this, he could still perform complex habitual tasks, like making a cup of tea, by relying on well-established routines stored in his brain.

What's important is that Eugene didn't consciously recall where the kettle was; instead, the familiar setting of his kitchen and the sequence of actions served as a kind of environmental context cue that triggered the entire habit. When researchers moved the kettle to a different location, Eugene was unable to complete the task because the usual environmental cues that prompted his habitual behaviour were disrupted.

This highlights how habits are closely tied to their environmental context—not just single cues—and how changing the surroundings can help break unwanted habits. For students, this suggests that even subtle changes to their learning environment can support the disruption of poor habits and the formation of better ones.

Make the Right Choice the Easy Choice

Environment plays a powerful, often underestimated role in shaping our behaviour in a way that is not helpful to us.

At school, I once moved offices to a space just above the sixth-form café. After break duty, I had to walk past it to get back to my office. At first, I'd stop in occasionally. But over time, it became automatic—even on days I wasn't on duty, I'd find myself heading in and buying a croissant.

I hadn't planned for this habit; it formed quietly, through nothing more than convenience and repetition. The cue was the route I took, the smell of food drifting out, the familiar pause. The response was buying the croissant. It felt harmless—just a small treat. But the habit stuck.

It wasn't until I moved to a new school that I broke it. This time, I deliberately chose a breaktime routine that didn't involve walking past the café. I took a different path—one that led through the staff room instead. Without the familiar sights and smells to cue the behaviour, the craving disappeared. I made it to lunch just fine.

What struck me wasn't just that I stopped buying food—I didn't miss it at all. That's when I realised: maybe it was never really about the croissant. Perhaps the real reward had been something else—like a moment of connection, a brief chat, or simply a break from the demands of the day. The food had just become part of the routine I used to seek that reward.

We can apply the same logic to encouraging new habits. If a student tends to go to their bedroom after dinner and immediately picks up their phone or PlayStation controller, we can create an alternative habit by changing the setting:

After dinner, do flashcards at the dining table.

The Power of Environment: A Case Study

The key is to consider how we can shape our surroundings to reduce unwanted behaviours and increase the likelihood of learning-focused ones.

Educators are already familiar with this idea. Think about seating plans—teachers constantly adjust them to minimise the negative impact that certain friendship groups can have on learning. Early in my career, I was focused on making my classroom visually inspiring. I covered the walls with colourful displays and motivational quotes like "Shoot for the moon. Even if you miss, you'll land among the stars." But over time, I realised that these well-intentioned decorations could become distractions. Now, I'm more deliberate about what goes on the walls. If I want students to focus on the board, I need to make sure it's the most visually appealing and attention-grabbing part of the room.

Environmental cues extend beyond the classroom too. If I want students to arrive on time, it's not enough to just expect it—we need to ensure staff are present in the corridors and at bottlenecks to gently steer students away from taking the scenic route. The beauty of investing in habit-building like this is that it's temporary. Once students have formed more effective routines, the habits begin to run themselves. And by then, it takes a conscious effort to break them.

At my last school, we faced a recurring challenge that couldn't be solved by staff merely patrolling the corridors. Between lessons, students routinely returned to their lockers to fetch their class books and then congregated to chat before heading to class. As a result, many students were consistently late despite our repeated instructions to carry their books with them throughout the morning. The behaviour persisted because it had become a habit: the cue was the bell signalling the end of a lesson, the routine was the trip to the locker, and the reward was a five-minute chat with friends. With our school being too large for us to monitor every corridor, the students always found a way to visit their lockers.

Our leadership team held several meetings to address this problem. One suggestion was to encourage personal responsibility; however, a few mentions in assemblies were not enough. Next, we split up friendship groups' locker areas so that students could no longer easily congregate with their friends. Unfortunately, the students simply reverted to their original meeting point, sharing lockers in the same location where the habit had been long established. Next, we tried imposing a disciplinary consequence for being in the wrong locker area. This approach soon became unmanageable—with over 50 detentions on the first day, many students skipped their assigned detentions, and we expended considerable time and resources following up. In an attempt to streamline the process, we reduced the sanction by declaring that being caught five times in the designated area would result in one detention. Yet, much like an alcoholic who can decline a drink when sober in the future but not in the moment, the students did not view the deferred consequence as a sufficient deterrent against the immediate reward of chatting with friends.

I wish I had read The Power of Habit before encountering the locker issue; in it Charles Duhigg recounts the story of an army sergeant in Afghanistan who was tasked with reducing riots in a town. By carefully observing, he identified that the unrest tended to start shortly after teatime—when crowds gathered around food trucks. By removing the food trucks, the cue for the rioting was eliminated, and the disturbances ceased.

In our case, the cue was the ringing bell—a factor we never initially considered changing. Instead, we tackled the problem by removing the lockers altogether. For the majority of our students, this environmental change broke the habit. However, for some, the craving for the reward was too strong; they simply devised a new routine, roaming the school to chat with friends instead.

Reflecting on the matter now, I've seen other schools successfully modify behaviour through removing a cue. For example, one school plays classical music for 60 seconds while students walked in orderly lines along painted corridors—a routine that, with repetition, became a habit in itself. Such strategies to replace and tighten the existing routine might have further reduced the disruption in our corridors.

This is just one example from school life. We also faced issues with students frequently leaving class to go to the toilet. To address this, we closed all but one toilet, making it more difficult for them to congregate or use their phones. This intervention, similar to our approach with the lockers, significantly reduced the number of students skipping lessons.

We encountered another challenge when we introduced slushes at lunchtime. Some students began throwing them, which quickly led us to remove the slush machines. Despite this, a minority still managed to create a disturbance in other ways.

In each of these instances, the reality remains: some students—often those who could benefit most from targeted support—need more than just a simple change in the environment.

This experience highlights a broader truth: not every individual struggling with habits will thrive without additional support. Despite Alcoholics Anonymous (AA's) proven success—which is based on principles like those I advocate in this book—some continue to drink. Often, those who fall off the wagon the most are also the ones who deserve the greatest support to break the cycle. If you have students lingering at their lockers when they should be in class, they are the first ones you should be trialling habit scorecards with. Likewise if you are a parent of a child who is likely to find ways to procrastinate you could have this conversation at home.

One of the biggest challenges we face in creating learning habits is that, by nature, learning is hard. This means that the activities that facilitate learning are often not inherently attractive. Compounding this issue is the fact that our brains are constantly competing with what psychologists call Supernormal Stimuli—things like social media, video games, and streaming content, which provide levels of excitement and stimulation far beyond those of everyday tasks.

So, how can something like flashcards possibly compete with these distractions? Social media, for instance, offers an amplified version of social interaction—endless likes, notifications, and dopamine hits. Video games provide instant gratification and excitement. In comparison, flashcards and traditional revision methods may seem dull.

One way to combat this is by removing or reducing distractions. For example, you could move your revision session to a different environment, like the dining table, which creates a clear boundary between study time and other activities. Alternatively, we can explore the role of cravings in the brain's feedback loop and use that knowledge to make learning more enjoyable.

Cravings are deeply tied to the brain's reward system, particularly the dopamine system. Dopamine, often referred to as the "feel-good" chemical, plays a crucial role in our desire to seek out rewards. It doesn't just create pleasure—it fuels the anticipation of pleasure, which triggers cravings for certain behaviours or experiences. When we engage in an activity that leads to a positive outcome, such as answering a question correctly, dopamine is released. This reinforces the behaviour and creates a desire to repeat it. Over time, our brains begin to predict rewards, releasing dopamine even before the reward is experienced.

In the classroom, this concept can be used effectively. For example, whole-class feedback, such as using mini whiteboards, allows educators to assess the room and respond to the students' needs. But there's a bonus—these techniques also create more opportunities for students to respond, providing them with the dopamine hit. Techniques like choral questioning where all students respond at once in unison provide a dopamine boost before any answers are given. While we can't necessarily make the retrieval process itself inherently exciting, we can enhance the experience with positive reinforcement through collective response.

There's also a valuable opportunity here for teachers and parents to work together. By helping parents understand how to support their child's learning outside of school, they can maximise their child's engagement with learning. A simple but effective approach could be using a technique called temptation bundling. For example, parents could encourage their child to bundle a necessary task with a pleasurable one: "When I get home and check my phone (current habit), I will first check my homework (new habit). After completing it, I will spend 10 minutes on social media (reward)." This technique uses dopamine to increase motivation. When we anticipate a reward, we are more likely to complete the task at hand. By pairing a task that feels less enjoyable with something that is inherently motivating, we can help create better habits.

However, parents should be mindful of the rewards they are using. They must ensure that the rewards are limited, monitored, and aligned with the goal of fostering better learning habits—not reinforcing negative behaviours.

The reward doesn't always have to be so obvious; one example comes from the story of Febreze. When Procter & Gamble first launched the product, its purpose was to make things smell odourless; they assumed people would be triggered to clean their homes when they noticed unpleasant odours. But it turned out that many people had become "nose blind" to the smells in their own homes and simply didn't notice the cue.

So, the company shifted strategy. Instead of relying on a cue people often ignored, they repositioned Febreze as a reward—the satisfying final step after cleaning. They created a pleasant smell to ensure everything smelt as nice as it looked. The new habit loop became clean the room (routine), spray Febreze (reward), and enjoy the fresh scent and feeling of accomplishment. This small change created a stronger habit by making the process feel rewarding, not just necessary.

Some study strategies—like highlighting or decorating a mind map—aren't the most effective for learning on their own, but they feel good and provide a sense of progress. Rather than removing them, we can place these more enjoyable tasks after a more effortful but effective strategy.

For example:

When I get home from school, I will "blurt" out everything I can remember from today's lesson without looking. Then, I'll highlight the key words and organise the information to make it look good.

The Power of Believe

One powerful technique for changing habits is to keep the cue and reward the same but alter the routine. This approach works because it leverages the brain's existing habit loop—something already familiar—without requiring a complete behavioural overhaul. By identifying the cue (what triggers the behaviour) and the reward (the benefit gained), we can substitute the routine with something more helpful or aligned with long-term goals.

For instance, if someone reaches for a sugary snack when feeling stressed, it's not just about the snack—it's about the comfort the sugar provides. Rather than trying to eliminate the habit altogether, we can shift the routine to something like a short walk or a cup of tea. The craving is still satisfied, but in a way that supports better wellbeing over time. In the scenario of my break time croissants, this was also the case: the cue, the bell ringing, and the real reward, the 15-minute escape, stayed the same; what changed was my route to this escape.

How does this apply in a school context? Imagine a student who feels low on energy before lunch.

- **Cue:** Feeling tired or unmotivated.
- **Old Routine:** Eating a lot of chocolate or sugary snacks at break.
- **Reward:** A quick energy boost and a mental break.

Now, we keep the cue and the reward the same but change the routine:

- **New Routine:** A brisk five-minute walk or a chat with a friend, followed by a healthier snack.

This new habit still delivers energy and a moment of mental reset—but without the sugar crash that comes later. It's a small shift, but one that builds self-awareness and self-regulation over time.

This method ties directly back to the core idea introduced at the start of this book: before we can expect students to change their habits, we must first teach them how to learn effectively. Understanding learning strategies and why they work gives students a sense of control—reducing anxiety and overwhelm, and paving the way for more productive routines.

For example:

- **Cue:** Sitting down to revise and feeling overwhelmed.
- **Old Routine:** Reaching for a phone and scrolling through social media.
- **Reward:** A short burst of relief and distraction.
- **New Routine:** Doing a quick "blurt" or mind dump of everything remembered on the topic to build momentum.

Again, the cue and reward remain the same—but the routine becomes one that supports learning, rather than avoidance.

However, these habit changes will only take root if students believe the new routine will help. If they doubt it will work or don't see themselves as capable learners, they'll struggle to commit. That's why belief lies at the heart of habit change.

We must first ensure students believe they can learn.

One of the most compelling demonstrations of the power of belief is the placebo effect. Research shows that when people believe they are receiving a helpful treatment—even if it's just a sugar pill—their brains can trigger real improvements. Pain decreases, mood lifts, and healing speeds up. This illustrates that belief is not just wishful thinking—it has real, physiological power. Our expectations and mindset shape our experience, even at a biological level.

This brings us to the concept of identity-based habits. Lasting change happens when new behaviours are seen not just as tasks but as expressions of identity. The goal of helping students understand how learning works is not just academic—it's transformational. We want them to move from thinking, "I want to do well," to believing, "I am a good learner."

When that shift happens, everything changes. Actions begin to align with the belief. Students are more likely to stay on top of homework, ask thoughtful questions, revise regularly, and engage with their learning—not because they're told to, but because it feels natural to who they are. This internal belief fuels motivation and makes positive habits more likely to stick over time.

This idea is supported by the work of psychologist Albert Bandura, who developed the theory of self-efficacy—the belief in one's ability to succeed in specific situations (Bandura, 1997). Bandura found that when individuals believe they can achieve something, they are far more likely to try, to persevere through difficulty, and to recover from setbacks. In the context of learning, this means students who believe they are capable of understanding and improving are more willing to engage with challenging material and persist when it gets hard. By supporting students to build both effective learning strategies and belief in their ability to use them, we lay the foundation for habits that are not only effective but enduring. Bandura's research reminds us that without belief, even the best learning techniques may go unused—because effort begins where belief begins.

I am sharing a personal story that might seem somewhat removed from the academic focus of this book. However, I invite the reader to consider this as a case study, illustrating how personal habits and identity shape behaviour in a very real way. This story highlights key concepts discussed throughout this book, and by reflecting on my journey, I aim to bring these theories to life, providing a tangible example of how habits, identity, and belief systems intertwine in the process of behaviour change.

Through my younger years, I was a heavy drinker, and this didn't come as a surprise. It was a normal occurrence in our household to see my father come home after a tough day at work, sit in front of the TV, and drink. Then, at the age of 15, I moved in with my grandparents, who also enjoyed a drink. I deeply admired my grandad; he was an extraordinary figure in my life. At his funeral, I met many people he hadn't seen in years, who shared touching stories about the amazing person he was. As you do when you admire someone so much you try to mimic their behaviours, both good and bad.

When I moved in with my grandparents, they were already retired. Looking back now, I can see the role that habits played in their decision-making. On Sundays, they would spend the whole day at the pub. Afterward, we'd have Sunday lunch, and they would sit in the conservatory my grandad had built, drinking and listening to Frank Sinatra all evening. Despite having all the free time in the world, they only drank on weekends—continuing a habit they had maintained for years. It wasn't until a few years later, when I left for university, that they moved to Spain. That's when they started drinking every day. My grandad used to joke that he wasn't an alcoholic because he chose to drink every day. Looking back, I see how the change in environment led to the shift in their drinking habits—from weekends to every day.

When I started drinking at 16, it was after rugby matches on weekends. I was simply copying what seemed normal to me, spending time with my grandparents in their conservatory while chatting, observing them socially enjoy a drink. But when I moved to university and my environment changed, it suddenly became an everyday occurrence.

In my second year at university, I had a medical exam for a job, and the nurse asked how much I drank each week. Not knowing the exact units, I estimated about five to six pints a day—seven days a week—around 35 pints a week. The nurse told me that was too much, but I shrugged it off, saying, "Don't worry, I'm just at uni." I was kind of right—my university years went by in a blur of drinking and partying, and despite the chaos, I managed to find my calling as a teacher. For the first time, I believed I was a different person. No longer did I identify as the fun-loving drinker; now, I was a teacher. I had changed my identity, and with it, my habits shifted naturally—drinking was confined to weekends again.

If we look at this through the lens of the cue-routine-reward model, drinking became the routine triggered by the cue, which was the weekend, and the reward was something I didn't fully recognise at the time, but I now understand. It was a detachment from the life I was living—a need for identity. When I found a new routine, going to work as a teacher, I achieved the reward I had been seeking without even realising it.

I share this story to highlight a crucial point about habit formation: new habits can crumble when faced with enough stress. Psychologists have studied this in depth, especially in the context of AA. They've found that the key to why some individuals remain sober while others relapse is not due to quiet, boring Sunday afternoons but rather the moments when people feel desperate—when things have gone badly wrong.

This happened to me. The first time I was told as a teacher that I wasn't very good, I turned to alcohol. I still remember it vividly, even after 20 years. My girlfriend—now my wife, Ceri—was making Sunday lunch, but I didn't come home. I found a drinking buddy, a man named Lennie, and ignored the missed calls from Ceri. She eventually turned up at the pub, upset, and I broke down. I apologised and confessed that I didn't think I could make it as a teacher. My belief in myself had collapsed, and with it, the new habit I had built.

Fortunately, I was transferred to a school where I received more support, and it didn't take long before I started seeing myself as a teacher again. As my career progressed, the drinking subsided, apart from the occasional social drink at gatherings.

It wasn't until years later, when my life changed completely, that I stopped drinking for a prolonged period of time. This change came after the birth of my daughter, who was diagnosed with an incurable disease. We were told she had less than six months to live unless she received a liver transplant. One option was for me to donate my liver, though it was a cross-blood type, and the risks were high. This was the moment I decided to quit alcohol altogether and focus on staying as healthy as possible in case we couldn't find a donor.

The next six months were incredibly difficult. My wife and I argued nearly every day, and we shared our concerns with a nurse who arranged for us to see a psychologist. It was the first time in weeks that we left our daughter, Mali, in the care of the nurses, but we both agreed it was important to speak to someone.

In our session, the psychologist asked us how we dealt with stress. I admitted that I closed off from the world, bottling everything up. She asked why I had adopted this strategy, and I explained that it had worked for me in the past. At 15, when I moved from living with my parents to my grandparents, I'd coped by shutting myself off. My wife, on the other hand, grew up on a farm, and her default was the opposite—she would throw things around for a few minutes and then feel fine. These were habits we had formed over time.

Before this, my wife and I had supported each other through tough times, but we'd never been stressed at the same time. Normally, I'd laugh off her breaking her mobile phone, but now, when things were tough, I couldn't support her because I wasn't supporting myself. We were stuck in our own stress responses—mine was to withdraw, hers was to explode and move on—and neither of us could reach the other.

The psychologist then asked, "Who do you want your daughter to be like when she grows up?" We looked at each other and said, "Neither of us." And then she gave us the best advice I've ever received: "Be the person you want your daughter to be."

A few months later, our daughter received her liver transplant, and as I write this book, she is a healthy ten-year-old girl. One thing that has changed since then is that I've never had a drink again. When people ask why I don't drink, I say it's for my daughter's sake, as her liver is so precious and I want to be a role model. But it's deeper than that.

As I mentioned earlier, my drinking reduced when I changed my identity to believing I was a teacher. However, this identity wasn't foolproof. I shared one story about a difficult day, but there were others. What I've come to realise through research and reflection is that the real turning point wasn't just about adopting a new role—it was about transforming the beliefs that underpinned my actions. My identity has since shifted to that of a father. And as the psychologist said, "Be the person you want your daughter to be."

Alcohol and shutting myself off were routines I had deeply embedded over the years. They gave me the reward I craved, which was simply survival—getting through the day.

But now, I've found a new routine that has stuck. The habit I've practised ever since is to open up—to talk about my feelings with my daughter, to check in with how she's doing, and to model emotional openness and vulnerability. The results have been remarkable. I haven't had a drink in ten years, and I don't even think about it anymore. That urge—once so strong—is gone, not because I resisted it, but because I replaced it with something more meaningful. The new habit of opening up is now fully embedded, and it's coupled with an unwavering belief and a deeply rooted identity: that I am a good father, and I am living in a way that I would want my daughter to learn from.

While deeply personal, this story encapsulates the very essence of this chapter. Habits, identity, belief systems, and environment do not exist in isolation—they constantly interact, evolve, and shape our behaviour in profound ways. What begins as a routine can become a refuge, and what we believe about ourselves determines how resilient those habits are when life becomes difficult. By understanding these forces, we not only gain insight into our own lives but also uncover ways to support meaningful, lasting change in others—whether they are our students, our children, or ourselves.

Belonging: The Missing Link in Habit Formation

Belonging is a powerful motivator—one that can be harnessed to build new habits and make rewards feel more desirable. It's not just a soft, emotional concept. Belonging is hardwired into our biology, and the effects of social inclusion—or exclusion—can profoundly shape behaviour.

Imagine being invited to play a game. It's simple: an online ball-tossing game with two other players. At first, everything seems fine. The ball is tossed between you and the others. Then something changes. The other players stop throwing the ball to you. You're left watching as they pass it between themselves, excluding you completely.

At first, it's confusing—maybe even amusing. But as time goes on, the discomfort grows. You feel isolated, unsure, maybe even hurt.

This was the experience of participants in a study by Eisenberger et al. (2003). The "players" in the game were computer programmes designed to simulate inclusion—and then exclusion. When participants were left out, they reported emotional pain like physical discomfort. Brain scans revealed that the experience activated the same regions associated with physical pain, particularly the anterior cingulate cortex.

The message is clear: social exclusion doesn't just feel bad—it physically hurts. The need to belong is not a luxury. It's a biological necessity, deeply tied to how we're wired as social beings.

This insight carries major implications for education. A growing body of research has shown that belonging plays a critical role in students' academic success and their willingness to adopt productive learning behaviours.

In one study, Walton and Cohen (2011) explored how reinforcing a sense of belonging could impact the performance of university students, especially those from minority backgrounds. Participants were divided into two groups. One group received a message reassuring them that feelings of social alienation were normal during the transition to university—and that those feelings would pass. The other group received no such message. The difference was stark: those who received the "belonging" intervention reported feeling more connected to their school and, crucially, went on to achieve higher grades and graduation rates.

Another study by Downey and Somers (2009) found that students who felt socially rejected—or who were particularly sensitive to rejection—performed worse academically and participated less in social and classroom activities. A lack of belonging doesn't just impact how students feel—it directly affects how they learn and engage.

Understanding the psychological need for belonging gives us insight into why some students—often those from working-class backgrounds—struggle to develop strong learning habits. These children may not arrive at school with the same sense of familiarity, confidence, or routine as their more advantaged peers.

Sociologist Annette Lareau's research into parenting styles shines a light on how home environments shape children's relationships with institutions like schools. Lareau identified two distinct approaches: concerted cultivation, typically found in middle-class families, and the accomplishment of natural growth, more common in working-class homes (Lareau, 2003).

In concerted cultivation households, children are enrolled in structured activities—music lessons, sports teams, drama clubs. Parents actively support their children's schooling, communicate with teachers, and encourage self-advocacy. These children learn how to navigate formal institutions confidently, which translates into smoother transitions into school routines and learning expectations.

By contrast, children in working-class families often experience more unstructured time. Their parents tend to adopt a hands-off approach, allowing children to grow naturally without pushing them into structured settings. While this fosters independence in some ways, it can leave them less familiar with the routines and expectations of school life.

This became real for me when visiting a secondary school open day with my daughter, Mali. As we walked the corridors, she was greeted several times—"Hi Mali!" I asked who these students were, and she'd casually reply, "That's Daisy from Drama." Because of her involvement in extracurriculars, she already had a sense of belonging. When my daughter starts school in September, she won't be arriving alone. She'll be walking into a place where she feels seen and connected. For other students, that journey might not be so smooth.

During the tour of the secondary school, we visited the English department. There was a task to write a poem. She confidently walked up to a teacher, asked for a pen and paper, and got on with the task at hand. Afterwards, she offered to read it aloud to the teacher in the room, proud of her accomplishment. This was not her first interaction with a new adult. In fact, her interactions with unfamiliar adults are normalised. Over her early years, my daughter has tried a variety of activities: drama, ballet, swimming, tennis, and art. Some she pursued for several years; others, like tennis, lasted two weeks. She has now found her passion, which is art. But what is important to note is the range of adults she has met and interacted with along the way. Lareau's case studies show that working-class children also spend time with adults, but these adults are much more likely to be family members, and the interactions are often much less formal. Lareau concludes that these more formal interactions with adults support middle-class students when they are in school and help create a greater sense that they belong there.

The importance of group dynamics is further supported by Solomon Asch's famous conformity experiments in the 1950s. In these studies, participants were asked to identify which of several lines matched the length of a target line. While the correct answer was obvious, most people in the room—who were secretly working with the researchers—deliberately gave the wrong answer. Many participants, despite knowing the truth, conformed to the group's incorrect response. The larger and more unified the group, the stronger the pressure to conform (Asch, 1955).

This tells us something crucial:

the more people we see following a behaviour, the more likely we are to follow it too—especially if we want to belong.

Schools spend a lot of time establishing behaviour norms. And rightly so. These norms are essential for creating a learning environment where students can focus their attention. But what I'm advocating for goes beyond behaviour—ensuring we build social norms around learning itself.

When students are given retrieval questions for homework, we can explicitly teach them to use the "cover, write, check" method (*a self-testing strategy where students read a piece of information, cover it up, try to recall or write it from memory, then check for accuracy*). Make it the norm. Praise it. Display it. Celebrate it. Let it become the social proof of effective learning. When routines like this are repeated and rewarded, they become part of a shared culture—and students begin to associate them with success and belonging.

As a parent, find out what the social norms for learning look like at your child's school so you can reinforce the same behaviours at home.

When we first introduced retrieval practice as our main homework strategy, we received many complaints from parents. There were widespread misconceptions about what effective learning looked like. Many parents preferred more "creative" homework tasks, believing these would better challenge their child. But as I've already shown through the concept of desirable difficulties, there is nothing easy about "cover, write, check." It may not be a glamorous homework strategy, but it is certainly challenging—because it highlights, in plain sight, the gaps in a student's knowledge. It holds up a mirror to their learning.

This is one of the reasons I've written this book: to build a bridge between parents and schools. If we want students to develop strong learning habits, they need to feel like they belong. And that goes for parents, too. Parents need to understand what effective learning looks like so they can reinforce the culture the school is trying to create.

The beauty of "cover, write, check" is its simplicity. With the right guidance, parents can support this approach at home and provide the encouragement and structure some students need to develop effective learning habits. Not every parent has the time, materials, or knowledge to help their child build a giant plant cell out of recycled materials—but every parent can quiz their child on the core knowledge they need in a subject. It's not about doing more; it's about doing what works.

At the same time, schools and parents need to avoid reinforcing unhelpful messages. If the work displayed on corridor walls is chosen mainly because it looks pretty, what message are we sending? Is aesthetics being valued over depth of thought? If students are praised for finishing first, are we unintentionally encouraging speed over quality?

Shared routines are more than a classroom management tool—they are the foundation of culture. Routines reduce cognitive load, freeing up working memory so students can focus on learning. But they also signal belonging. When students walk in line, answer in full sentences, or follow a clear homework process, they are not just complying—they are becoming part of a collective.

> If you want a learning habit to become embedded with students, you must first teach it explicitly, then reward it visibly, and finally embed it socially.

The more that routine is seen, recognised, and celebrated, the more likely it is to spread—until it becomes not just a routine, but a shared identity.

The Role of Social Norms in Habit Formation

Just as belonging to a community can create a powerful sense of responsibility and shared values, it can also establish social norms that guide our behaviour, sometimes in unexpected ways. Social norms—unwritten rules that govern our behaviour—hold a remarkable power to influence the choices we make every day, including how we approach learning.

Take, for instance, the example of the speed limit on the UK's motorways. The law sets the official speed limit at 70 miles per hour, but many drivers know that travelling at 75 miles per hour is widely tolerated. This unwritten norm, formed by a combination of shared behaviour and unspoken expectations, influences how drivers act. Even though the legal limit is 70, the social norm subtly encourages a small deviation. Drivers conform to this social understanding, not necessarily because it is explicitly allowed, but because it has become the "accepted" behaviour in the context of motorway driving. In the same way, social norms can shape how students approach their studies, often leading them to adopt certain learning habits based on what they perceive as the "acceptable" level of effort or engagement within their peer groups.

By harnessing the power of belonging, we can establish social norms that encourage good learning habits. When students feel connected to a group that values hard work, persistence, and effective study techniques, those norms can become the driving force behind their actions. Just as people drive at 75 miles per hour because it feels like the social norm, students can be guided to adopt better learning behaviours when these behaviours are reinforced by the group they belong to. Understanding how social norms influence habits allows us to create environments where positive behaviours, like effective studying, become the standard. When students see their peers engaging in productive learning practices, they are more likely to adopt similar behaviours themselves, reinforcing a cycle of positive habit formation.

When covering a recent class that had experienced several long-term supply teachers, I witnessed the negative impact of a newly established social norm. When I set the students off on a task, only a few began working at a pace I would consider acceptable—instead, many chose to chat with their peers about their weekends. However, when I reviewed the answers with the class, the students suddenly became fully "engaged": they eagerly recorded every answer from the board and strove to compile a flawless set of notes.

To an outsider, the class might have appeared as a group of students deeply immersed in their learning. Though, this behaviour was a poor proxy for learning. For these students, the process had become an ingrained habit. The PowerPoint slides, centrally produced by the head of department, had come to symbolise the lesson itself. Over time, the students came to prioritise simply having a complete set of notes—the correct answers—over actively listening to the teacher or thinking deeply about the material. Whether it was due to a build-up of distrust towards the various cover teachers or an ingrained routine, the outcome was the same: instead of challenging themselves, they conformed to a norm that merely emphasised passive notetaking.

In order for students to understand how social norms can shape their lives, a good place to start is by sharing some famous studies.

The Milgram Experiment: How Social Norms Shape Our Decisions

In 1961, psychologist Stanley Milgram set out to understand how ordinary people could commit extraordinary acts of harm under certain social conditions. What he discovered revealed the disturbing power of social norms and authority over individual decision-making (Milgram, 1963).

Milgram's experiment was set up as a study of memory and learning, where participants—who were unaware of the true purpose of the experiment—were asked to administer increasingly severe electric shocks to another person, whom they believed was a fellow participant. In reality, the person receiving the shocks was an actor, and no real harm was ever done. The true focus of the study was to observe how far the participants would go in obeying commands from an authority figure, even when they believed they were causing extreme pain to another person.

As the "learner" (the actor) screamed in pain and begged for mercy, many of the participants showed signs of distress, some even hesitating or showing signs of guilt. But when the experimenter—a figure of authority in a lab coat—told them to continue, most participants did. They were following the norm of obedience to authority, a social influence deeply ingrained in our behaviour. Despite the clear discomfort of their actions, the overwhelming majority continued to administer shocks, with some even reaching the highest level, where the "learner" was no longer responding at all.

The results were shocking. Over 60% of participants went all the way to the maximum shock, illustrating how powerful social norms and authority figures can be in influencing decision-making, even when it goes against an individual's personal morals. Milgram's experiment revealed that under the right conditions, people will often follow the instructions of an authority figure—an uncomfortable but significant lesson in how social norms and the pressure to conform can override personal ethical judgements.

The Milgram experiment serves as a chilling reminder of how easily individuals can be swayed by authority and social norms, even when those norms encourage harmful behaviour. It shows us the lengths to which people will go to fit in or obey authority and underscores the importance of questioning the decisions that societal norms ask us to make.

The Bystander Effect: Social Norms and Inaction

In the early 1960s, the tragic murder of Kitty Genovese in New York City became a powerful example of the impact of social norms on human behaviour. Kitty was attacked in the courtyard of her apartment building, and, despite her screams for help, reports claimed that dozens of people heard the commotion but did nothing to intervene. The case shocked the public and prompted psychologists to study why so many witnesses failed to act in a situation where immediate help was needed.

Psychologists Bibb Latané and John Darley conducted a series of experiments in the 1960s to investigate this phenomenon, which they called the bystander effect (Larané & Darley, 1968).

> In one experiment, participants were placed in a room where they believed they were working on a group project. During the experiment, smoke began to pour into the room from under the door. When participants were alone, most immediately sought help or notified the experimenter. However, when participants were in the room with others who did nothing—who either ignored the smoke or acted like nothing was wrong—participants were far less likely to seek help themselves. In fact, when there were more people present, the likelihood of any individual acting to alert the authorities dropped.
>
> The reason for this, Larané and Darley concluded, is that individuals often look to others to determine how to behave in ambiguous or emergency situations. When everyone around them remains passive, it creates a social norm of inaction. People, unknowingly, conform to what they perceive as the "correct" response, which, in this case, was doing nothing. The social pressure to conform to the behaviour of others can override our own instincts to act, even when we know something is wrong.
>
> The bystander effect illustrates how powerful social norms can be in shaping behaviour. When surrounded by others who are passive or unconcerned, we tend to follow their lead, even if it means failing to intervene in critical moments. It's a stark reminder that our actions are often driven by the desire to conform to the behaviour of those around us, even if it leads to negative or harmful outcomes.

Reflective Questions

1. Can you think of a time when you followed what others were doing—even if you felt it might be wrong or unhelpful? What made you go along with the group?

2. Have you ever hesitated to speak up or act because no one else around you was doing anything? What was the outcome?

3. In your learning, have you ever avoided trying hard, asking questions, or showing interest because it didn't seem "normal" in your peer group?

4. Are there times when you've accepted an idea or answer just because a teacher or textbook said it, without thinking it through for yourself? Why do you think that happened?

Cristina Bicchieri's work on social norms offers powerful insights into how people's behaviour is shaped not just by personal beliefs but by what they think others do and expect (Bicchieri, 2006). In her 2006 research, she explored how harmful practices like female genital cutting (FGC) in parts of Africa were maintained—not because individuals necessarily supported them—but because of strong social expectations. People continued the practice because they believed others were doing the same and that others expected them to do it. Crucially, Bicchieri found that effective interventions didn't rely on condemnation or punishment but on *positive framing*. Campaigns emphasised that an increasing number of families were choosing healthier alternatives and that respected leaders supported these choices. This allowed communities to view the new behaviour as socially acceptable—and even admirable—paving the way for a shift in what was seen as normal. This approach aligns closely with the principles of nudge theory discussed earlier in this book: real change often comes not from enforcing rules, but by subtly reshaping the environment and expectations so that people make better choices by default. Just as a cafeteria layout can nudge students towards healthier food choices, changing perceived social norms can nudge entire communities towards healthier, more ethical behaviours. In education, we can apply the same principle—creating the perception that effective learning habits are not just valued but expected—so that positive behaviours become the new normal.

As a school or parent, if you don't already have them, a valuable step might be to develop a few clear, memorable mottos that reflect how learning really happens. Better still, involve students in this process. When students help create the language of learning, they're more likely to internalise it and act on it.

Here are a few examples:

Think hard now, remember more later.
Make it stick by making it effortful.
Learning that lasts takes effort that matters.

I have a simple phrase I often use with my eldest daughter—one that many parents will recognise. Whenever she's reluctant to keep going with her schoolwork, I ask, "What does practice make?" Almost instinctively, she replies, "Practice makes perfect?"

But this isn't just a throwaway line. Behind it are many conversations we've had about learning—about effort, growth, and the reality that progress isn't always immediately visible. If her response feels half-hearted or lacking conviction, I sometimes bring up the *kettle analogy* mentioned previously in this book. It's a useful way to remind her that just because she can't see the results yet doesn't mean nothing's happening. She may simply be stuck in the *valley of disappointment*—that difficult stretch when she is not seeing the benefits of her effort.

When these phrases are used consistently and visibly across a school or in the home, they begin to shape the culture. Over time, they help establish new social norms—norms that quietly but powerfully signal the kinds of behaviours that are expected, valued, and rewarded.

That's why it's so important to praise the things that really matter. If we want effortful learning to become the norm, then it's effort that should be recognised. A teacher saying, "Well done, Katy—you gave that work a lot of effort. I'm hopeful that learning will stick," sends a much stronger message than praising a student simply for finishing first. The former reinforces a norm that learning takes time and focus. The latter risks rewarding speed over substance, and may unintentionally encourage surface-level work.

The importance of consistent language in shaping norms was clear to me during an interview. Throughout the day, staff regularly used the word candour whenever I offered a particularly honest or open reflection. Each time, others in the room responded with subtle approval—a nod, a smile, a note taken. Even in a high-pressure setting, I quickly picked up on this pattern. Their repeated use of a single, meaningful word created an atmosphere where honesty wasn't just accepted—it was encouraged. As a result, I felt at ease. I answered challenging questions with greater openness and authenticity.

That small but intentional use of language shaped my behaviour. It showed me, in real time, how social norms can be purposefully crafted—and how powerful they can be, even when you've only been in a school for a few hours.

Tipping Points

We can speed up the rate of change of habit formation by considering tipping points. In his book *The Tipping Point*, Malcolm Gladwell (2000) introduces the concept of the "glass window effect" through a story that illustrates how subtle environmental factors can influence behaviour in unexpected ways. He refers to a study in which researchers looked at the way people in a neighbourhood responded to crime. The study focused on how environmental cues—specifically, the condition of buildings—affected crime rates.

Gladwell recounts how researchers found that areas with broken windows or buildings in disrepair were more likely to experience higher crime rates, while neighbourhoods with well-maintained buildings had fewer incidents of crime. This effect was tied to the idea that the physical condition of a space subtly communicated to people what was considered "acceptable" behaviour. In places where windows were broken and buildings were neglected, it was as though the environment was sending a message that it was acceptable to disregard rules, leading to an increase in criminal behaviour. In contrast, well-maintained spaces signalled a higher standard, prompting people to behave more appropriately.

The "glass window effect" highlights the power of environmental cues and how they can create a subtle, often unnoticed influence on people's actions. When the physical environment suggests that certain behaviours are acceptable, people may unknowingly adapt to fit those cues, even if they aren't consciously aware of them. This is why a well-kept environment can foster positive behaviours, while a neglected one can encourage negative outcomes.

As a senior leader, I sometimes have to cover lessons for absent staff. Recently, I found myself covering a class that had unfortunately experienced several different supply teachers due to a long-term absence. When I walked in, the front desk was cluttered with paperwork dating back weeks, and the desks to the side of the room were piled high with worksheets. Understandably, as a supply teacher, you may only be in a school for a few days, often across multiple classrooms, so you might not have the time or inclination to fully settle into the space.

This experience, though, occurred shortly after reading *The Tipping Point*, and it made me reflect on what this room was saying about our school culture and what we were tacitly communicating about what was acceptable. If we expect our students to work at home in a distraction-free environment, are we, in turn, creating barriers within our schools that prevent the very learning habits we want to cultivate?

In a school setting, when new ideas about how learning happens are introduced, you'll often see a small group of *early adopters*—students who are curious and willing to try out strategies like retrieval practice or spacing. These students can become powerful connectors, helping to spread effective learning habits among their peers.

Parents also play an important role in supporting their child's engagement with these strategies. One simple but powerful way is by showing genuine curiosity about school life and learning. However, it's common for children to be dismissive when asked general questions like "How was your day?", often replying with "Not much happened." To get more meaningful responses, parents might find it more effective to ask about specific aspects of the school day. School assemblies, for example, provide an ideal entry point.

Assemblies are more than just routine gatherings—they're a vital part of school culture. Schools use them to communicate important messages about values, expectations, and wider social or ethical issues. They help shape the identity of the school community and aim to support the development of well-rounded, thoughtful young people.

When parents ask targeted questions about assemblies—what was discussed, whether anything stood out, or how it made their child think—it not only increases the likelihood of meaningful conversation but also helps reinforce the sense of belonging and purpose that assemblies aim to build. This also creates opportunities for retrieval and reflection, both of which are known to strengthen memory and understanding—making it more likely that students will remember and apply what they've heard.

While these early adopters are important as a parent you would hope to find your child in this category, they are not necessarily the ones who will create social change within the school. This group represents the "connectors." I've mentioned before our school's big debate about lockers. This debate became more complex when we considered the role of our college council. When we surveyed them about the potential removal of lockers, they unanimously told us that students didn't want this change to happen. However, when we later surveyed all students across the school, the results didn't align. The problem was that our school council consisted of volunteers—students who had put their hands up at the beginning of the school year. In hindsight, looking at Lareau's work on class differences, it's easy to see why most of these students were more confident in this role due to their upbringing. These students, advocating for their peers, were not representative of the whole school population and gave us a skewed perception of what the student body wanted. These students, while important, were not the connectors within the school community—they were the early adopters.

To truly accelerate changes in school culture around learning habits, you must focus on finding the connectors. Connectors are individuals who possess an extraordinary ability to build networks and connect with people across diverse social circles. In a school setting, they are the students who know everyone—those who can get people to interact, share ideas, and collaborate. As an educator If you're looking for one, simply observe a school lunch. You'll likely see a student moving seamlessly from one social group to another. These are the students who can influence learning habits across the school, either increasing or decreasing the "noise" in the school environment, depending on their understanding and engagement with learning.

In *The Tipping Point*, Malcolm Gladwell illustrates the power of connectors through the story of Paul Revere's midnight ride. Revere's famous ride is an excellent example of how connectors, people who are well-connected across different social circles, can influence the spread of information. On the night of 18 April 1775, Revere set out to warn the colonial militias that the British were coming. But instead of going it alone, he worked through a network of individuals—people with far-reaching social ties—who could pass along the message quickly. These connectors helped ensure that the news spread rapidly, leading to the preparation for the American Revolution. Revere's strategic use of connectors to amplify his message shows how influential these individuals can be in spreading information and sparking a tipping point.

Consider a student named David, who is a well-connected figure across various groups in his school. He's part of the football team, the debate club, and a close-knit group of academically focused friends. David, being influential among his peers, often offers advice on how to manage schoolwork, but his study methods are based on habits that are less than optimal. He might rely on cramming the night before a test, re-reading notes passively, or procrastinating until the last minute. These methods become ingrained in David's social circles. One day, after sharing how he managed to pass an exam by studying late into the night, his friends in the debate club and on the football team start adopting the same approach. They believe that because David, with his busy extracurricular schedule, can manage to succeed with these strategies, they too can do the same.

David, as a connector, spreads these ineffective study habits across various groups in the school. While he might not intend to do so, his influence causes students to adopt subpar study methods, believing that they're the key to academic success.

Just like Paul Revere's ride, David's influence shows the power of connectors to spread ideas, but it also highlights the potential consequences when those ideas are not grounded evidence. In schools connectors like David can either be a force for positive change or inadvertently reinforce ineffective habits.

Chapter Summary

- Habits operate through a four-stage loop: Cue → Craving → Response → Reward. Understanding this cycle is key to building or breaking any habit.

- To change a habit, the first step is to identify the cue—the trigger that sets the behaviour in motion. Once you know the cue, you can work on shifting the response by introducing new routines or strategies.

- Effective techniques for adapting habits include:
  - Pointing and calling—saying your intended action out loud to increase awareness.
  - Habit scorecards—tracking daily behaviours to make patterns visible.
  - Habit stacking—linking a new habit to an existing one to create momentum.
  - Implementation intentions—planning when, where, and how you'll act.
  - Starting small—making the new habit so easy it feels almost effortless.

- If a craving is making a habit hard to break, try changing the environment. This can reduce temptation and make it easier to choose differently.

- Developing strong learning habits begins with belief. You must believe that your efforts will lead to meaningful change. This belief is grounded in understanding how learning works and seeing yourself as someone capable of learning well.

- Finally, habits are easier to build when you feel you belong. Being part of a group or culture that supports your desired habits can give you the motivation and accountability to stay on track.

References

Asch, S. E. (1955). Opinions and social pressure. *Scientific American, 193*(5), 31–35. https://doi.org/10.1038/scientificamerican1155-31

Bandura, A. (1997). *Self-efficacy: The exercise of control*. W.H. Freeman and Company.

Bauer, E., & Beske-Janssen, P. (2012). Pointing and calling in healthcare: The verbalization of action in routine medical tasks. *Performance Improvement Quarterly, 25*(2), 5–24. https://doi.org/10.1177/25160435221078099

Berridge, K. C. (2007). The debate over dopamine's role in reward: The case for incentive salience. *Psychopharmacology, 191*(3), 391–431. https://doi.org/10.1007/s00213-006-0578-x

Berridge, K. C., & Robinson, T. E. (1998). What is the role of dopamine in reward: Hedonic impact, reward learning, or incentive salience? *Brain Research Reviews, 28*(3), 309–369. https://doi.org/10.1016/S0165-0173(98)00019-8

Bicchieri, C. (2006). *The grammar of society: The nature and dynamics of social norms*. Cambridge University Press.

Downey, G., & Somers, C. L. (2009). Rejection sensitivity and academic achievement: Mediating processes and implications for interventions. *Journal of Social Issues, 65*(1), 169–183. https://doi.org/10.1111/j.1540-4560.2008.01597.x

Duhigg, C. (2012). *The power of habit: Why we do what we do in life and business*. Random House.

Eisenberger, N. I., Lieberman, M. D., & Williams, K. D. (2003). Does rejection hurt? An fMRI study of social exclusion. *Science, 302*(5643), 290–292. https://doi.org/10.1126/science.1089134

Gladwell, M. (2000). *The tipping point: How little things can make a big difference*. Little, Brown.

Graybiel, A. M. (2008). Habits, rituals, and the evaluative brain. *Annual Review of Neuroscience, 31*, 359–387. https://doi.org/10.1146/annurev.neuro.29.051605.112851

Japan Industrial Safety and Health Association (JISHA). (2009). Zero accidents with point and call. Retrieved from https://www.jisha.or.jp/english/

Larané, B., & Darley, J. M. (1968). Group inhibition of bystander intervention in emergencies. *Journal of Personality and Social Psychology, 10*(3), 215–221. https://doi.org/10.1037/h0026570

Lareau, A. (2003). *Unequal childhoods: Class, race, and family life*. University of California Press.

Milgram, S. (1963). Behavioral study of obedience. *Journal of Abnormal and Social Psychology, 67*(4), 371–378. https://doi.org/10.1037/h0040525

Milne, S., Orbell, S., & Sheeran, P. (2002). Combining motivational and volitional interventions to promote exercise participation: Protection motivation theory and implementation intentions. *British Journal of Health Psychology, 7*(2), 163–184. https://doi.org/10.1348/135910702169420

Schultz, W. (2016). Dopamine reward prediction-error signalling: A two-component response. *Nature Reviews Neuroscience, 17*(3), 183–195. https://doi.org/10.1038/nrn.2015.26

Schultz, W., Dayan, P., & Montague, P. R. (1997). A neural substrate of prediction and reward. *Science, 275*(5306), 1593–1599. https://doi.org/10.1126/science.275.5306.1593

Skinner, B. F. (1938). *The behavior of organisms: An experimental analysis*. Appleton-Century.

Smith, K. S., & Graybiel, A. M. (2013). A dual operator view of habitual behavior reflecting cortical and striatal dynamics. *Neuron, 79*(2), 361–374. https://doi.org/10.1016/j.neuron.2013.05.038

Squire, L. R. (1992). Memory and the hippocampus: A synthesis from findings with rats, monkeys, and humans. *Psychological Review, 99*(2), 195–231.

University of Lincoln. (2023). NHS Couch to 5K Running App boosts mental health and exercise. Retrieved from https://www.lincoln.ac.uk/news/2023/09/2393.asp

Walton, G. M., & Cohen, G. L. (2011). A brief social-belonging intervention improves academic and health outcomes of minority students. *Science, 331*(6023), 1447–1451. https://doi.org/10.1126/science.1198364

5 AI: Can We Outsource Effort without Losing Learning?

The Hidden Cost of AI Convenience

In this book, I've dedicated a significant portion to helping students overcome procrastination and develop lasting habits that support their ability to retain knowledge. This chapter focuses on the role of artificial intelligence (AI), we must be mindful that "if AI is used in ways that replace thinking and effort with convenience, it could reinforce unproductive behaviours."

The study Impact of Artificial Intelligence on Human Loss in Decision Making, Laziness, and Safety in Education (2023) raises an important concern: AI could amplify laziness and diminish motivation. With nearly 69% of students reporting that AI made them lazier, this highlights a real danger. Students who struggle with procrastination or maintaining focus might become even more reliant on AI tools for shortcuts, leading to passive learning rather than the active engagement needed to form productive, long-lasting study habits.

If AI is used in ways that replace thinking and effort with convenience, it could reinforce unproductive behaviours. This is particularly worrying when students are already struggling to build the motivation and awareness required to succeed academically. The study serves as a reminder that, while AI can be a helpful tool, it's crucial that we ensure it doesn't inadvertently undermine the very habits and strategies that help students overcome their challenges.

A study by Burnett and Lee (2005) explored how vehicle navigation systems affect the formation of cognitive maps—the mental representations we build of our surroundings. Using a driving simulator, participants navigated a virtual town either with traditional paper maps or voice-guided GPS-like instructions. Those using paper maps showed better spatial understanding, remembered more landmarks, and produced more accurate mental maps than those guided by GPS. The findings suggest that while modern navigation tools reduce immediate effort, they can undermine deeper spatial learning by limiting engagement with the environment—highlighting a trade-off between convenience and long-term cognitive development.

Just as GPS navigation can hinder the development of cognitive maps by removing the need for active engagement with the environment, the growing use of AI tools in education may similarly reduce students' ability to build strong, well-connected schemas of subject knowledge. When learners rely too heavily on AI to generate answers, summarise content, or solve problems, they risk bypassing the cognitive effort needed to organise and integrate information meaningfully. This mental effort is crucial for constructing robust mental models that support deep understanding and long-term retention. While AI can offer valuable support, overdependence may short-circuit the very processes that lead to learning—highlighting the need to balance technological assistance with tasks that require students to think, reflect, and make sense of knowledge for themselves.

A study titled *"The Retention of Manual Flying Skills in the Automated Cockpit"* by Casner et al. (2014) investigated how prolonged use of cockpit automation affects pilots' manual flying skills. In a Boeing 747-400 simulator, 16 airline pilots performed both routine and nonroutine flight scenarios with varying levels of automation. The findings revealed that while pilots' basic manual control and instrument scanning skills remained largely intact—even with infrequent practice—there was a notable decline in cognitive tasks essential for manual flying. Specifically, challenges arose in tasks such as tracking the aircraft's position without map displays, determining subsequent navigational steps, and recognising instrument system failures.

The rise of the automated cockpit may have unintentionally undermined some of the very characteristics that define true expertise in aviation. Experts typically rely on a deep, intuitive understanding of their environment, built from years of active engagement and pattern recognition. In a highly automated cockpit, however, many of the tasks that once required constant attention, judgement, and adaptation are now handled by systems. This reduces opportunities for pilots to actively practice and reinforce the cognitive processes that underpin expert performance. By removing pilots from the loop during routine flight, automation may limit the real-time decision-making and situational analysis that allows expertise to flourish. As a result, pilots may become less responsive and less able to act fluidly in unexpected situations, weakening the very internalised knowledge and instinct that define expert performance.

This tension between automation and expertise is vividly illustrated in the film *Sully*, starring Tom Hanks as Captain Chesley "Sully" Sullenberger. The movie recounts the real-life emergency landing of US Airways Flight 1549 on the Hudson River after both engines failed. While post-incident investigations focused heavily on what automated systems and simulators suggested Sully *should* have done—such as returning to the airport—the film highlights how his deep, intuitive expertise as a pilot overrode theoretical models. Drawing on decades of experience, Sully made a split-second decision based not on checklists or automation, but on his real-time judgement of what was actually possible. This decision saved all 155 people on board. The film underscores a central theme of expertise: that true professionals, when faced with novel, high-stakes situations, rely on internalised patterns and gut instinct developed over years of active, hands-on engagement—something that over-automation risks eroding.

In an article for Science.org, Betsy Sparrow explores how the internet, particularly search engines like Google, influences human memory. The author argues that the ease of accessing information online has transformed the internet into a form of "transactive" memory, a theory first introduced by sociologist Daniel Wegner and colleagues in the 1980s. They proposed that in groups, memory is not solely the responsibility of individual members but is shared and distributed across the group. Each person becomes an expert in a specific domain, and the group functions as a collective memory system, drawing on individual expertise when needed. In the context of the study, it showed that when individuals anticipate future access to information, they tend to remember less of the information itself but better recall where to find it. If we use an earlier principle that memory is the residue of thought, this makes sense: if people are focusing their thinking on where to find information rather than on the content of the information itself, then they are less likely to remember the information (Sparrow et al., 2011).

Concerns identified in other fields are now being seen in education. Studies are starting to show that a reliance on AI can have a negative effect on learning. A recent study exploring the impact of generative AI tools, such as ChatGPT, on student performance found that students who used these tools performed worse on exams compared to their peers who did not. The research suggested that reliance on AI for completing assignments may hinder deeper learning (Li & Wang, 2023; Zhou & Xu, 2024; Zhu & Liu, 2023). Early commentary in the scientific community has also cautioned that unchecked AI use could stunt students' ability to internalise material, emphasising the need for policies that encourage AI as a supplement to effort rather than a replacement (Nature Editorial, 2023).

So, how widespread is the use of AI in education? It is hard to tell. A 2025 survey by the Higher Education Policy Institute revealed that 92% of UK undergraduates have used generative AI tools for essay writing, up from 66% the previous year. When asked why they use AI, students most often said it saves them time and improves the quality of their work. The same question was asked about when the participants were in high school, and it was found that just under half (45%) of students had used AI, with 40% saying they felt that the use of AI would help them get a good grade in their subject (Freeman, 2025).

Concerns about AI use are not limited to essay completion but also extend to problem-solving processes. Krupp et al. (2023) conducted a study to examine the impact of ChatGPT-assisted problem-solving on physics students' performance and behaviours. The research involved two groups: one using ChatGPT (27 students) and the other using traditional internet search engines (12 students) to solve physics exercises. The experiment was intentionally designed to be too difficult for ChatGPT to provide an immediate answer but structured in a way that would allow it to give a response with carefully applied prompts.

The results were revealing. Throughout the process, students were asked to confirm if they thought the answers provided by ChatGPT were correct. Nearly half of the solutions generated by ChatGPT were mistakenly believed by students to be accurate, suggesting an overreliance on the AI tool, even among students with expertise in the subject. Moreover, students using ChatGPT frequently relied on copy-paste methods for 42% of their queries, compared to only 4% in the search engine group. This highlights significant differences in interaction styles and underscores the lack of critical reflection when students engaged with ChatGPT.

These challenges highlight why the ideas in this book—are more important than ever. As AI tools become more accessible and integrated into everyday learning, without explicit teaching about how learning happens, students risk becoming passive consumers of answers rather than active builders of knowledge, which risks them developing expertise in their intended field.

Not only could AI negatively affect the development of expertise, but it could also amplify some of the challenges students face—particularly those related to bias. While I advocate for the use of nudge theory to help students make better decisions, AI could unknowingly use similar techniques to steer students towards their own existing biases or towards biases embedded within the AI itself.

Ask the Algorithm

Aisha was a curious and ambitious Year 11 student. With GCSEs approaching, she'd discovered a powerful new AI study assistant. It could answer questions, summarise articles, and even tell her which sources were "more reliable." It felt like having a personal tutor on demand.

At first, she used it to check her work and get feedback. But over time, she noticed a trend: every time she asked for historical context or political analysis, the AI gave certain perspectives more weight than others. For example, when researching colonialism, it frequently downplayed the harms or framed the topic through a very specific Western lens.

When Aisha wrote her coursework, her arguments increasingly reflected those viewpoints. She didn't question them—they were polished, confident, and "sounded right." When her teacher suggested a few alternative readings, Aisha was surprised. "But the AI said..." she began, before stopping short.

She realised she hadn't just been using the AI to learn—she had been absorbing its voice, values, and biases without noticing.

This kind of quiet influence isn't just a theoretical risk—it's backed by evidence. In the 2024 study *How human–AI feedback loops alter human perceptual, emotional and social judgements*, researchers found that even subtle AI feedback can shift how people think, feel, and judge—especially when the AI is seen as an expert.

Students, like Aisha, often treat AI tools as neutral sources of truth. But these systems are trained on data that can reflect and reinforce biases. Over time, the AI doesn't just help shape *what* students learn—it shapes *how* they think.

Reflective Questions

- How might relying on AI tools affect the diversity of perspectives you consider when researching a topic?
- In what ways might relying too much on AI affect your own learning?

Harnessing AI for Learning: Principles Grounded in Cognitive Science

Despite the challenges AI presents, it's clear that the technology is here to stay. However, it's not all bad news. A growing number of educators and EDtech organisations are exploring how AI can be used to enhance, rather than detract from, learning in the classroom—by applying principles rooted in cognitive science.

If you're considering introducing AI into your classroom or school or as a parent want to support your child with the use of AI, a good place to start is by establishing a set of guiding principles that align with cognitive science. These principles can help ensure that AI tools are used effectively to support learning, rather than undermining it.

Promote Active Thinking	Support Cognitive Load	Provide Feedback	Scaffold Learning	Promote Retrieval	Promote Spaced Repetition and Interleaving

- **Promote active thinking:** AI should be used to enhance, not replace, active engagement with knowledge. Encourage students to interact with material, rather than passively absorbing information. This helps build deeper understanding and retention.

- **Support cognitive load:** AI can help reduce unnecessary cognitive load by taking care of time-consuming tasks, such as organising study schedules or providing quick access to information. This frees up mental effort for more complex thinking and problem-solving. It can also reduce time students spend procrastinating on tasks that are necessary but do not directly support learning.

- **Provide meaningful feedback:** AI tools can assist in offering feedback, but they should never replace the need for students to truly understand the material. Feedback from both AI and educators should guide students to think and self-reflection.

- **Scaffold learning:** AI can be a valuable tool for scaffolding students' learning, providing prompts, hints, and guided practice that help them build confidence in a topic. By gradually increasing the level of difficulty, students can develop a strong foundation and build motivation before tackling more complex material independently.

- **Promote retrieval:** While AI can support research and fact-finding, it should not replace the essential processes of memorisation and recall. These cognitive processes are crucial for long-term retention. AI should encourage students to engage in active recall and spaced repetition, rather than bypassing these processes altogether.

- **Value interleaving and spaced repetition**: AI should ensure it does not make "learning" too easy and should have an element of desirable difficulty to ensure learning sticks.

In the remainder of this chapter, I will delve into a series of case studies that illustrate how these principles are applied in real-world educational settings. By examining these examples in more detail, we can gain a deeper understanding of how AI tools can be effectively integrated into the classroom, supporting student learning while adhering to the cognitive science-based guidelines we've discussed.

Applying Cognitive Science Through Adaptive Flashcards

At a recent conference, I met Andrew Cohen, founder of Brainscape—a flashcard-based learning app grounded in the science of learning. After my presentation on themes explored in this book, Andrew approached me to discuss how Brainscape was designed around many of the same principles. It was clear we shared a passion for applying cognitive science in ways that help students learn more effectively. We continued our conversation after the event, and I invited Andrew to share a summary of how Brainscape leverages AI and evidence-informed strategies to support student progress.

Brainscape is a web and mobile flashcard platform that uses AI to personalise learning. Students or teachers can create flashcards manually, or upload class notes, slides, or even photos of textbook pages for the AI to convert into high-quality flashcards. This feature reduces the friction involved in getting started with revision, allowing students to quickly generate study materials tailored to the content they're learning.

But more than just a digital flashcard app, Brainscape integrates several key principles from the learning sciences:

- **Spaced repetition**: Based on how confident students feel after each flashcard, Brainscape intelligently spaces out the review of concepts. Lower-confidence material reappears more frequently, helping reinforce weaker areas and avoid the illusion of mastery.

- **Retrieval practice**: Flashcards require students to recall information actively, rather than passively recognising it. This promotes deeper learning and long-term retention.

- **Metacognition**: After reviewing each answer, students rate their confidence on a scale. This reflection helps them become more aware of what they know and where they need to focus.

- **Cognitive load management**: The system avoids overwhelming students by gradually introducing new content based on their confidence levels. Combined with a simple interface and centralised "Study" button, it lowers the barrier to consistent practice.

- **Critical thinking and collaboration**: When students create their own flashcards—or review and improve AI-generated ones—they engage in deeper thinking. Brainscape even allows peers to suggest edits to shared decks, encouraging thoughtful engagement with the material and peer accountability.

To build stronger habits, Brainscape incorporates streaks, study goals, and estimated time-to-mastery features, helping students overcome procrastination and develop a regular study rhythm. Importantly, the platform also provides teachers with detailed dashboards to monitor student usage and identify areas where additional support might be needed.

Brainscape demonstrates how technology, when designed around evidence-based principles, can make study more efficient, engaging, and aligned with how memory and learning actually work.

Promote Active Thinking	Support Cognitive Load	Provide Feedback	Scaffold Learning	Promote Retrieval	Spaced Repetition and Interleaving
Yes	Yes	Yes	Yes	Yes

There are many similar apps available on the market, and this is not an endorsement of any one over another. Whatever app a student chooses to use, encouraging them to justify how it aligns with each of the guiding principles will help them evaluate its effectiveness.

AI Tutors in Education: Promise with Precautions

Dr Gregory Kestin, Associate Director of Science Education at Harvard University, created an AI tutor to support students in his physics class in a study carried out by him. The results provide evidence of the potential of AI in education. The study involved 2,000 university-level physics students over a four-week period. Participants were randomly assigned to either an AI tutoring system or a traditional lecture. Students using the AI tutor learned over twice as much in a shorter time frame compared to their peers in the active learning setting. Additionally, students who engaged with the AI tutor reported higher levels of motivation and engagement throughout the process (Kestin & Miller, 2024).

The AI tutor was carefully designed to integrate key cognitive science principles to enhance student learning. It aimed to manage cognitive load by breaking material into manageable segments and offering personalised feedback. To minimise common AI errors, such as giving incorrect answers or misjudging responses, the system was programmed to guide students through each problem step by step. Additionally, it was provided with detailed solutions to ensure that the AI delivered precise and high-quality explanations to support students effectively.

I was fortunate to gain early access to a trial of an AI tutor programme called GCSEtutor.ai. It covers a range of subjects, but I chose to explore GCSE Science, given my background in the subject. This allowed me to engage more critically with the system's pedagogical design and evaluate how it aligned with key learning principles.

I selected the topic of Bonding, and the tutor's first prompt was straightforward: "Tell me what you already know." I decided to test its ability to diagnose misconceptions by deliberately including a partially correct, but flawed, response:

Ionic bonding is metals and non-metals, and covalent bonding is only gases.

What happened next was telling. The tutor immediately responded with a prompt asking for a clearer definition of ionic bonding. It didn't pick up on the misconception about covalent bonding being limited to gases—something that some students wrongly believe. Still, it rightly challenged the surface-level nature of my definition.

I replied with:

A chemical reaction between metal and non-metal elements.

This was met with praise, followed by a deeper question about electron transfer, an essential part of understanding ionic bonding. When I replied, "No idea," the tutor provided a concise explanation of how electrons are transferred from metals and then posed a follow-up question asking me to apply this knowledge to non-metals.

This kind of dialogic exchange continued, mirroring the back-and-forth of a well-structured dialogue with a teacher. The system prompted me to think, to apply, and to retrieve knowledge—exactly the kind of cognitive engagement we want from effective learning environments.

But then came a twist. Rather than returning to my earlier misconception about covalent bonding, the tutor suddenly introduced a new topic: metallic bonding. It shifted the focus entirely, asking me a series of questions on this new concept. At that point, my original error seemed forgotten.

To be fair, this is an early-stage programme still in development. It's entirely possible that this oversight will be addressed in future iterations. But it also serves as a reminder: even in the classroom, students can—and do—leave lessons with misconceptions, despite our best efforts. AI tutors, like human teachers, need to be attuned not only to *what* is said but also to *what is missed*.

Curious to compare experiences, I then posed the same misconception to ChatGPT. Its response was direct and accurate, but it lacked the scaffolding, follow-up questions, and motivational nudges (like points and streaks) that the AI tutor had provided. ChatGPT gave me a polished explanation—but I didn't have to think very much to get it.

This small experiment captures something vital. ChatGPT was more efficient, but it bypassed the kind of struggle that strengthens memory. The AI tutor, on the other hand, encouraged retrieval, prompted reflection, and supported the construction of understanding—key ingredients for long-term retention.

The takeaway? Even if two systems deliver the same *answer*, the process by which that answer is arrived at matters deeply. For learners, the productive struggle—especially when supported by timely feedback and guidance—is where the real learning takes place.

This is not to say ChatGPT is not useful; however, the programme is better used when the learner has a deeper understanding to ask the appropriate prompts to ensure they are developing the reflectiveness that is needed. Over the past couple of months, I've been helping my daughter with her SATs revision. She brings home practice papers, and we go through the questions she got wrong together. In maths, I can easily identify where she made a mistake, help her understand it, and then create several solutions for her to check her understanding. However, when she makes a mistake in English, my lack of knowledge of primary school English means I struggle to provide the same level of support.

For example, she was recently asked to identify the determiners in a text. Instead of struggling on my own, I turned to ChatGPT:

A determiner is a word that introduces a noun and gives information about which one, how many, or whose. It helps to clarify what the noun refers to. Determiners are always placed before a noun (and before any adjectives describing the noun).

After reading the definition out to my daughter, she immediately remembered that she had covered this topic some time ago.

ChatGPT also provided some examples, which I used to test her understanding:

- *The cat sat on a mat.* → (The and a are determiners.)
- *My brother saw some birds.* → (My and some are determiners.)
- *Which route did you take?* → (Which is a determiner.)

I then followed up with a prompt to ask for a few more complex examples, which it provided:

- *This book was placed on that shelf for a reason.* → (This and that are determiners.)
- *Her three older brothers all participated in the charity event.* → (Her and three are determiners.)
- *Those many books on the shelf belong to my sister.* → (Those and many are determiners.)

As someone who uses ChatGPT regularly and has a solid understanding of the English education system, I found this process relatively straightforward. However, for many parents and students, the potential of such tools remains untapped. With the right guidance and training, parents could be empowered to better support their children, unlocking new opportunities for learning and engagement. Providing parents with the skills to navigate these resources effectively could transform their ability to actively contribute to their child's educational journey.

In an earlier chapter, I explored the role of heuristics and how they can influence students' decision-making, often without them realising. These cognitive shortcuts are not easy to overcome, which is why AI has the potential to act as a valuable temporary scaffold—helping students slow down and reflect more carefully. One practical application is using AI to prompt reflective thinking; for example, by asking how heuristics might be affecting their judgement during essay writing. The example below shows a prompt and AI-generated response based on an A-level Environmental Science essay question.

Prompt: I need to write an essay about the dangers of mining for cobalt. Can you give specific examples of the heuristics that could affect my essay?

Confirmation Bias

- **Definition:** Looking for evidence that supports what you already believe and ignoring conflicting data.
- **In your essay:** If you're critical of cobalt mining, you might focus only on negative aspects and ignore efforts to improve conditions—such as fair trade initiatives or companies investing in ethical sourcing. A balanced essay shows awareness of *both* the dangers *and* the ongoing efforts to address them.

Availability Heuristic

- **Definition:** Judging the importance or frequency of something based on how easily examples come to mind.

- **In your essay:** Graphic images or high-profile news stories about child labour in the Democratic Republic of Congo (DRC) might lead you to think this is the *only* or *most* widespread issue in cobalt mining. While serious, it's important to balance this with data on less visible problems, like environmental degradation or long-term health impacts on miners.

There are a couple of important things to ensure here. First, like all scaffolds, this needs to be temporary. In an actual exam, students will not have access to ChatGPT or other AI tools. Therefore, educators need to ensure that any such tool is phased out when the student is ready. The goal is for students to eventually have enough cognitive capacity to consider the heuristics themselves before essay writing, as they become more familiar with the process.

Promote Active Thinking	Support Cognitive Load	Provide Feedback	Scaffold Learning	Promote Retrieval	Spaced Repetition and Interleaving
Yes	Yes	Yes	Yes		

Feedback: Why It's Not What AI Says, But What Students Do

One of the most powerful long-term applications of AI in education may be its role in delivering meaningful, consistent feedback to students.

In her blog post "*So, can AI assess writing?*", (Christodoulou 2025) Daisy Christodoulou examines the findings of a large-scale trial by No More Marking, which tested the reliability of AI in assessing student writing using Comparative Judgement. Over 5,000 eleven-twelve year olds students participated in the study, where both human teachers and an AI system compared writing samples to judge quality. The AI agreed with human decisions 81% of the time—remarkably close to the 87% agreement typically seen between human markers.

Interestingly, most disagreements occurred when the quality difference between two pieces of writing was marginal. A closer look revealed that many of these discrepancies were due to human error—such as being influenced by neat handwriting or making accidental misclicks. Notably, the AI focused on the substance of students' arguments, rather than superficial features like word count or repeated phrases. Christodoulou concludes that AI has significant potential to support teachers by offering consistent, scalable feedback—particularly when paired with thoughtful human oversight.

One teacher exploring this potential is Gareth Edwards, Head of History, who has integrated the AI platform TILF.io into his classroom practice. As Gareth describes:

> The platform itself is incredibly intuitive and easy to use. Teachers or students simply type in the exam question they are answering, select the level of course (GCSE or A Level), exam board, and the name of the unit the question belongs to.
>
> TILF.io is directly linked to mark schemes for each GCSE and A Level subject. Once a student submits their response, the AI scans it and provides detailed feedback—highlighting what was done well and offering precise suggestions for improvement. It also estimates the likely mark the answer would receive, clearly aligning this judgment with the appropriate assessment objectives (AOs).

An example.

Paragraphs Feedback

In the first paragraph, while you provide a clear agreement with Interpretation 2, you could enhance your analysis by including specific examples of Nazi propaganda or campaigns that garnered public support. This would strengthen your argument about the importance of mass support in Hitler's rise to power. Consider discussing specific events or slogans that resonated with the German populace.

The second paragraph effectively links the economic context to the rise of the Nazis, which is a strong point. However, you could improve it by more explicitly connecting the economic hardships to the increase in Nazi support. For instance, you could elaborate on how the Nazis' promises directly addressed the fears and needs of the populace during the Great Depression.

In the third paragraph, your evaluation of Interpretation 1 is good, but it could benefit from a clearer distinction between the roles of political manoeuvrings and public support. You mention that Hitler's personality and support gained him power later on; however, providing a specific example of a political decision or event that illustrates this point would enhance your analysis.

The conclusion summarises your views well, but it could be more impactful if you briefly restate the key points that led you to favour Interpretation 2. This would reinforce your argument and provide a clearer closure to your evaluation.

What Went Well

The essay demonstrates a clear understanding of both interpretations and effectively uses historical context to support the analysis. The connections made between public support, economic conditions, and Hitler's rise to power are particularly strong, showing a good grasp of the complexities involved in this historical event.

> **Even Better If**
>
> To achieve a higher mark, the essay should include more specific examples and details to support the claims made. Enhancing the analysis with direct references to Nazi propaganda, specific events, and clearer distinctions between the roles of public support and political manoeuvrings would strengthen the overall argument.
>
> **Overall Feedback**
>
> The essay provides a thoughtful evaluation of the interpretations regarding Hitler's rise to power, with a strong emphasis on the role of mass support. While the analysis is generally solid, it would benefit from more specific examples and a clearer structure in some areas. Overall, it demonstrates a good understanding of the historical context and the differing views on Hitler's appointment as Chancellor.

Crucially, Gareth has gone a step further by providing a structured framework to guide students in how they engage with the feedback. For each suggestion, students are asked to not only revise their answer but also explain the reasoning behind their changes. This reflective process turns feedback into an opportunity for deeper learning.

> **Example**
>
> In the first paragraph, while you provide a clear agreement with Interpretation 2, you could enhance your analysis by including specific examples of Nazi propaganda or campaigns that garnered public support. This would strengthen your argument about the importance of mass support in Hitler's rise to power. Consider discussing specific events or slogans that resonated with the German populace.
>
> **Student Response**
>
> *Original Text*
>
> "Mass support gave Hitler a key to unlocking the door to power" suggests that the main reason for Hitler becoming Chancellor in 1933 was support from the public.
>
> *Rewritten Example*
>
>> Mass support, exemplified by the Nazi slogan 'Work, Freedom, and Bread', gave Hitler a key to unlocking the door to power, as it resonated deeply with the struggling German populace during the Great Depression.

> **Reasoning**
>
> By including a specific slogan, the argument becomes more concrete and illustrates how the Nazis effectively communicated their message to the public, enhancing the analysis of mass support.

If AI feedback continues to improve and reaches a level comparable to that of teachers, it could transform how feedback is delivered in schools. As Dylan Wiliam (Wiliam, 2016) notes in his article *"The Secret of Effective Feedback"*:

The only important thing about feedback is what students do with it.

AI can free teachers from the time-intensive task of marking and enable them to focus their energy on what matters most: helping students understand and apply the feedback they receive. Gareth Edwards' case study exemplifies this shift—by providing question prompts and encouraging active reflection, students are more likely to retain the improvement and apply it across contexts.

In this way, AI isn't replacing teachers—it's amplifying their impact.

Promote Active Thinking	Support Cognitive Load	Provide Feedback	Scaffold Learning	Promote Retrieval	Spaced Repetition and Interleaving
Yes	Yes	Yes	Yes		

Chapter Summary

- Without clear guidance, AI tools risk reinforcing unproductive learning habits.
- Excessive dependence on AI can hinder the development of expertise.
- It is essential to establish a set of principles for using AI effectively, grounded in robust cognitive science.
- Seek out AI applications that align with how learning happens to maximise educational impact.
- Use AI primarily to generate timely, personalised feedback, enabling educators to focus on supporting students in how to interpret and apply that feedback.

References

Ahmad, S. F., Han, H., Alam, M. M., Rehmat, M. K., Irshad, M., Arraño-Muñoz, M., & Ariza-Montes, A. (2023). Impact of artificial intelligence on human loss in decision making, laziness and safety in education. *Humanities & Social Sciences Communications, 10*(1), Article 311. https://doi.org/10.1057/s41599-023-01787-8

Burnett, G. E., & Lee, K. (2005). The effect of vehicle navigation systems on the formation of cognitive maps. In G. Underwood (Ed.), *Traffic and transport psychology: Theory and application* (pp. 407–418). Elsevier.

Casner, S. M., Geven, R. W., Recker, M. P., & Schooler, J. W. (2014). The retention of manual flying skills in the automated cockpit. *Human Factors, 56*(8), 1506–1516. https://doi.org/10.1177/0018720814535628

Christodoulou, D., & Wheadon, C. (2025, March 31). So, can AI assess writing? Results of our large-scale AI-enhanced Comparative Judgement trial. *No More Marking*. Retrieved from https://substack.nomoremarking.com/p/so-can-ai-assess-writing

Freeman, J. (2025, February 26). Student generative AI survey 2025. *Higher Education Policy Institute & Kortext*. Retrieved from HEPI website.

Kestin, G., & Miller, K. (2024, September 5). Professor tailored AI tutor to physics course. Engagement doubled. *Harvard Gazette*. Retrieved from https://news.harvard.edu/gazette/story/2024/09/professor-tailored-ai-tutor-to-physics-course-engagement-doubled/

Krupp, D., Lu, X., Fang, F., & Singla, S. (2023). The impact of ChatGPT-assisted problem-solving on physics students' performance and behaviors. In *Proceedings of the 2023 Conference on Learning at Scale (L@S '23)* (pp. 45–56). https://doi.org/10.1145/3576091.3576112

Li, J., & Wang, H. (2023). Academic integrity and AI: Implications for student learning and assessment. *International Journal of Educational Integrity, 19*(2), 1–12. https://doi.org/10.55016/ojs/cpai.v7i3.78123

Nature Editorial. (2023). The double-edged sword of AI in education. *Nature, 613*, 393. https://doi.org/10.13140/RG.2.2.31891.45609

Sparrow, B., Liu, J., & Wegner, D. M. (2011). Google effects on memory: Cognitive consequences of having information at our fingertips. *Science, 333*(6040), 776–778.

Wiliam, D. (2016). The secret of effective feedback. *Educational Leadership, 73*(7), 10–15. Retrieved from https://www.ascd.org/publications/educational-leadership/apr16/vol73/num07/The-Secret-of-Effective-Feedback.aspx

Zhou, M., & Xu, L. (2024). Effects of generative AI on higher education: Challenges for gifted learners. *Journal of Educational Technology & Society, 27*(1), 45–59.

Zhu, Y., & Liu, S. (2023). The influence of AI-assisted learning on student academic performance: A meta-analysis. *Computers & Education, 196*, 104696. https://doi.org/10.15354/sief.24.re395

The Path to Expertise: Accelerating Learning Habits

How Novices and Experts Think Differently

When we examine how novices and experts approach learning, it's clear that their thinking differs in significant ways. Often, when students compare their test scores to others, they may find themselves wondering what it takes to achieve the top scores in the class. Many will then form misconceptions about the traits or behaviours that lead to such outcomes.

To challenge these myths, it's helpful to explore what students think is required for success. After reading through each of these common misconceptions, I encourage you to pause and reflect on how the ideas in this book can help dispel these misconceptions.

Myth	What Students Often Believe	Addressing the Myth
1. Natural talent	Top grades come from being naturally gifted. Success is about innate ability, not effort.	Remind students that working memory is limited. The more knowledge you build, the easier it becomes to learn new material. High achievers often rely on accumulated knowledge, not raw talent.
2. Memorisation skills	Some students just have "better memories" and can effortlessly remember everything.	Memory strength is less important than strategy. Techniques like retrieval practice, spacing, and elaboration help improve memory retention—regardless of natural ability.

(Continued)

Myth	What Students Often Believe	Addressing the Myth
3. Studying for long hours	More study hours = better results. Sleep and well-being can be sacrificed for longer revision.	Quality beats quantity. Twenty minutes of focused retrieval is more effective than hours of passive re-reading. Fatigue also affects decision-making and learning efficiency. One study found that judges made harsher decisions later in the day as mental resources declined (Danziger et al., 2011).
4. Perfect notes	Neat, detailed, and aesthetically pleasing notes lead to better understanding and top grades. Students may rewrite notes, add colour-coding, or focus on formatting to make their work look polished.	While organised notes can help with review, the *process* of note-taking matters far more than how the notes look. Mueller and Oppenheimer (2014) found that students who typed notes verbatim on laptops performed worse on conceptual tests than those who wrote by hand. Handwriting forces students to summarise and process ideas in real time—an act that deepens understanding.
5. No mistakes or failures	High achievers don't make mistakes. Failure signals a lack of ability.	Carol Dweck's research on mindsets (2006) shows that students with a fixed mindset see mistakes as proof of inadequacy, while those with a growth mindset view them as learning opportunities. By normalising error and modelling productive responses to setbacks, teachers and parents can help dismantle this harmful myth and promote resilience.

In this chapter, I will compare the decision-making processes of novices and experts. The goal is twofold: first, to help students understand that as they gain expertise, many aspects of learning become easier; and second, to explore what we, as educators and parents, can do to accelerate the development of learners in becoming experts. This will involve looking at how we can build students' mental models of learning and address the challenge of overconfidence.

I once visited a school where each classroom featured a simple graph on the wall. The x-axis was labelled "time," and the y-axis was labelled "independent learning." The concept was clear: over time, the goal was to foster greater independence in its students, helping them become more self-directed learners; however, there was no road map.

A framework for understanding what this developmental process might actually look like comes from the work of Dreyfus and Dreyfus, particularly in their book *Mind Over Machine: The Power of Human Intuition and Expertise in the Age of the Computer* (Dreyfus & Dreyfus, 1986). I initially read this book as part of my research for the chapter on the role of artificial intelligence (AI) in learning, as it challenges the notion that expert performance can be fully replicated by computers or AI. However, the Dreyfus brothers' work offers a clear explanation of how individuals progress through various stages of skill acquisition, from novice to expert. It also outlines how their thinking and approach to problems evolve as they develop expertise.

The Five Stages Are as Follows

Stage	Characteristics	Thinking Process	Choosing Study Materials	Approach to Assignments	Time Management
1. Novice	New to a task, relies on rules and step-by-step instructions. Limited context or understanding.	Focuses on isolated features without understanding context. Rigid and rule-bound.	Follows teacher instructions exactly (e.g., specific textbook or worksheet).	Copies text verbatim, believing this ensures success.	Studies for long hours without considering effectiveness or efficiency.
2. Advanced beginner	Gaining experience; starts to recognise patterns but still relies on rules.	Begins to see the "big picture" but still heavily dependent on guidelines.	Begins selecting resources for specific struggles (e.g., videos for difficult topics).	Attempts application but may mismatch examples or concepts.	Experiments with strategies (e.g., setting time limits) but struggles to prioritise effectively.
3. Competent	Can prioritise and act more independently; analyses situations.	Makes deliberate, strategic decisions; may feel stress from weighing options.	Chooses materials based on needs (e.g., textbooks for theory, past papers for practice).	Breaks down tasks and connects ideas across topics.	Starts prioritising tasks by importance or deadline but may overfocus on comfort topics.

(Continued)

Stage	Characteristics	Thinking Process	Choosing Study Materials	Approach to Assignments	Time Management
4. Proficient	Grasps broader perspective; anticipates outcomes; works fluidly.	Relies on pattern recognition and experience; decision-making is faster, still thoughtful.	Selects materials aligned with goals (e.g., past papers for exam prep).	Synthesises information, makes broader connections (e.g., real-world or cross-topic).	Allocates time strategically, focusing on high-impact areas.
5. Expert	Intuitive, automatic, and adaptive; deep, internalised understanding.	Decisions guided by intuition and deep expertise; rarely needs explicit analysis.	Uses highly tailored or advanced resources (e.g., academic papers, niche tools).	Integrates complex ideas effortlessly; anticipates problems.	Balances study, rest, and commitments; knows how to avoid burnout and when to push.

The Dreyfus and Dreyfus model explains how people move from following strict rules to developing flexible, intuitive expertise. Whether you're a teacher or a parent, you can often identify where a learner is along this journey. At each stage, the way students make decisions about their learning becomes more thoughtful and adapted to the situation. Beginners depend heavily on clear instructions and step-by-step processes, while experts use their deep knowledge to adjust and respond intuitively to new challenges.

I have applied the Dreyfus and Dreyfus framework specifically to the development of expertise in learning itself. The goal of becoming an expert learner is to speed up the process by which students develop expertise in specific subjects like physics or geography. While it's possible for students to become expert biologists—or excel in any domain—without first becoming expert learners, this involves a longer journey filled with more trial and error and many bumps along the way. When students apply effective learning habits to a particular subject, they begin to develop expertise in that domain more efficiently. Once they have mastered a subject, their perspective and decision-making in that domain will also change.

> ### CASE STUDY: Problem-Solving in Physics
>
> In Chi et al.'s (1981) study, the researchers examined how expert and novice physics students approached a specific type of problem—a free-falling object under the influence of gravity.
>
> The Problem:
>
> The physics problem presented to both groups involved calculating the velocity of an object in free fall after a certain period of time. The problem required knowledge of Newton's laws of motion and the equations of motion.

Aspect	Novices	Experts
Problem categorisation	Focus on **surface features** (e.g., "free fall," "motion problem"). Grouped problems based on the context or vocabulary used.	Focus on **underlying principles** (e.g., constant acceleration). Categorised based on deep structure and physics concepts.
Use of equations	Applied formulas **mechanically** (e.g., $v = g \times t$) without considering context or initial conditions. Often made errors or misapplied equations.	Considered **conceptual meaning** behind formulas. Thought about relationships (e.g., between velocity, acceleration, time) before choosing an equation.
Mental representation	Viewed the problem in a **fragmented, step-by-step** way. Solved parts without fully grasping the whole situation.	Formed a **coherent, holistic** model of the situation. Integrated understanding of motion and forces.
Use of context	Focused on **numbers** and surface cues. Struggled to interpret what was physically happening.	Considered the **real-world context**, including object motion and environmental factors.
Problem-solving efficiency	Slower, more prone to **errors** due to limited understanding. Relied on guesswork or trial-and-error.	**More efficient** and accurate. Quickly identified relevant principles and applied appropriate strategies.

This clear distinction between novice and expert thinking is also evident in research across other subjects. For example, in history, Wineburg (1991) found that novice learners often focus on surface details of historical texts and accept information at face value, whereas experts critically analyse sources, situate them within broader historical contexts, and actively question their reliability.

Similarly, in English, Bereiter and Scardamalia's (1987) research on writing expertise reveals a comparable pattern. Novice writers typically follow a knowledge-telling approach, relying on linear, step-by-step processes and focusing on surface-level details, much like novices in physics who focus on formulas and numbers. In contrast, expert writers engage in knowledge-transforming processes, critically reflecting on and reorganising their ideas, adapting flexibly to the demands of the writing task.

Together, these studies highlight a fundamental pattern: beginners depend heavily on explicit instructions and clear, rigid procedures, while experts develop deep, flexible knowledge that allows them to adapt intuitively to new and complex challenges. What is also important to note is that not only do experts take very different steps than novices, but these steps also allow for reduced cognitive load and increased speed of completion.Schneider and Shiffrin (1977) investigated how people process information when performing tasks. They found that:

Novices engaged in controlled processing, meaning that they had to devote conscious attention and effort to every step of the task. For example, when detecting patterns or searching for information, novices had to manually process each individual piece of data, one at a time. This required more cognitive resources and led to slower performance.

Experts, on the other hand, had developed automatic processing skills. This meant that they could detect patterns, search for relevant information, and direct attention to key elements of the task with little or no conscious effort. Their mental frameworks were so well developed that they could process information quickly and efficiently, freeing up capacity to focus on more complex aspects of the task, such as problem-solving.

To summarise.

Experts not only know more, but because the basics are automated, they have more mental space to take on new and harder ideas.

Let's return to the scenario at the start of this book—the expert learner sitting in a university lecture. If you don't recall it clearly, you may want to revisit it, as it sets the foundation for what follows.

At first glance, it might seem that the learner quickly recognised they were experiencing cognitive overload due to the volume of new information being presented.

In fact, that's not what happened. Had they truly reached cognitive overload, they wouldn't have been able to continue making effective decisions about their next steps. What actually occurred was an almost automatic recognition—not that they were overwhelmed, but that they wouldn't be able to elaboratively integrate the new material or connect it meaningfully to what they already knew. As a result, they adapted in the moment, shifting their focus to extract just the key vocabulary.

After the lecture, not only did they demonstrate expert knowledge of how to learn the new material efficiently, but they also showed at least proficient knowledge of the subject matter. This allowed them to create concept maps and link the new knowledge from the lecture to what they already knew, continuing to strengthen and expand their schema.

Let's now look at the example of the plumber and how their growing knowledge of plumbing and expertise as a learner allowed them to work through the problem.

Area	Expert	Plumber Example
1. Knowledge organisation	Experts can quickly recognise patterns and apply their knowledge to new and varied situations, because their knowledge is well integrated and deep.	They recognised the system must have an inlet valve and used their prior knowledge to identify where it would be.
2. Problem-solving approach	Experts can see the underlying structure of problems and often solve them more efficiently. They use their deep understanding to make intuitive leaps and adapt their methods based on context.	They worked out that the float was controlling the inlet valve.
3. Cognitive load	Experts experience lower cognitive load due to their ability to chunk information into meaningful units, freeing up mental space for higher-level thinking.	At no point did they become overawed by the challenge; they worked through the problem steadily.
4. Flexibility in application	Experts are flexible in their approach. They can apply their knowledge across contexts, adjusting strategies and exploring new methods as needed.	The outcome of the scenario shows this—they completed a problem different from their usual tasks, with some support.
5. Metacognition (thinking about thinking)	Experts are highly metacognitive. They monitor their thinking, adjust strategies when needed, and use self-regulation to improve.	They recognised their limitations, asked for help, and wanted to try it themselves to ensure they learned and improved.

The Case of Overconfidence

So how can we accelerate the rate of students becoming experts' learners and what barriers are in the way.

One well-known barrier to the development of expertise is the Dunning-Kruger effect—a cognitive bias where individuals with low ability in a particular domain tend to overestimate their competence. In contrast, those with more experience and knowledge are often more aware of the limits of their understanding. This means that novice learners may feel overly confident in their abilities, believing they have mastered a topic when, in fact, they have only scratched the surface. This false confidence can reduce the motivation to study further, seek feedback, or engage in deeper learning—all of which are essential for genuine expertise.

An example of this in action is a student who completes a unit on photosynthesis and feels confident they "get it." They tell their teacher, "I don't need to revise—it's easy." On the test, they perform poorly, unable to explain key processes or apply the concepts in unfamiliar contexts.

What's Happening?

Their limited grasp of the topic leads them to overestimate their understanding, because they lack the depth of knowledge to see what they're missing. Their confidence isn't based on mastery—it's based on surface familiarity.

A detailed study on this phenomenon was conducted by Lawson (2006) at the University of Liverpool. In the experiment, participants were first asked to rate their knowledge of how bicycles work, with many believing they had a solid understanding of the subject. After this self-assessment, they were then asked to draw a bicycle from memory. Despite their high self-ratings, many participants produced drawings with significant inaccuracies—such as misplacing the chain or missing key components entirely. This mismatch between their perceived knowledge and their actual performance clearly demonstrates the Dunning-Kruger effect, where individuals with limited knowledge tend to overestimate their abilities. The study highlights how confidence in one's understanding doesn't always align with reality.

I had the chance to experience this task myself at a conference last year during Bradley Busch's presentation on his five favourite cognitive science studies. Despite knowing the outcome of the experiment in advance—having read about it prior to the conference—I was still shocked that I couldn't draw the bicycle accurately.

This exercise is a valuable one to use with students, as it vividly illustrates how easy it is to be overconfident in one's knowledge. It also provides an opportunity to explore a key theme in this book: why is it that people struggle to draw a bike, despite potentially spending countless hours riding one? The answer lies in how our focus shifts when we're engaged in an activity. When riding a bike, your attention is on the road, the route, and the surroundings—not on the inner workings of the gear system. If you're not actively thinking about something, it's much less likely to stick in your memory.

One way to reduce people's estimation of their own knowledge is to have them provide a functional explanation. Rozenblit and Keil (2002) found that people often overestimate their understanding of how everyday objects, like coffee makers or toasters, work. While participants were confident in their knowledge, they struggled to provide detailed explanations of the mechanisms behind these devices. The researchers suggested that this discrepancy occurs because, in everyday life, people are rarely required to think about or explain how the objects they use function. As a result, they develop superficial knowledge, understanding what the device does without comprehending the intricate processes involved. This lack of need to articulate functional explanations leads individuals to overestimate their competence.

Some students will have overconfidence in their learning habits for this very reason: they have never had to justify them. As has already been discussed, learning habits can feel counterintuitive because they may contradict our natural impulses or assumptions about how learning works.

To reduce these intuitive beliefs, ask students to rank each of the intuitive beliefs according to which ones they think are effective learning habits. For those that they rank highest, ask them to provide an explanation behind their answer based on what they know about the science of learning. The counterintuitive reality for each has been provided below.

Student Task: Justify Your Learning Beliefs

Many students feel confident in their learning habits without ever having had to explain or justify them. This task will help you examine whether that confidence is well-placed.

1. **Belief Ranking**
   Below is a list of commonly held beliefs about learning. Rank them from 1 (most effective) to 5 (least effective) based on how effective you believe each one is for long-term learning.

Belief	Your Rank (1–5)
Re-reading notes is the best way to revise	
Testing yourself is only useful once you feel ready	
Highlighting helps you remember key content	
You need to fully understand a topic before you can try to recall it	
The harder learning feels, the less effective it probably is	

2. **Justification Challenge**
   Now choose the two beliefs you ranked the highest. For each one:

   ○ Write a brief explanation of *why* you believe it is effective.

- Then, compare your explanation with what the science of learning says (the counterintuitive reality provided below). Are your beliefs supported by evidence, or do they need rethinking?

3. **Counterintuitive Reality**

    - **Re-reading notes is the best way to revise.** Re-reading makes information feel familiar, which creates the illusion of knowing it, but it doesn't strengthen memory. Real learning happens when you try to recall information rather than just review it. The effort of remembering helps your brain store knowledge more deeply and retrieve it more easily later.

    - **Testing yourself is only useful once you feel ready.** Testing isn't just a way to check what you know — it's one of the best ways to learn. Trying to recall information before you feel ready actually strengthens memory and highlights what still needs work. Even getting answers wrong helps your brain learn more effectively the next time.

    - **Highlighting helps you remember key content.** Highlighting feels productive but doesn't do much on its own. It can draw attention to important ideas, but unless you actively engage with that information — by explaining it, summarising it, or testing yourself on it — it doesn't improve memory or understanding.

    - **You need to fully understand a topic before you can try to recall it.** Understanding and recall develop together. Trying to recall something you don't fully understand helps you see what you do and don't know. This process strengthens learning and helps you build a clearer, deeper understanding over time.

    - **The harder learning feels, the less effective it probably is.** Learning that feels easy often isn't very effective — it just feels comfortable because it's familiar. When learning feels effortful, it's usually because your brain is working to create stronger connections. That challenge is a good sign that real learning is happening.

4. **Reflection Questions**

    - Were you surprised by any of the counterintuitive truths?
    - Did your confidence in any of your learning habits change as a result of this task?
    - What changes (if any) will you make to how you study?

How Do We Make Decision?

One of the most influential figures in the study of decision-making is cognitive psychologist Gary Klein. His work focuses on how people make decisions in real-world, high-pressure situations, often when time is limited and information is incomplete. Unlike traditional models that emphasise slow, analytical thinking, Klein was interested in how experts make quick, effective decisions without always consciously weighing up all the options. Through his fieldwork with firefighters, military personnel, and emergency responders, Klein developed the recognition-primed decision (RPD) model, which shows that experts often rely on intuition and pattern recognition built up through years of experience. His research highlights the shift from rule-based reasoning in novices to intuitive, experience-driven judgement in experts, making his work central to understanding how learning and expertise develop over time (Klein, 1998).

Klien states that novices rely on rules because

- They lack experience, so they don't have patterns to draw from.
- As a result, they must consciously follow rules, guidelines, or procedures they've been taught.
- Their decision-making is analytical, step-by-step, and often slower.

Klein observed that novices often compare multiple possible options because they don't yet recognise what a good solution "looks like." Their reasoning tends to follow a step-by-step process, where they:

- Evaluate different choices or actions,
- Consider pros and cons,
- Apply explicit rules or instructions,
- And only then make a decision.

An example of a novice learner in action is Liam is a Year 10 student who's just started preparing for his GCSE exams. It's a Tuesday evening, and he knows he has a science test next week. Unsure of the best way to revise, he tries to remember what his teacher said in class and what he's seen in school resources. He mentally runs through his options: he could re-read the textbook, make flashcards, watch a YouTube video, or try a past paper. He compares the options one by one, weighing up which might be most useful. Eventually, he decides to re-read the chapter and then make notes as he has seen other people's notes in his class, and they do well on tests. He follows the steps carefully but isn't fully confident it's the most effective approach. He's relying on rules and advice he's heard, rather than experience or instinct.

The problem is when evaluating his choices and considering the pros and cons, his limited understanding of how learning happens has resulted in a poor choice, things Liam could have considered.

Principle	What Liam Did	What Liam Could Have Done Instead
1. Retrieval practice works better than re-reading	Re-read his textbook and made a mind map.	Started with a short quiz or flashcards to actively recall information.
2. Spaced practice beats cramming	Revised reactively rather than planning over several days.	Reviewed the topic that evening and planned to revisit it later in the week.
3. Cognitive load should be managed	Took in a lot of information at once by re-reading and then making a mind map.	Broke revision into smaller chunks, like doing ten retrieval questions on a single subtopic.
4. Metacognition and self-regulation	Didn't reflect on whether his chosen strategies were actually helping him learn.	Asked himself questions like, "Do I really understand this?" or "What helped me last time?" to guide his revision choices.

If Liam were functioning more like an expert learner, his decision-making would be much more intuitive and efficient. Rather than consciously weighing up multiple revision strategies, he would instantly recognise the type of situation he was in: *a short window of time before a test on a topic he had some, but not full, understanding of.* Based on previous experiences that had worked, his brain would quickly match the situation to a familiar pattern—for example, "When I've had a test the next day and needed to quickly reinforce my memory, retrieval practice helped most."

From this recognition, Liam wouldn't spend time deliberating or comparing options. Instead, he'd jump straight into a strategy that he knew would be effective—perhaps doing a self-quiz or trying to write out everything he knew from memory, then checking gaps. If he ran into difficulty, he'd adapt quickly, perhaps switching to a spaced flashcard app or using past paper questions to test himself further. This kind of fast, flexible decision-making, rooted in experience and pattern recognition, is the hallmark of the recognition-primed model.

Liam didn't compare options; he saw the right course of action because their experience allows them to *recognise the situation and respond accordingly.*

When students are developing learning habits, a hopeful starting point would be to see them make decisions by comparing strategies based on sound reasoning—deliberately weighing the evidence before moving towards faster, experience-driven judgements, as seen in recognition-primed decision-making. However, without a firm understanding of how learning works, their choices may not be based on rational comparison at all. Instead, students may simply go with what feels right or familiar, even if it's ineffective.

This pattern mirrors what Soelberg (1967) observed in his study of business students making job decisions after graduation. At the time, it was widely assumed that students would make rational, deliberate decisions—listing pros and cons, rating options, and carefully weighing their choices. But Soelberg's findings told a more complex story.

Even when students engaged in a formal decision-making process—identifying criteria, scoring job offers, and comparing alternatives—many had already made their decision. One composite example involved a student choosing between a prestigious consulting firm and a smaller startup that aligned more closely with his values. On paper, the consulting role was objectively stronger: higher salary, stronger reputation, better career prospects. Yet the student chose the startup. When asked why, he said something along the lines of, "It just felt right from the beginning."

Soelberg referred to this as a pre-decision—an instinctive choice made early on, often without conscious awareness, which people then justify through later analysis (Soelberg, 1967). This means that even when decision-making appears rational on the surface, it may be driven by fast, intuitive judgements underneath.

While this *resembles* Klein's recognition-primed decision-making on the surface, there's a key difference: Klein studied experienced professionals who had developed reliable mental models through repeated exposure to high-stakes situations. Soelberg's students, by contrast, were novices with little prior experience to draw on. Their intuitive decisions weren't grounded in expertise but rather in gut feelings—which were then rationalised after the fact.

That's what makes Soelberg's findings so compelling. They reveal just how easily we can convince ourselves that we've been logical, when in fact we've simply backed up a pre-existing preference with post-hoc reasoning.

In this book, I argue for giving students a strong foundation in cognitive science, especially when it comes to decision-making and expertise. Knowledge is essential—it's the foundation of expert thinking. But as any experienced teacher will tell you, simply having the theory isn't enough. Most of us spent a year in teacher training, learning the frameworks and methods of good teaching. Yet no one feels like an expert teacher on day one. Knowing what to do and being able to do it fluently in real time are very different things.

That's why I return to the idea—popularised by Anders Ericsson—that it takes around 10 years or 10,000 hours of deliberate practice to truly become an expert. But that doesn't mean we can't help learners along the way. There are strategies we can teach students that can speed up their development, not by cutting corners, but by building better awareness of how decisions are made.

Take Liam, for example. Faced with how to revise for a test, he decides to re-read the chapter and make notes—something he's seen other students do. And because those students tend to do well, he reasons that this must be a good strategy. But it's very possible that Liam had already made that decision instinctively and only afterwards justified it by pointing to what others had done. In other words, his reasoning came after the decision—not before.

If we want to help students like Liam become more strategic, we need to help them recognise these patterns in their own thinking. Teaching them about pre-decisions, gut feelings, and the difference between intuition and analysis can give them the tools to pause, reflect, and eventually make more deliberate, informed choices.

Addressing Poor Decision-Making in Novices

In a study by Essex and Healy (1994), researchers aimed to assess the effectiveness of a set of rules designed to improve decision-making skills in medical students and general practitioner (GP) trainees. The researchers created a rule base by analysing clinical data from thousands of patients over eight years in a general practice setting. This rule base was intended to capture expert judgement and help guide decision-making in clinical scenarios.

The experiment involved 93 fourth-year medical students and 179 GP trainees. Participants were presented with a series of clinical scenarios—hypothetical patient cases that required decision-making. They were asked to record their thoughts and management plans both before and after being introduced to the rules derived from the rule base. Each participant's responses were assessed by a panel of independent experts, who evaluated whether their decisions were good, acceptable, or poor. The results showed that when participants were exposed to the rules, they were better able to identify the right course of action and improve their decision-making.

It would be useful to have your own set of learning rules in your school or classroom or as a parent at home as a starting point to reduce inconsistency among novice learners. Here is a suggested starting point.

Thinking is key	Engage with the material actively—don't just read or listen passively. Interrogate new knowledge and try to link it to knowledge already in your long-term memory.
Use spaced repetition	Review material regularly over increasing intervals. Spacing out your study sessions helps solidify your memory.
Apply knowledge to real-life scenarios	Relate what you learn to real-world situations. This not only helps with understanding but also makes learning more relevant.

(Continued)

Test yourself frequently	Self-testing, or retrieval practice, strengthens your memory and helps identify areas where you need more focus.
Break tasks into manageable chunks	Avoid feeling overwhelmed and reaching cognitive overload by breaking down larger tasks into smaller, more achievable goals.
Embrace mistakes as learning opportunities	Don't be afraid to make mistakes. Use them as opportunities to learn and improve your understanding.
Don't rely on just one source	Cross-check your information and look for different perspectives to deepen your understanding of the topic. Be aware of the role of heuristics in decision-making.
Ask for feedback regularly	Seek feedback from teachers, peers, or tutors. Constructive feedback can help you see where you need to improve.
Take breaks for better focus	Take short, regular breaks during study sessions to refresh your mind and maintain focus.
Stay organised and plan ahead	Decide in advance what you want to achieve during each study session to keep yourself focused and motivated. Use tools like calendars or planners to stay on top of deadlines, assignments, and revisions.

Developing Better Mental Models

The "knowing-doing" gap refers to the disconnect between knowing what needs to be done and actually putting that knowledge into practice. This gap can arise in many fields, as individuals may understand the theory behind a task but struggle to implement it effectively. Educators, in particular, are familiar with this concept, as teachers often know which strategies could improve student outcomes but face challenges in consistently applying them in the classroom. Bridging this gap highlights the need for ongoing support and reflection to turn theoretical knowledge into tangible results.

One way to understand this is through the concept of mental models—internal, simplified representations of how the world works. These models help individuals make sense of complex systems and guide their decisions and problem-solving. Mental models are not fixed; they are dynamic, shaped and reshaped by experience, learning, and reflection.

Different mental models can shape how people interpret problems, make decisions, and take action—even when they are looking at the same situation. Mental models can influence what we notice, what we prioritise, and what we believe will solve the issue. Consider a city experiencing heavy traffic. A civil engineer, whose mental model centres on infrastructure, may propose widening roads or improving signal systems. An urban planner, with a model based on human behaviour and city design, might suggest investing in public transport or creating more walkable spaces. Both are experts, yet their different mental models lead them to diagnose and solve the same problem in very different ways.

I saw this firsthand when I took a group of 12 students to the UK Space Design Competition held annually at Imperial College London. The task was to design a space settlement for 2,000 people on the surface of Mars. Our team included students from a range of subject backgrounds. Within the competition, students were divided into specialist teams, each responsible for different aspects of the design. Those studying physics and maths gravitated towards designing the structural shell of the settlement, ensuring it could withstand the harsh conditions of Mars. Meanwhile, students with a background in biology focused on food production systems. Their subject choices shaped the roles they took on—and more importantly, the mental models they brought with them.

This difference in mental models quickly became apparent. The structural team, made up mainly of physicists and mathematicians, designed a compact, minimal settlement to keep costs and material use low. They spent the first morning calculating radiation shielding requirements, estimating material quantities, and optimising oxygen supply systems. But when they shared their design with the teams responsible for human needs and infrastructure, problems arose. One psychology student, tasked with assessing the social and psychological needs of the inhabitants, took one look and asked, "You're going to put eight people in a tiny room with bunk beds? How would you feel about that if you were living there?" Half a day's work was suddenly in question. The engineering-focused team had prioritised physical survival but had not considered the lived experience of the people inhabiting the space.

This example perfectly illustrates how different mental models shape the way problems are framed, and solutions are proposed. Just as the physicists focused on systems and constraints, the psychology student brought a human-centred model that highlighted social and emotional well-being—something the others had unintentionally overlooked.

The same is true in the classroom. When a student fails a test, one student with a fixed mental model of ability might conclude, "I'm just not good at this," and give up. Another, whose model of learning includes effort and strategy, might think, "I didn't prepare effectively next time I'll revise differently." The event is the same, but the mental model behind the interpretation drives two very different outcomes.

I was fortunate enough to attend a presentation by Sarah Cottinghatt at a conference last year, where she discussed how strengthening mental models plays a crucial role in reducing the knowing-doing gap. During Sarah's talk, she asked the audience to consider how they would respond if a student put their head on the desk. The range of answers was wide, depending on various factors. For example, if the teacher was in the middle of a detailed explanation, they might not want to stop and address it immediately. However, if students were answering questions in silence, it could be the ideal moment to intervene.

Additionally, how much the teacher knows about the student affects their response. If it's a common occurrence, the teacher might take a more relaxed approach, such as a quick "David, head up," while a more out-of-character behaviour might prompt a different strategy. The class context also matters—if the class is particularly challenging, the teacher might choose not to address the issue straight away, as doing so could disrupt the attention of the whole group. In a more focused class, however, a brief pause and a purposeful walk over to the student might be more effective.

This exercise highlights how teachers use their mental models to make split-second decisions based on context, knowledge, and experience. These mental models are often tacit—intuitive frameworks built over time through experience and practice. While they guide decisions, they can also be difficult to articulate.

By placing a "microscope" on our decision-making process, reflecting on why we make the choices we do, we can better understand and refine these models. In some cases, this reflection can help close the knowing-doing gap, allowing us to shift from simply knowing strategies to consistently applying them in the most effective ways. This process of actively engaging with our mental models helps to clarify, strengthen, and expand our ability to make more informed, confident decisions.

In education we improve teachers' mental models through instructional coaching. Instructional coaching is a collaborative, reflective process in which a coach works closely with a teacher to refine their teaching practices. This approach focuses on observation, feedback, and dialogue, with the goal of helping teachers understand and improve their decision-making processes in real time. It is particularly helpful in drawing out the tacit knowledge that teachers have built up over years of experience—knowledge that may not always be explicitly articulated but influences the way they respond to various classroom situations.

Through coaching, teachers are encouraged to reflect on the choices they make in the moment, considering why they took a particular action, how it aligned with their broader teaching goals, and how it impacted student learning. For example, a coach may observe a teacher managing classroom behaviour or facilitating a lesson, then engage in a conversation afterward to explore the teacher's reasoning behind their decisions. This reflection helps the teacher become more aware of their mental models and provides a space to test out new strategies or refine existing ones. Over time, this reflective process helps to strengthen the teacher's mental models, enabling them to make more informed, effective decisions in the classroom. Instructional coaching is powerful because it doesn't just focus on giving teachers answers; it helps them develop the skills to critically assess their own practices and improve their teaching in a way that feels meaningful and sustainable.

For the students that need the most support in developing their learning habits, a coaching approach may be required to break ingrained habits.

One way of doing this is mapping students' decision-making with them (Figure 6.1).

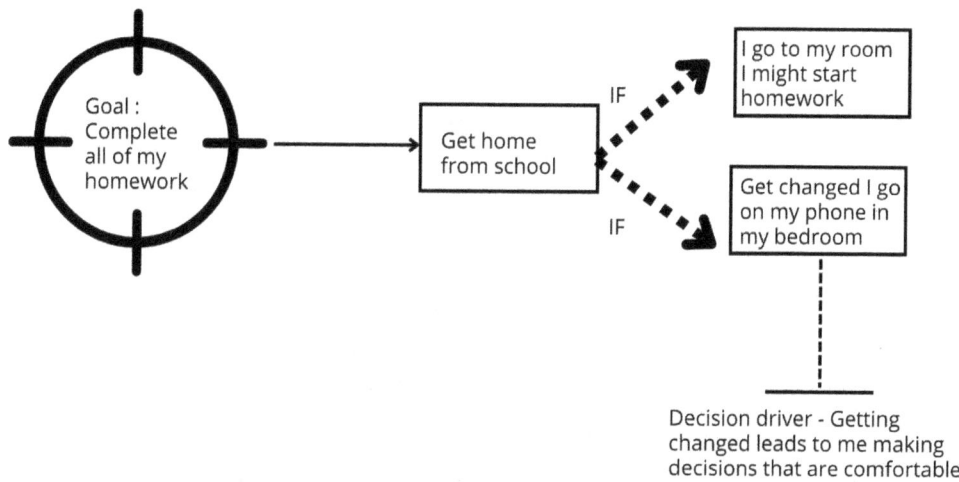

Figure 6.1 Mapping student decision-making—completing homework

The example above shows how we can map a student's decision-making when they regularly avoid homework. By talking through the steps they take after school, we can identify a pivotal moment—the point when they get home and immediately reach for their phone. This is the key cue we want to interrupt.

Now let's explore how some principles from this book could help shift this habit. One approach is to use an implementation intention:

When I get straight home from school, I will complete my homework.

Another is habit stacking, where you attach the new habit to an existing one:

When I change into my comfy clothes, I will check what homework I have.

However, comfy clothes may cue relaxation too strongly, reinforcing the craving for comfort and leading to more procrastination. In this case, a change in environment might help disrupt the cycle:

When I get home from school, I will complete my homework at the dining table.

Or you could take a more dramatic step to break the habit loop entirely by making the old behaviour impossible:

When the school day ends, I will go straight to the library to do my homework.

At this stage, it's important to map out possible future scenarios. You don't want to replace one unhelpful habit with another (Figure 6.2). For example, if comfort was the original reward, the craving might still be there—and they may simply take their phone out in the library.

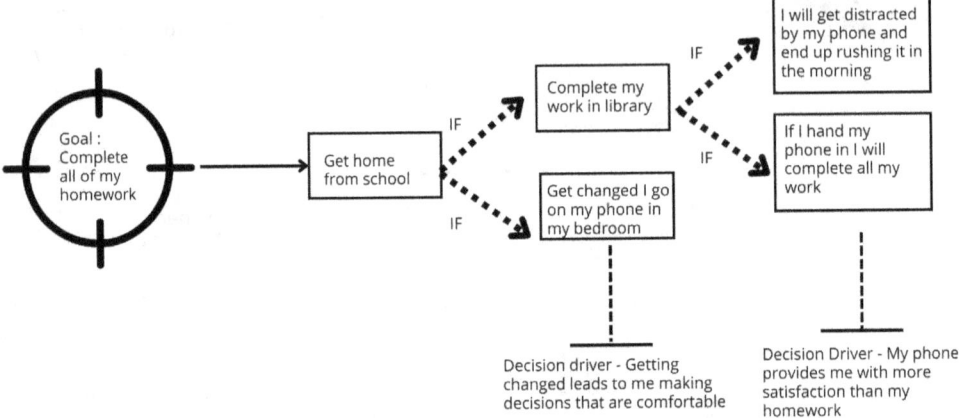

Figure 6.2 Mapping student decision-making—changing environment

As I discussed in the leadership debate about removing lockers, sometimes the most effective solution is to remove the trigger altogether. In this case, that might mean putting the phone away completely (Figure 6.3).

Now let's return to the same student a couple of weeks later. They've been completing their homework regularly and are now turning their attention to revision for upcoming exams.

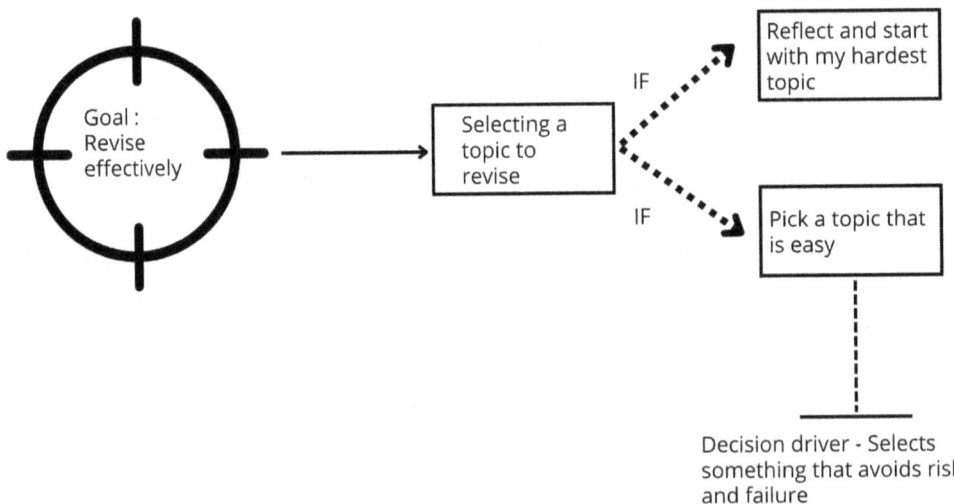

Figure 6.3 Mapping student decision-making—effective revision

As you talk through their current approach, it becomes clear that they're choosing to revise only the easier topics. They suspect this is linked to a lack of confidence and a fear of failure.

This could be a helpful moment to read the story of Netflix and Blockbuster together—an example of risk avoidance that can open up a meaningful conversation about the role fear plays in decision-making (Figure 6.4).

The student agrees to challenge themselves by tackling more difficult topics, and you begin discussing what that might look like in practice. If fear of failure is driving their choices, it's likely that even if they select a harder topic, they might give up too soon—or persist with strategies that feel comfortable but aren't effective, reinforcing the belief that they're not capable.

To prepare for this, they create an implementation intention:

When I find myself reaching for my phone, I will take a five-minute break and grab a healthy snack instead.

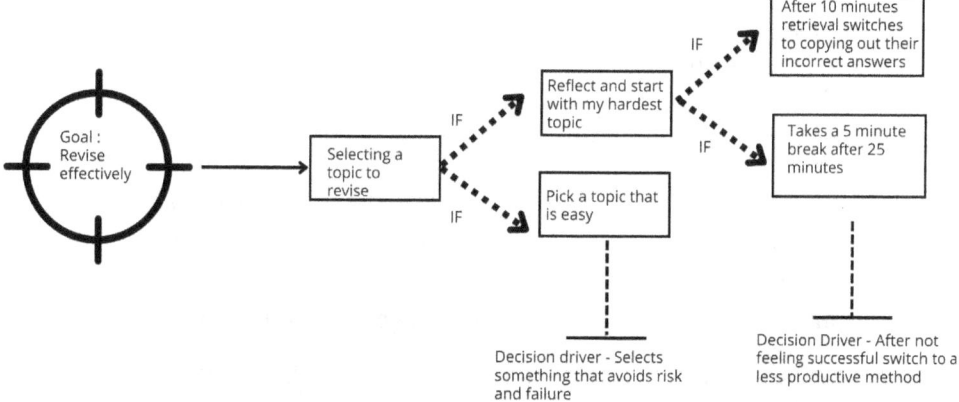

Figure 6.4 Mapping student decision-making—giving up

Both of these examples—avoiding homework and choosing easy revision topics—show how building better habits goes hand in hand with developing stronger mental models. Habits help automate helpful behaviours, while mental models guide decision-making in more complex moments. By reflecting on the cues, motivations, and choices involved, students can start to understand not just *what* to change, but *why*—making their learning behaviours more intentional, resilient, and effective.

Using Scenarios to Accelerate Learning Habits

Scenarios are a powerful way to build mental models because they help learners visualise abstract concepts in concrete, relatable contexts. By embedding ideas in realistic situations, scenarios make it easier to understand how principles work in practice. They reveal cause-and-effect relationships, encouraging learners to mentally simulate outcomes and engage actively with the material. This kind of thinking deepens understanding and supports the flexible application of knowledge across different settings. Scenarios also surface hidden assumptions, allowing learners to reflect on and sometimes revise their beliefs based on the outcomes they observe. In this way, scenarios do more than illustrate—they invite exploration, reflection, and deeper learning.

Scenarios help build mental models by:

- Making abstract concepts tangible through concrete examples
- Showing cause-and-effect relationships in action
- Encouraging mental simulation, prediction, and active engagement
- Revealing and challenging hidden assumptions or beliefs

The scenarios provided in this book are designed to help you bring abstract concepts to life. Each scenario will have two or three guiding principles from this book. In each case, some of the principles will be clearly used by the learner, while other principles may not be as evident. The goal is to unpick with students how the guiding principles are at play within the scenario.

Some suggested rules to follow:

- **Activate prior knowledge:** Before presenting each scenario, ask students to reflect on what they already know about the guiding principles. This helps them approach the scenario with a foundation of prior knowledge, allowing them to make connections and predictions as they engage with the material.

- **Encourage critical thinking:** As students work through the scenarios, challenge them to analyse the situation from different angles. Encourage them to consider multiple perspectives and outcomes, fostering critical thinking and problem-solving skills. Ask guiding questions such as, "What do you think would happen if…?" or "How could this scenario play out differently?"

- **Promote reflection:** After working through a scenario, prompt students to reflect on their learning. Ask them to consider how the scenario has shaped their understanding of the concept and whether it has challenged or confirmed their previous ideas. This reflection helps solidify the mental models they're building.

- **Adapt scenarios to your context:** While the scenarios provided in this book are flexible, feel free to adapt them to fit the needs of your students. Adjust the details or complexity of the scenarios to match your context, or link them to real-world events to make the learning experience even more relevant.

Prior to introducing scenarios to students, below is a short story as an introduction to provide context.

When Something Doesn't Feel Right: Building Mental Models Through Experience

Imagine you're PC Reyes. You've patrolled the streets of Manchester for over a decade. By now, your instincts are like your warrant card or your hi-vis jacket—just part of who you are.

On paper, it's just another routine stop: a silver Vauxhall Astra going 15 mph over the limit on a quiet B-road just after dusk. You flick on your siren. The car pulls over smoothly—no drama.

As you walk up, you do your standard visual: hands on the wheel, solo driver, reg plates check out, nothing to flag backup for.

But your gut doesn't sit right.

There's nothing screamingly wrong. The driver is courteous, the documents all in order. But his grip on the wheel is overly firm. His eyes—restless, flitting—not wild, but enough to raise your inner alert.

It's that calm that gets to you. Everything *looks* routine but *feels* off. Years of beat work have honed your mental map—this fits the usual script, but it doesn't *feel* like the usual.

You don't go heavy. Instead, you ask the driver to step out while you recheck his details. Your partner looks confused but backs you up.

Then you see it—wedged behind the front passenger seat, a small sports bag with the zip half-open. Inside: a stolen handgun and a forged Met Police ID.

Turns out, the bloke's been wanted in connection with a string of armed burglaries across Greater Manchester. You'd stepped into something that could've gone another way.

Later, your partner asks, "How did you clock it?"

You shrug. "I didn't know. It just didn't feel right."

Now, picture yourself as Jordan, captain of the Eastbourne Eagles Basketball team. Final minute of the match. Your side's two points down in a tough school basketball league fixture. The sports hall's echoing with stomping feet, shouts from benches, whistles from coaches.

The ball's in your hands at the halfway line, palms slick with sweat. You glance around—Sam, your quickest winger, is dashing up the right flank.

He's open.

Too open.

That inner flicker returns—not doubt exactly, but something that whispers: *No. Not now.*

Sam's waving. "I'm free!"

You almost sent it. Almost.

But instead, you twist left and offload to Jaden, just trailing the play. He catches it, drives into the lane, and nails the layup as the buzzer blares.

The gym erupts.

You're still not celebrating. You glance back and see it—a defender had been marking Sam tight, just out of your peripheral view. One pass that way, and it was interception city. Match over.

Back in the changing rooms, your coach claps you on the shoulder. "That was class. How'd you know?"

You just say, "Didn't. Something felt off."

But deep down, you know it's that model in your mind—the sum of years on the court, drills, late games, and instinctive pattern recognition. It told you what looked open wasn't safe. And you listened.

These aren't just "lucky guesses." Both PC Reyes and Jordan were guided by internal models shaped by years of experience. These models help us act when things don't line up—even when everything looks okay on the surface.

You can develop your own mental models too—not for traffic stops or basketball necessarily, but for learning, decision-making, and life. Trusting that quiet nudge when something doesn't sit right can be the start of thinking critically, not just reactively.

Think of it this way: you might already know strategies like spaced repetition, retrieval practice, or interleaving. These are the tools. But mental models help you figure out *when* to use them. For example, if you're re-reading a chapter over and over and it's not helping you retain the information, your mental model of learning should help you realise that this approach isn't working. Real learning takes effort, active engagement, and often discomfort. The more you build and reflect on your mental models—by looking at what worked, what didn't, and adjusting your approach—you'll become more efficient in your learning. You'll be able to recognise when something doesn't feel right, and use that moment to make a better decision.

Mental models grow from experience, feedback, and reflection—especially when you take the time to think, "What would I have done differently?" Embrace that discomfort. It's a sign that you're learning, growing, and adapting to be even better the next time.

One way to improve your mental models is by engaging with scenarios—whether from case studies, real-life examples, or problem-solving exercises. By reflecting on different situations, analysing what worked and what didn't, you build your internal framework of understanding. The more you practice recognising patterns and evaluating outcomes, the sharper your mental models become, helping you make better decisions, faster.

The scenarios are designed to unfold over several weeks, with each one exploring two or three guiding principles. At the start of each new week, these principles are revisited before introducing the next scenario. This repetition is intentional—helping to deepen students' understanding by encouraging them to reflect on and apply the principles across different contexts.

Guiding Principle	Explanation
Heuristics can play a role in students' decision-making	Heuristics are mental shortcuts that help people make decisions quickly. While useful in some situations, they can lead to biased or suboptimal choices, particularly in complex or unfamiliar scenarios.
Memory is the residue of thought	The more you think about something, the more likely you are to remember it. This highlights the importance of active engagement and repetition in securing information in long-term memory.
Self-gratification can lead to poor decision-making	Prioritising immediate rewards can interfere with long-term goals, often resulting in poor decisions. Recognising this can help students make more thoughtful, future-oriented choices.
Habits are hard to break	Consistently making poor choices may be a sign of ingrained habits. Changing these requires intentional effort and the use of effective strategies.
To transfer knowledge to your long-term memory, you need to practice retrieving it	Actively recalling information, rather than just reviewing it, strengthens memory and supports deeper learning.
Motivation doesn't lead to success; success leads to motivation	Taking action and achieving small wins builds confidence and fosters motivation, creating a positive feedback loop.
Overconfidence can lead to poor decisions	When learners become overconfident in their abilities or strategies, they may skip important steps, underestimate challenges, or fail to prepare properly.
Organising ideas helps build schema	Structuring and connecting new information to what you already know creates mental frameworks that make it easier to understand and recall knowledge later.

Scenario 1—Shortcut Thinking: When Quick Answers Undermine Deep Understanding

Character

- **Ava**—A Year 10 student working on her own

Scene: Home—Evening

> Ava sits at her desk with her laptop open. Her history homework is to write a short essay answering the question: "What were the main causes of World War II?"

Ava: (sighs) I don't have time to read all this. Let's just Google it.

She types "What caused World War II?" into the search bar and clicks on the first link that pops up.

Ava: (reading aloud) "Hitler invaded Poland in 1939, and that started the war." Okay, great—easy. That's my opening.

She starts typing, quickly summarising the article without much thought.

Ava: I remember my uncle saying the war was basically all Hitler's fault anyway. That sounds right.

She spots a paragraph in the article mentioning the Treaty of Versailles and the Great Depression but skips over it.

Ava: That stuff sounds complicated. Not really the main point. Let's stick with the Hitler bit. Everyone says that anyway.

Ava finishes the essay quickly and submits it with a proud smile.

Ava: Done in 25 minutes. Nailed it.

Discussion Points

Heuristics Can Play a Role in Students' Decision-Making

Ava's decision-making in completing her essay is influenced by several cognitive biases. She falls into anchoring bias by focusing solely on the first piece of information she finds—Hitler invading Poland—and uses it as the foundation for her essay without seeking alternative perspectives. She also exhibits availability bias by relying on easily accessible sources, such as a recent comment from her uncle and a quick online search, instead of conducting deeper research. Additionally, Ava shows confirmation bias by dismissing information that doesn't align with her existing belief that Hitler was the primary cause of the war, ignoring the economic and political causes. Finally, her overconfidence bias leads her to believe she fully understands the topic after minimal effort, assuming her quick and simple answer is both complete and accurate. These biases prevent her from engaging critically with the material and ultimately result in a shallow and incomplete understanding.

Memory Is the Residue of Thought

Ava doesn't engage deeply with the material. She skips over important details (such as the Treaty of Versailles and the Great Depression) and doesn't take the time to think critically about the content. As a result, she doesn't have the opportunity to retain meaningful information. She doesn't think enough about the topic to form lasting memories, instead only remembering a simplistic version of the cause of World War II based on surface-level details.

Self-Gratification Can Lead to Poor Decision-Making

Ava seeks immediate gratification by quickly completing the task in 25 minutes, focusing on the easiest answer that requires minimal effort. While this quick completion feels rewarding in the moment, it leads to poor decision-making in terms of the quality of her learning. She avoids the more challenging aspects of the task, which would have required more time and thought, sacrificing a deeper understanding for the sake of instant satisfaction.

Scenario 2—Beyond the First Idea: Embracing Change in Writing

Scene: English Classroom—Essay Writing Week

The assignment is to write a persuasive essay based on a novel the class has studied: *Of Mice and Men*.

MR. EVANS: You can choose your own angle, but make sure your argument is clear and backed up by the text. If your idea isn't working, don't be afraid to rethink it.

Chloe sits at her desk, frowning at her notebook. She's been working on an essay arguing that Curley's wife is the true villain of the novel—but it's not going well.

CHLOE: (whispering to herself) I've already written 600 words. But it's not convincing. I'm running out of quotes… and honestly, it doesn't even feel true anymore.

She glances at the planning sheet Mr. Evans handed out.

CHLOE: (sighs) I could start over and write about loneliness, like I originally thought… but I've already spent two evenings on this. I can't just waste all that time.

Scene: Next Day—Peer Review

Mr. Evans pairs students up to give each other feedback. Chloe reads her draft aloud to her partner, who looks confused.

PARTNER: I mean… you've written a lot, but I'm not sure the argument works. Didn't the teacher say the story's more complex than just "good guys vs. villains"?

Chloe is frustrated; she knew she had made a poor decision but decided to stick with it. She had been told this before by other teachers, so she decided to write an implementation intention.

If I feel frustrated after wasting time completing work, I will look at my journal.
She then writes the following in her journal:

The frustration I feel now is temporary. If I make changes now, I will get a better grade in the end and will feel better.

Discussion Points

Heuristics Can Play a Role in Students' Decision-Making

Continuing with poor decisions: Chloe's decision to continue with her argument about Curley's wife being the true villain is an example of the sunk cost fallacy. She has already invested time and effort into this approach, and even though she recognises it's not working, she feels compelled to stick with it. This fallacy occurs when people persist in a course of action because they've already invested resources (in this case, time) that they don't want to "waste," even though continuing may not be the best choice.

Habits Are Hard to Break

Recognising a pattern: After Chloe recognises that she has faced this struggle before, it's clear that her tendency to persist with a flawed idea has become a habit. She's repeating the same pattern—sticking with an argument that isn't working because she's invested too much time in it. This kind of habitual thinking can be difficult to break, especially when she feels emotionally attached to the work she's already done.

Implementing strategies for change: Chloe's decision to write an implementation intention is a step in the right direction. By planning how she will respond to frustration (looking at her journal), she's starting to develop a strategy to break the habit of persevering with ineffective work. Recognising the need for change and actively seeking strategies to make that change—such as rethinking her argument—will help her build better decision-making habits moving forward.

Scenario 3—Caught between Doubt and Effort: Paul's Homework Dilemma

Character: Paul—Year 9 student

Scene: Evening, at home—after school
Paul slumps into his chair at the kitchen table. His science homework is to revise key terms about photosynthesis using a set of flashcards his teacher gave the class.
He flips through the cards slowly, reading each one like a shopping list.

Paul (reading aloud with little interest):
"Chlorophyll—green pigment that absorbs light…"
"Glucose—a type of sugar made during photosynthesis…"
After about ten minutes, he sighs and pushes the cards away.

Paul (to himself):
I don't even know if I remember any of that. I always forget it anyway. What's the point? I'm just bad at science. Homework doesn't help.
He pulls out his phone and scrolls through videos instead.
The next day, the teacher does a quick recap quiz.

Teacher:
Let's see how much you remember—no notes!
Paul stares blankly at the paper. Some words look familiar, but he can't recall the definitions.
Paul looks around and sees his classmates confidently joining in and thinks to himself they get it because they are clever than me.

Discussion Points

Memory Is the Residue of Thought

Paul doesn't remember the content from the lesson as it was unlikely he was actively participating in the lesson.

Practicing Retrieval Strengthens Memory

Paul looked at his flashcards but didn't actually try to recall the answers—he just read them. This kind of passive review feels easier but doesn't help information stick. To strengthen memory, students need to **actively practise retrieving** information.

Motivation Doesn't Lead to Success; Success Leads to Motivation

Paul feels demotivated because he hasn't experienced success. Paul needs to start small—taking action, even in small steps, can lead to progress and renewed motivation.

Scenario 4—When Life Gets Tough: Maya's Classroom Comeback

Character: Maya—Year 10 student

Scene: Friday morning—English lesson
Maya walks into class a little quieter than usual. It's been a hard week—things at home have been stressful, and sleep has been patchy. But this isn't the first time

she's felt this way, and she's learned that how she responds in class can make a big difference to how much she takes in.

As the teacher begins to explain a new topic about persuasive writing, Maya feels that familiar wave of fuzziness. The words are floating past her, and the urge to zone out grows.

Maya (internally noticing the cue):
This is when I usually drift off and don't take anything in.

She glances down at the sticky note in her planner—an implementation intention she wrote last month after a similar week:

> If I notice I'm not following the explanation, I will take a breath, focus my eyes on the teacher, and try to connect what I'm hearing to something I already know.

She shifts in her seat, straightens her posture, and begins to listen more actively.

As the teacher gives an example about persuasive language used in advertising, Maya silently links it back to the campaign project they did last term. She jots a quick note in the margin: "Same techniques as media unit."

Later that day, Maya realises she hasn't been doing much revision lately—retrieval practice had slipped as life at home got overwhelming. She opens her flashcard app and quizzes herself gently, not aiming for perfection, just getting back into the rhythm. It feels like a small win.

Discussion Points

Memory Is the Residue of Thought

Maya supports her memory by making meaningful links during the lesson.

Habits Are Hard to Break

She recognises an old habit (switching off in class) and uses a strategy to interrupt it.

To Transfer Knowledge to Long-Term Memory, Practise Retrieving It

She had fallen out of the habit due to outside stress, which may have been part of the reason she struggled in the lesson. Maya makes a conscious effort to re-engage with retrieval practice and rebuild that routine.

Scenario 5—From Confidence to Carefulness: Amina's Revision Story

Amina is revising for her maths exam. She's feeling a bit anxious, but she remembers how well she did in her last test. She thinks:

I revised the night before last time, and I got 8 out of 10. Plus, I was really focused that night, had snacks, and even listened to my chill playlist. I'll do the same this time. I revise best when it's last minute and I have music and snacks.

She spends a couple of hours the night before the exam re-reading her notes and going through some example questions she feels confident with. It feels familiar and comfortable, and the playlist helps her stay calm.

A few days later, when the results come back, Amina is surprised—and disappointed. She scored 4 out of 10.

Her teacher hands the paper back with a comment: "You clearly understood the methods but made lots of avoidable mistakes—check your working carefully!"

Looking through the paper, Amina sees what her teacher meant. She rushed some of the questions, misread others, and didn't double-check her answers. She had relied on her intuition to guide her, just like last time, but this time the problems were harder and needed slower, more deliberate thinking.

Discussion Points

Memory Is the Residue of Thought

Amina's revision focused more on comfort and familiarity (re-reading, chill environment) rather than deep engagement with the material. She likely didn't think hard enough about the maths problems, which meant less was stored in long-term memory. The lack of active thought during revision made it easier to forget steps and make mistakes during the test.

Heuristics Can Play a Role in Students' Decision-Making

Amina used a substitution heuristic when answering the questions on her test. Instead of carefully analysing the problems, she quickly substituted them with similar questions she had seen before in class or during her previous revision. This quick, automatic thinking led her to make assumptions about what the correct answers were without fully engaging with the specific details of each question. As a result, she made a number of silly mistakes.

Overconfidence can Lead to Poor Decisions

Amina's overconfidence in her revision strategy led her to believe that just replicating the approach that worked last time would guarantee success. She assumed that since she had done well before with a similar strategy, she would automatically perform well again, without considering that this time might require a different approach. This overconfidence in her method led her to rush through her revision and not take the time to work through the problems carefully.

Scenario 6—When Good Plans Come Too Late: Liam's Last-Minute Flashcard Rush and Mind Map Attempt

Character: Liam—Year 11 student

Scene: Saturday evening—at home, revising for his history exam

Two weeks before his history exam, Liam had created a detailed set of flashcards covering all the key topics from the term. He knew flashcards were a great way to test himself and strengthen memory.

However, life got busy, and Liam didn't start using the flashcards right away. For the first 12 days, the cards just sat on his desk.

Scene: Forty-eight hours before exam—Liam's rush to revise

Feeling anxious as the exam approached, Liam finally picked up the flashcards. He spent two solid hours going through them rapidly, trying to cram all the information into his head at once.

After this, feeling a bit overwhelmed by the amount of information, Liam decided to make mind maps to organise his ideas into logical sequences and connections. He hoped this would help him see the bigger picture and understand how topics are linked together.

Liam (thinking):

> I'm behind, but maybe the mind maps will help me make sense of everything before the exam.

Scene: Exam day—history exam

In the exam, Liam could recall some facts but struggled with questions that required deeper understanding and quick recall of details. He found gaps where information hadn't fully "stuck," especially on questions needing detailed knowledge or connections between events.

After the results came back, Liam's score was lower than he hoped.

Discussion Points

Organising Ideas Helps Build Schema

Although Liam made mind maps after his flashcard session, he didn't use them to truly organise and connect ideas. Instead of linking new information to his existing knowledge or seeing how concepts related to each other, he simply copied facts from the flashcards onto the mind maps. This required little deeper thinking or effort, so the mind maps became a simple list of recently covered points rather than meaningful learning.

Habits Are Hard to Break

Although Liam knew what to do, breaking the habit of procrastination and starting early was difficult. Perhaps Liam could consider a change in environment the next time he prepares to revise for an exam to break the old habit.

To Transfer Knowledge to Long-Term Memory, Practise Retrieving It

Effective revision requires starting early and spreading retrieval practice over time, not rushing it at the last minute.

Scenario 7—Small Wins, Big Progress: Sarah's Flashcard Habit

Character: Sarah—Year 10 student

Scene: After school, at home

Sarah is preparing for her upcoming biology exam. Knowing that spaced practice is key, she creates a set of flashcards two weeks before the exam.

She decides to commit to reviewing them every other day and tracking her engagement on a chart stuck to her bedroom wall. Every time she completes a flashcard session, she colours in a box on the chart.

Over the next two weeks, Sarah:

- Reviews her flashcards consistently, spacing her sessions roughly every 48 hours.
- Monitors her progress visually, which gives her a sense of achievement and structure.
- After completing seven sessions, she rewards herself with a small treat—a favourite snack or watching an episode of her favourite show.

Sarah notices that each session feels easier, and she remembers more information than before. The visible progress and rewards keep her motivated, even on days when she feels tired or distracted.

Exam Day

Sarah feels confident walking into the exam room. Her steady, spaced revision means she can recall key concepts quickly and with ease.

Discussion Points

To Transfer Knowledge to Long-Term Memory, Practice Retrieving It

Sarah spaced out her flashcard sessions, strengthening memory over time.

Motivation doesn't Lead to Success; Success Leads to Motivation

By tracking her progress and rewarding herself, Sarah built momentum and kept motivated through positive feedback loops.

Scenario 8—Jayden's Library Habit: Changing Place, Not Strategy

Jayden used to revise at home, but it was always a struggle. The distractions were constant—his phone buzzing with messages, the TV playing in the background, and family members chatting nearby. Even when he tried to focus, his mind would drift away or he'd find himself scrolling through social media without realising it. After getting a disappointing result in his mock exams, Jayden knew something had to change.

Determined to improve, he decided to change his environment. Starting the next week, he began going to the school library after lessons. The library was quiet, calm, and felt serious—everything Jayden thought he needed to focus properly. He brought his notes, textbooks, and a highlighter, feeling motivated and ready to make the most of this new habit.

However, although the setting was different, his revision approach stayed the same. Jayden's strategy was simple: he re-read his notes over and over, hoping that by repeatedly looking at the information, it would stick in his memory. He highlighted key points and occasionally made some annotations but didn't try to test himself or actively engage with the material.

After several weeks, Jayden's test scores were not improving. Despite spending long hours in the library, he still struggled to recall important facts and apply concepts in exams. This left him feeling frustrated and discouraged. Eventually, he gave up on revising altogether and slipped back into his old habits of revising at home, often distracted and unmotivated.

Discussion Points

Habits Are Hard to Break

Jayden's story shows how difficult it is to change not just *where* you revise, but *how* you revise. Moving to the library was a positive change in environment, which helped reduce distractions and gave him the right mindset to focus. However, Jayden's underlying habit—the way he revised—remained the same. He continued to rely on re-reading his notes, a passive strategy that often feels productive but doesn't deeply engage the brain.

Memory Is the Residue of Thought

This principle emphasises that memory strengthens not just through exposure but through *active thinking*. Jayden spent hours re-reading his notes, but re-reading is mostly a passive activity. His brain wasn't forced to retrieve information, make connections, or apply concepts, so the "residue" of his thought was weak. This meant the material didn't move effectively into his long-term memory.

Heuristics Can Play a Role in Students' Decision-Making

Even though Jayden changed his revision location, his decision-making was influenced by common mental shortcuts, or heuristics, that can sometimes lead to unhelpful patterns. One such heuristic is the sunk cost fallacy—because Jayden had already spent weeks re-reading notes in the library, he felt compelled to continue this strategy despite poor results, unwilling to "waste" the time and effort he had already invested.

Additionally, confirmation bias and overconfidence played a part. Jayden believed that simply changing his environment would solve his revision problems, and he selectively focused on the quietness and seriousness of the library as evidence that his new habit was working. This led him to overlook or dismiss the fact that his actual revision strategy—re-reading notes—was ineffective. His overconfidence in the idea that location alone was the key prevented him from critically evaluating or trying different, more effective approaches like self-quizzing or active recall.

Together, these heuristics kept Jayden stuck in a cycle where he changed location but not approach, limiting the effectiveness of his revision despite his good intentions.

Scenario 8—Tom's Turnaround with Point, Call, Check

Tom was known around school as a bit of a troublemaker. He often disrupted lessons—calling out, fidgeting, and sometimes ignoring instructions. His teachers found it hard to keep him focused, and his behaviour was affecting his learning and that of others.

One day, Tom's teacher introduced a simple strategy called *Point, Call, Check*. The idea was that whenever Tom felt distracted or was about to act out, he should:

- **Point** to what he was supposed to be doing (like the question on the board or the task in his book),
- **Call** out the key instruction or rule for that task ("I need to read the question carefully" or "I should put my hand up to speak"),
- **Check** that he was actually following the instruction before continuing.

At first, Tom thought this sounded a bit childish, but he agreed to try it for a week. During lessons, whenever he felt like messing around, he stopped, pointed at the task, said the instruction out loud to himself, and then checked if he was doing it properly.

Slowly, Tom noticed he was getting less distracted and more engaged. He found he was listening to the teacher's explanations better because he was actively reminding himself what he needed to do. The *Point, Call, Check* routine helped him slow down and think harder about what he was supposed to do.

Over time, Tom also noticed that he was doing better in the short retrieval questions his teacher gave the class. He was able to recall information more quickly and answer confidently, which made him feel more successful and motivated to keep improving.

Discussion Points

Motivation Doesn't Lead to Success; Success Leads to Motivation

At the start, Tom wasn't very motivated to behave or focus in class. But by using *Point, Call, Check*, he took deliberate action—even when he didn't feel like it. As he started experiencing small wins, like listening better and answering retrieval questions more confidently, those successes boosted his confidence and motivation. This shows how taking action and seeing progress can create a positive cycle, where success fuels motivation rather than the other way around.

Memory Is the Residue of Thought

Tom's improved focus meant he was thinking more deeply during lessons. By consciously reminding himself what to do, he engaged more actively with the teacher's explanations and class tasks. This deeper thinking helped information stick better in his memory, as shown by his improved performance in retrieval questions. The principle highlights how actively processing information, rather than passively hearing it, strengthens learning.

Habits Are Hard to Break

Tom's disruptive behaviour was a well-established habit that didn't change overnight. The *Point, Call, Check* strategy gave him a practical way to interrupt his usual impulses and make better choices step-by-step. His story illustrates how changing habits requires conscious effort and strategies to support self-regulation. Recognising that habits take time to shift is important for maintaining patience and persistence during behaviour change.

Scenario 9—Ethan's AI Shortcut

Ethan had always found English homework a bit of a chore. One evening, while struggling to write an analytical paragraph for his homework on *Macbeth*, he decided to try something new. He opened an AI writing tool, typed in the question, and within seconds had a well-structured response.

The result was impressive. His teacher praised his work, commenting on his use of vocabulary and the clarity of his argument. Encouraged by the feedback, Ethan started using the AI more often. He'd tweak the outputs slightly to make them sound more like his voice, but most of the work was done for him. His marks went up, and his confidence grew.

When it came to revising for the upcoming in-class assessment, Ethan didn't do much. After all, he'd been getting strong feedback on his homework all term—he assumed he was on track. But when he sat down to write in timed conditions, without AI to help, he froze. He struggled to recall quotes, couldn't structure his response clearly, and found it hard to develop ideas on his own.

His test result was disappointing. Ethan was surprised and frustrated. It felt unfair—he'd worked hard on his homework. But in reality, he hadn't been practising the skills he needed to retrieve and apply knowledge independently. The AI had made the homework easier, but it hadn't helped him *think* deeply or remember key content.

Discussion Points

Memory Is the Residue of Thought

Ethan's use of AI to complete his homework meant he wasn't actively engaging with the material. While the final answers looked impressive, the thinking—the struggle, retrieval, and effort to organise his ideas—was outsourced. As a result, he wasn't forming strong memory traces because he wasn't doing the cognitive work himself.

Self-Gratification Can Lead to Poor Decision-Making

Ethan's decision to rely on AI was driven by the immediate reward: quicker completion, high-quality output, and praise from his teacher. This short-term gratification felt good, so he repeated the behaviour without considering the long-term consequences. Because he was being rewarded in the moment, he saw no need to change. However, this strategy ultimately backfired when he underperformed in a high-stakes assessment. Ethan prioritised ease and praise over genuine understanding, and it affected his long-term success.

Scenario 10: Aaliyah's Struggle to Adjust

Aaliyah had always been a high achiever. At GCSE, she earned a string of top grades, especially in English, science, and history. Her teachers praised her work ethic, and her peers saw her as someone who just "got it." Encouraged by her success, Aaliyah enrolled in A-levels with high hopes of going on to study law at university.

But the jump in difficulty between GCSE and A-level took her by surprise. The lessons moved faster, the texts were harder, and the expectations for independent study were much higher. In her first history essay, she got a grade that she'd never seen before—an E. Her teacher said the ideas were vague and lacked depth. In chemistry, she struggled to keep up with the pace of the lessons and couldn't seem to follow the logic of multi-step calculations that had once come easily.

At first, Aaliyah tried to keep up appearances. She told herself it was just a shaky start. But after receiving more disappointing results in her initial assessments, her confidence took a hit. She began to feel like maybe she wasn't "naturally academic" after all. The identity she'd built—of being one of the smart ones—started to unravel.

This knocked her motivation. She felt embarrassed in class, stopped putting her hand up, and started missing deadlines. Eventually, the fear of failing became so overwhelming that she began skipping lessons altogether. Her attendance dropped, and her teachers struggled to get her to re-engage. What had started as a confident, capable student spiralled into disconnection and self-doubt.

Discussion Points

Motivation Doesn't Lead to Success; Success Leads to Motivation

Aaliyah began her A-levels assuming that the same motivation and study habits that worked at GCSE would be enough. But when her early assessments went poorly, her sense of competence took a hit. Instead of seeing those early struggles as part of the learning curve, she saw them as signs that she wasn't good enough. As a result, her motivation collapsed. This highlights an important truth: motivation often comes *after* success, not before it.

If Aaliyah had been supported to track small wins—improvements in classwork, mastering part of a complex topic, completing independent reading—she might have experienced the sense of progress that builds confidence. Success, even in small amounts, creates a positive feedback loop: doing well builds belief, which fuels effort, which in turn leads to more success. Without that loop, Aaliyah spiralled instead.

Memory Is the Residue of Thought

Aaliyah's early success at GCSE may have been influenced by a curriculum that was more structured and revisited key ideas more frequently. At A-level, she was expected to make more of the thinking happen independently—linking concepts, applying ideas to unfamiliar contexts, and recalling information over longer periods. But Aaliyah hadn't yet developed the habits of deep thinking and active engagement that A-level success demands.

Her poor performance wasn't simply due to a lack of ability but a lack of cognitive engagement. Reading notes, passively listening in lessons, or doing the bare minimum of homework doesn't lead to durable memory. Real understanding—especially at a higher level—requires effortful thought: testing yourself, making connections, revisiting content, and reflecting on feedback. Because Aaliyah wasn't engaging in that kind of thinking, her memory of key content was weak, which compounded her difficulties.

Metacognition and Self-Regulation

Coaching students on effective learning habits and giving them scenarios to analyse can play a powerful role in developing their mental models—and, in turn, their expertise about how learning works. These conversations help students see patterns, make better decisions, and understand what strategies are most effective in different situations. However, if our ultimate goal is to prepare the student sitting in a university lecture theatre or the apprentice on a job site, we need to go one step further. The final stage in this journey is supporting students to develop their **metacognitive skills**. Metacognition is the ability to think about one's own thinking—to plan how to approach a task, monitor progress, and evaluate whether a strategy is working. A student with strong metacognitive skills is able to make independent decisions, adjust when things aren't going well, and take ownership of their learning. It's what turns a set of good habits into lifelong learning competence and evaluate their approach to a task, making adjustments when needed. This means they're not just working hard—they're working smart.

Thomas Edison: The Power of Reflection and Perseverance

Thomas Edison, the inventor of the light bulb, is often celebrated for his groundbreaking success, but his journey was paved with countless failures. What set him apart, however, was his ability to use metacognitive strategies—planning, monitoring, and evaluating—to learn from each setback and keep improving.

Planning: Setting a Clear Goal

When Edison set out to invent a practical electric light bulb, his first step was meticulous planning. He wasn't just trying to make any bulb; he wanted one that could last long enough for widespread use. Planning involved not just designing a working bulb but figuring out how to make it affordable and efficient.

Edison's early plan was to experiment with various filaments, including cotton and bamboo. He also knew he needed to create a reliable vacuum inside the bulb to prevent the filament from burning too quickly. His goal was clear: create a long-lasting light bulb that could revolutionise the way people lived.

Monitoring: Reflecting in Real Time

Despite his planning, Edison faced numerous failures. Early filaments would burn out almost instantly, and the bulbs weren't durable enough for everyday use. Yet, Edison didn't give up. Instead of blindly repeating the same experiment, he continuously monitored the results of each trial and made adjustments based on his observations.

For example, after his early attempts with carbon filaments failed, he switched to experimenting with different materials. He tried over 6,000 different materials, ranging from hair to plant fibres. Each time one failed, Edison would assess what went wrong. He would examine how long the filament lasted, whether the filament's conductivity was sufficient, and whether the vacuum inside the bulb was effective. If a material failed, he reflected on why it failed and quickly adjusted his strategy—an example of self-monitoring.

Evaluating: Learning from Setbacks

The process was incredibly taxing and frustrating, but Edison believed in evaluating his work critically. After each failure, he didn't just think, "That didn't work." Instead, he took the time to evaluate what happened, asking deeper questions:

- Why did the filament burn out so quickly?
- Was the vacuum inside the bulb properly sealed?
- Did the material have the right electrical conductivity?

With each failure, he refined his methods. After many months of trial and error, Edison discovered that carbonised bamboo was an effective filament, lasting much longer than previous materials.

His breakthrough didn't just come from blind repetition. It was the result of constant reflection and evaluation—taking the time to assess each failure, adjust his methods, and continue refining his process.

The Final Breakthrough

Edison's constant monitoring and evaluating of his experiments ultimately led to success. After experimenting with various filaments and vacuum techniques, he finally developed a practical, long-lasting light bulb. The key wasn't just the amount of work he put in, but how he reflected and adjusted with each failure. Edison knew the importance of evaluating his progress—recognising that each failure was a learning opportunity, not an endpoint.

Thomas Edison's journey is a prime example of how metacognitive strategies—planning, monitoring, and evaluating—can turn failure into eventual success. Rather than being discouraged by setbacks, he used them as opportunities to learn, refine his approach, and keep moving towards his goal. Through constant self-reflection, Edison didn't just invent a light bulb; he invented the process of innovation itself.

Reflective Questions

- **Planning:**
  - How did Edison's initial plan help him set clear goals for his invention? What strategies did he use to refine his plan after each failure?

- **Monitoring:**
  - Edison constantly monitored his progress and made adjustments. How can you apply this idea of self-monitoring to your own learning or study habits? What would happen if you just continued without checking your work or progress?

- **Evaluating:**
  - After each failure, Edison evaluated what went wrong and adjusted his methods. Think about a time when something didn't work as you expected. How did you evaluate the situation, and what changes did you make moving forward?

Just like Thomas Edison didn't rely on luck but adjusted his approach after each failure, students can improve their learning habits through the Planning, Monitoring, and Evaluating framework.

Planning involves setting clear goals and choosing strategies that are likely to work. Monitoring is about staying aware during the task, checking if your strategy is effective, and making adjustments if necessary. Evaluating allows for reflection after the task to see what worked, what didn't, and how to improve next time.

By applying this framework, students can become more intentional and adaptive in their learning, just as Edison adapted his methods until he succeeded. The following sections break down each phase with examples, helping students build better habits and stronger mental models for learning.

Phase	Focus	Guiding Questions	Example
1. Before a task—planning phase	Setting goals and preparing strategies	• What is the goal of this task? • What strategies have worked for me before in similar situations? • What challenges might I face, and how will I deal with them?	Before starting revision, a student sets a goal: "I want to be able to explain the causes of World War I without using my notes." They choose retrieval practice and plan to quiz themselves using flashcards, anticipating that alliances will be the trickiest part to remember.

(Continued)

Phase	Focus	Guiding Questions	Example
2. During a task—monitoring phase	Staying aware and adapting	• Am I staying focused? • Is this strategy helping me learn? • Do I need to adjust what I'm doing?	While revising, the student notices they keep checking their phone. They switch to studying at the dining table instead of their room and put their phone in another room—adjusting their environment to stay focused.
3. After a task—evaluation phase	Reflecting and improving	• What worked well, and why? • What didn't work, and how can I change that next time? • Did I achieve my learning goal?	After a mock exam, the student notices they performed well in a section they revised the night before. At first, they feel confident—but on reflection, they realise this was likely due to short-term memory. Despite using retrieval practice, the knowledge hadn't fully transferred to long-term memory, and they struggled to apply it in different contexts. Next time, they plan to start retrieval practice earlier and use past paper questions to practise application.

Self-Regulation

Self-regulation refers to the ability to manage your emotions, thoughts, and behaviours in a way that helps you achieve your long-term goals. In the context of learning, it means staying focused, managing distractions, and regulating your emotional responses when faced with challenges. For instance, when a student feels frustrated with a difficult task, self-regulation enables them to calm themselves down, persevere, and keep going rather than giving up. It also involves setting clear goals, monitoring progress, and adjusting strategies when necessary. Self-regulation is crucial for maintaining motivation, managing time effectively, and handling stress—key factors in becoming an independent and successful learner. By developing self-regulation skills, students learn to control their impulses and emotions, stay on track, and continue making progress towards their learning objectives.

From Prison to the Classroom: Using Self-Regulation to Overcome Challenges

Tom was struggling at school. His grades were slipping, and no matter how hard he tried, he couldn't stay focused in class or keep up with his assignments. Every night, he'd sit down to study but would quickly feel overwhelmed, unsure of where to start. It wasn't that he didn't want to do well—it was that he was constantly battling his frustration, feeling like no matter what he did, it wasn't enough.

Tom realised that in order to move past this, he needed to take a step back and think about how to regulate his emotions and focus. He decided to set a goal: he would study for short, 20-minute bursts, focusing fully on one task at a time. To avoid distractions, he moved his study space to the kitchen, away from his usual cluttered desk, and made sure his environment was quiet and organised.

At first, it was tough. He'd still feel the urge to stop and check his social media, but Tom reminded himself that this was part of the process: he needed to stay calm and stick to his plan. Slowly but surely, the 20-minute sessions started to work. He felt less anxious and more in control. He also found that when he took a short break after each study session, he came back to his work feeling refreshed and able to concentrate more.

However, Tom's test scores didn't improve as quickly as he had hoped. He was frustrated but reminded himself that learning is not always proportional to effort—it takes time. He realised that in some subjects, his schema was lacking depth, and this itself was a barrier to understanding new material. Despite the setbacks, Tom remained hopeful. He knew that as his schema built and his understanding deepened, learning would become easier.

Tom isn't the only person to discover the power of self-regulation. Nelson Mandela, one of the greatest leaders in history, spent 27 years in prison under brutal conditions, but what led him there was a life spent fighting for justice and equality.

Mandela's early life was shaped by the racial segregation and systemic injustice of apartheid in South Africa. As a young lawyer, he saw firsthand how the system oppressed black South Africans, and he became an active member of the African National Congress (ANC). He was part of a movement that sought to challenge the racist policies of the apartheid regime. This was not an easy decision. Mandela knew that standing up for equality meant facing violence, imprisonment, and even death. But he also understood that ignoring the situation meant surrendering to injustice.

In the 1960s, after years of advocating for peaceful protests and negotiations, Mandela and his comrades were forced to take more direct action. He became involved in sabotage campaigns against government installations. This led to his arrest in 1962, and in 1964, Mandela was sentenced to life in prison for his role in the struggle against apartheid. During his trial, he famously said, "I have fought against white domination, and I have fought against black domination. I have cherished the ideal of a democratic and free society in which all persons live together in harmony and with equal opportunities."

The years that followed were incredibly difficult for Mandela. Isolated on Robben Island, cut off from his family and the outside world, he was subjected to harsh conditions—forced labour, little food, and barely any contact with fellow prisoners. He was often tempted to give in to anger, frustration, and despair. But Mandela understood something crucial: to remain focused on his ultimate goal, he had to regulate his emotions and not let them dictate his actions.

In his autobiography, Mandela describes how he learned to control his anger and not let the brutal treatment diminish his spirit. He understood that reacting with rage or bitterness would not help him achieve his long-term goal of freedom for his people. He often spoke about the importance of maintaining hope and focusing on the future, even when the present seemed impossible. It was during this period that he cultivated an inner resilience and patience that would carry him through the years to come.

Mandela's ability to regulate his emotions didn't mean he never felt anger or frustration—it meant that he knew how to channel those feelings into something productive. He once famously said, "Do not judge me by my successes, judge me by how many times I fell down and got back up again." He was able to keep his eyes on the bigger picture: not just for his own freedom, but for the freedom of all South Africans. His emotional self-regulation allowed him to endure years of hardship and stay true to his cause, leading to his eventual release in 1990 and his election as South Africa's first black president in 1994.

Mandela's story shows the immense power of self-regulation. It wasn't just about controlling his emotions—it was about staying focused, patient, and resilient in the face of overwhelming odds. Much like Mandela, Tom knew that setbacks were part of the journey. By regulating his emotions, staying patient, and keeping his focus on his long-term goals, Tom believed that with enough time, he too could overcome his challenges and succeed.

Determined to stay on track, Tom decided to tell a few friends about his new goal. By sharing it, he created a sense of accountability, and it felt like a commitment he didn't want to let go of. He remained confident that with patience and continued effort, his knowledge would eventually grow stronger and more connected.

Reflective Questions

- How do you manage your emotions when you face challenges in your learning or personal life? What strategies help you stay focused and calm?

- Think about a time when you had to push through frustration or setbacks. What actions did you take to keep yourself on track and maintain control over your behaviour?

- How can setting specific goals and breaking tasks into smaller steps help you regulate your actions and stay motivated, even when things don't go as planned?

This chapter has explored the deeper architecture that underpins effective, independent learning. At its core is the idea that students need more than strategies—they need structured ways of thinking. Through coaching and the use of carefully designed scenarios, we can help students surface and refine their mental models: the invisible frameworks that shape how they approach learning. By making their thinking visible, challenging misconceptions, and guiding reflection, we help them replace flawed or shallow models with richer, more accurate ones.

But improved thinking alone is not enough. As students begin to understand how they learn, they must also develop the metacognitive skills to plan, monitor, and evaluate their progress. These are the hallmarks of expert learners—those who don't just work hard but work smart. And woven through all of this is the need for self-regulation: the ability to manage emotions, persist through setbacks, and adjust behaviour in pursuit of long-term goals. Whether it's the anxiety before a test, the temptation to avoid difficult tasks, or the frustration of slow progress, learners must be equipped to face these internal challenges head-on.

Together, these elements—coaching, mental models, metacognition, and self-regulation—form the backbone of any powerful learning journey. When we teach students to think about their thinking, regulate their effort and emotion, and reshape the way they approach problems, we move closer to our ultimate goal: learners who are not just capable but self-directed—ready to take ownership of their development and meet the future with confidence.

Chapter Summary

- Novices follow rules and focus on surface details, while experts think flexibly and focus on deeper principles.

- Novices often overestimate their understanding due to the Dunning-Kruger effect, but encouraging reflection helps expose knowledge gaps and build true expertise.

- Creating simple, evidence-based learning rules helps novices make better decisions by guiding them when experience and intuition are lacking.

- Developing better mental models helps bridge the knowing-doing gap by enabling students to interpret situations more effectively, make wiser decisions, and apply strategies with greater consistency.

- Scenarios accelerate learning habits by turning abstract ideas into concrete experiences, helping learners build and test mental models through relatable situations, active reflection, and guided exploration of key principles.

- Metacognition and self-regulation help students think more clearly and act more deliberately, turning effort into effective, independent learning.

References

Bereiter, C., & Scardamalia, M. (1987). Knowledge telling and knowledge transforming in written composition. In S. Rosenberg (Ed.), *Advances in applied psycholinguistics, volume 2: Reading, writing, and language learning* (pp. 142–175). Cambridge University Press.

Chi, M. T. H., Feltovich, P. J., & Glaser, R. (1981). Categorization and representation of physics problems by experts and novices. *Cognitive Science, 5*(2), 121–152. https://doi.org/10.1207/s15516709cog0502_2

Danziger, S., Levav, J., & Avnaim-Pesso, L. (2011). Extraneous factors in judicial decisions. *Proceedings of the National Academy of Sciences, 108*(17), 6889–6892. https://doi.org/10.1073/pnas.1018033108

Dreyfus, H. L., & Dreyfus, S. E. (1986). *Mind over machine: The power of human intuition and expertise in the age of the computer.* Free Press.

Dweck, C. S. (2006). *Mindset: The new psychology of success.* Random House.

Essex, B., & Healy, M. (1994). Evaluation of a rule base for decision making in general practice. *British Journal of General Practice, 44*(382), 211–213.

Klein, G. (1998). *Sources of power: How people make decisions.* MIT Press.

Lawson, R. (2006). The science of cycology: Failures to understand how everyday objects work. *Memory & Cognition, 34*(8), 1667–1675.

Mueller, P. A., & Oppenheimer, D. M. (2014). The pen is mightier than the keyboard: Advantages of longhand over laptop note taking. *Psychological Science, 25*(6), 1159–1168. https://doi.org/10.1177/0956797614524581

Rozenblit, L., & Keil, F. (2002). The misunderstood limits of folk science: An illusion of explanatory depth. *Cognitive Science, 26*(5), 521–562.

Schneider, W., & Shiffrin, R. M. (1977). Controlled and automatic human information processing: I. Detection, search, and attention. *Psychological Review, 84*(1), 1–66. https://doi.org/10.1037/0033-295X.84.1.1

Soelberg, P. (1967). *Unprogrammed decision making* (PhD dissertation). MIT Sloan School of Management.

Wineburg, S. (1991). Historical problem solving: A study of the cognitive processes used in the evaluation of documentary and pictorial evidence. *Journal of Educational Psychology, 83*(1), 73–87. https://doi.org/10.1037/0022-0663.83.1.73

7 Conclusion

Throughout this book, we've explored the foundational principles that underpin successful learning—how students can understand how learning happens, slow down their thinking and challenge their biases, and develop habits that allow them to thrive academically and beyond. At the heart of it all is a powerful idea: with the right knowledge, strategies, and habits, anyone can become an expert learner.

We began by discussing how students learn best, emphasising that the key to academic success is not just about how much information they can cram into their minds, but about understanding how they retain long-term knowledge. We explored why learning is so challenging and often counterintuitive to how students want to learn.

Next, we examined the role of thinking—how important it is to develop a habit of thinking hard about what we want to remember. By understanding these biases and the limits of our thinking, we can take more intentional steps to challenge our assumptions and break free from patterns that don't serve us.

Then, we focused on the practical side of developing expert learners—how to form and sustain habits that foster growth. This is where insight must meet action. Understanding how we learn is only the first step; the real challenge lies in translating that understanding into consistent, productive behaviour. That's why so much of this book has centred on building habits—because success in learning isn't just about what we know, but what we repeatedly do.

Yet forming new habits is never easy. It means working against the brain's natural wiring, which favours comfort, shortcuts, and the path of least resistance. Our decision-making is often shaped by emotional triggers, and the desire for instant gratification. It's why students scroll instead of study and avoid difficult tasks. Without structure, support, and reflection, even the most motivated learners can fall into unhelpful patterns.

To overcome this, we must help students create environments that prompt better decisions, routines that reduce cognitive load, and systems that make success more likely. The strategies shared in this book—like implementation intentions, habit stacking, and scenario-based coaching—are designed to do just that. They allow students to consciously shape the small, daily behaviours that, over time, build expertise.

Ultimately, this is about giving students control—not just over their work, but over how they think, behave, and grow. In doing so, we prepare them not only to succeed in school but to thrive in life. With the rapid rise of technologies like AI, it's more important than ever that students understand how they learn. We've already seen the consequences of giving young people powerful tools like smartphones before they were equipped to use them wisely—an explosion of distraction, procrastination, and dependence on validation. If we do the same with AI, handing over tools before building the habits and judgement to use them, we risk repeating the same mistakes.

As educators or parents, our role is to guide students through this journey. We help them identify the habits that will serve them in the long run. But ultimately, the responsibility for learning rests with the student. Through self-regulation, reflection, and a commitment to continuous improvement, they will be equipped not just to succeed in their studies but to thrive as independent, lifelong learners.

By developing the skills outlined in this book, understanding how they learn, challenging biases, forming better habits, and adopting the mindset of an expert learner, students can become the architects of their own success. They will be ready to face the complex challenges of the future with confidence, curiosity, and the tools to keep growing.

This is the essence of independent learning: not just mastering content, but mastering the ability to learn, adapt, and thrive in an ever-changing world.

Glossary of Stories

Jessie Diggins: The Power of Struggling to Grow (page 31) This story shows how embracing struggle and desirable difficulties fosters deeper, lasting growth beyond quick fixes or short-term performance.

When Evidence Isn't Enough: A Story of Confirmation Bias (page 51) Ignaz Semmelweis's rejected discovery highlights how powerful confirmation bias can blind us to truth, even when lives depend on it.

Comfort versus Courage: Lessons from Blockbuster and Bill Gates (page 81) The contrasting paths of Blockbuster and Bill Gates demonstrate how clinging to comfort leads to failure, while embracing discomfort and risk drives growth and innovation.

Kamal's Turning Point: Tracking the Invisible Work (page 89) Kamal's shift from vague effort to consistent revision shows how habit tracking can transform identity and empower control over learning.

Cracking the Habit Code: What a Cat in a Box Can Teach Us (page 92) Inspired by Thorndike's puzzle box, this story reveals how trial and error learning and reward reinforcement shape habits in both animals and humans.

The Habit Loop: Uncovering the Science behind Our Behaviours (page 96) Research with animals uncovers that habits form through a four-stage loop—cue, craving, response, and reward—where anticipation drives automatic behaviour.

The Hidden Cue: How a Film on Your Teeth Became a Habit (page 100) Marketers leveraged the subtle cue of a film on teeth paired with the reward of freshness to engineer toothbrushing into a widespread daily habit.

The Milgram Experiment: How Social Norms Shape Our Decisions (page 121) Milgram's study reveals how social norms and obedience to authority can compel ordinary people to act against personal morals under social pressure.

Ask the Algorithm (page 132) Aisha's experience shows how reliance on AI study tools can subtly shape students' perspectives and reinforce biases, influencing not just learning content but thought patterns.

Thomas Edison: The Power of Reflection and Perseverance (page 181) Edison's invention success stemmed from persistent metacognitive strategies—planning, monitoring, and evaluating—that transformed failure into breakthrough learning.

From Prison to the Classroom: Using Self-Regulation to Overcome Challenges (page 185) Tom's progress through self-regulation—goal-setting, emotional control, environment adjustment, and patience—reflects the resilience exemplified by Nelson Mandela's journey.

Glossary of Experiments

Access downloadable versions of these experiments at www.routledge.com/9781041096382

Exploring Working Memory Limits and the Role of Prior Knowledge This experiment reveals the limited capacity of working memory and shows how prior knowledge helps us chunk information to remember more effectively.

Memory Through Different Eyes: How Perspective Shapes What We Remember This experiment demonstrates how our perspective and focus during learning shape what details we remember, highlighting that memory is influenced by what we actively think about rather than just what we are exposed to.

How Schemas Shape Memory: The Reconstruction of Unfamiliar Stories This experiment demonstrates how our existing knowledge and cultural background (schemas) influence the way we interpret, recall, and reconstruct unfamiliar information, often leading to altered or simplified memories.

Substitution Bias: How Intuitive Thinking Leads to Systematic Errors This experiment reveals how people often replace complex problems with simpler, intuitive ones—resulting in quick but incorrect answers—and highlights the need to engage deliberate analytical thinking to avoid common cognitive errors.

Anchoring Bias: How Initial Information Shapes and Skews Our Judgements This experiment demonstrates how people's estimates and decisions are heavily influenced by an initial reference point or "anchor," leading to biased judgements even when the anchor is arbitrary or irrelevant.

Testing Confirmation Bias This experiment reveals how people tend to seek evidence that confirms their existing beliefs while neglecting information that could disprove them, illustrating the cognitive bias known as confirmation bias.

Index

advanced organiser 26
anchoring bias 44–46, 55–58, 168
Ausubel, D. 3, 26, 34, 36

Bartlett, F. 3, 21–22
behavioural insights team 66–68
belief 112–116
belonging 116–117
bystander effect 121

Clear, J. 4, 85–87
cognitive overload 12, 26, 36, 85, 119, 133, 149, 155, 158
concerted cultivation 117
confirmation bias 50–55, 138, 168, 176
cue 18, 63, 96–101, 161, 172

desirable difficulties 30–32, 119, 134
Dreyfus & Dreyfus model 4, 146–147
Duhigg, C. 4, 100, 109
Dunning–Kruger effect 150–151, 173, 176

elaborative interrogation 35
environment 107, 109–110, 114, 124

fast thinking 17–18, 39–40, 42–46, 55, 58–59, 63, 83

Gladwell, M. 3–4, 124, 126
goals 84–86, 90
growth, natural 116

habit scorecard 101–104
habit stacking 104, 106, 161, 177

implementation intentions 103–104, 106–108, 163, 170
interleaving 33, 133, 166

Kahneman, D. 4, 16, 44, 49, 59, 65, 69–70
Klein, Gary 153–156

Lareau, A. 117–118, 125
learning lag 86
long-term memory (LTM) 5, 8, 13–16, 18, 20, 36

mental models 4, 56, 145, 156, 158–160, 165
metacognition 150, 155, 181
Miller, G. 3, 9, 11, 15
motivation 82, 167, 171, 176, 178
Murdock, B. 3, 14–15

naturalistic decision-making 4
noise 69–76, 126
nudge theory 63–64, 123

placebo effect 113
point and call 101–102
procrastination 82, 88–89, 91, 129, 135

retrieval practice 33, 88, 101, 119, 125, 132–133, 144, 155, 158, 167, 171–172, 175
rewards 96–99

schemas 21–22, 24–29, 34, 83–84, 86, 130, 167, 175
self-efficacy 113
self-explanation 36
self-gratification 43, 46, 77–78, 167, 169, 179
self-regulation 184, 187
short-term memory (STM) 15–16

social norms 120–122
spacing / spaced repetition 32, 125, 132–133, 144, 155, 157
statistical literacy 61
substitution bias 40–43, 173
sunk cost fallacy 46–49, 176
supernormal stimuli 110
slow thinking 17, 39–40

temptation bundling 111

Willingham, D. 5, 8, 17
working memory (WM) 9–13, 85, 119

For Product Safety Concerns and Information please contact our EU representative GPSR@taylorandfrancis.com
Taylor & Francis Verlag GmbH, Kaufingerstraße 24, 80331 München, Germany

www.ingramcontent.com/pod-product-compliance
Lightning Source LLC
Chambersburg PA
CBHW080412170426
43194CB00015B/2789